# Computing Myths,
# Class Realities

# Conflict and Social Change Series

### Series Editors
Scott Whiteford and William Derman
*Michigan State University*

*Computing Myths, Class Realities: An Ethnography of Technology and Working People in Sheffield, England,* David Hakken with Barbara Andrews

*The Culture of Protest: Religious Activism and the U.S. Sanctuary Movement,* Susan Bibler Coutin

*Literacy, Power, and Democracy in Mozambique: The Governance of Learning from Colonization to the Present,* Judith Marshall

*Gender, Sickness, and Healing in Rural Egypt: Ethnography in Historical Context,* Soheir A. Morsy

*Life Is a Little Better: Redistribution as a Development Strategy in Nadur Village, Kerala,* Richard W. Franke

*¡Óigame! ¡Óigame! Struggle and Social Change in a Nicaraguan Urban Community,* Michael James Higgins and Tanya Leigh Coen

*Manufacturing Against the Odds: Small-Scale Producers in an Andean City,* Hans C. Buechler and Judith-Maria Buechler

*The Bushman Myth: The Making of a Namibian Underclass,* Robert J. Gordon

*Surviving Drought and Development: Ariaal Pastoralists of Northern Kenya,* Elliot Fratkin

*Harvest of Want: Hunger and Food Security in Central America and Mexico,* edited by Scott Whiteford and Anne E. Ferguson

*Singing with Sai Baba: The Politics of Revitalization in Trinidad,* Morton Klass

*The Spiral Road: Change in a Chinese Village Through the Eyes of a Communist Party Leader,* Huang Shu-min

FORTHCOMING

*"I Am Destroying the Land!" The Political Ecology of Poverty and Environmental Destruction in Honduras,* Susan C. Stonich

*The Myth of the Male Breadwinner: Women and Industrialization in the Caribbean,* Helen I. Safa

# Computing Myths, Class Realities

## An Ethnography of Technology and Working People in Sheffield, England

David Hakken
with Barbara Andrews

Westview Press

BOULDER • SAN FRANCISCO • OXFORD

305.562
H15c

*Conflict and Social Change Series*

Copyright © 1993 by Westview Press, Inc.

Published in 1993 in the United States of America by Westview Press, Inc., 5500 Central Avenue, Boulder, Colorado 80301-2877, and in the United Kingdom by Westview Press, 36 Lonsdale Road, Summertown, Oxford OX2 7EW

TP

Library of Congress Cataloging-in-Publication Data
Hakken, David.
   Computing myths, class realities : an ethnography of technology
and working people in Sheffield, England / David Hakken with Barbara
Andrews.
      p.   cm. — (Conflict and social change series)
   Includes bibliographical references.
   ISBN 0-8133-8135-5 — ISBN 0-8133-8312-9 (pbk.)
   1. Working class—England—Sheffield—Effect of automation on.
2. Employees—England—Sheffield—Effect of automation on.
3. Computers—Social aspects—England—Sheffield.   4. Ethnology—
England—Sheffield.   5. Sheffield (England)—Social life and
customs.   I. Andrews, Barbara, 1944–      .   II. Title.   III. Series.
HD8400.S52H35   1993
305.5'62'0942821—dc20

                                                            92-44799
                                                            CIP

Printed  and bound in the United States of America

∞    The paper used in this publication meets the requirements
     of the American National Standard for Permanence of Paper
     for Printed Library Materials Z39.48-1984.

10    9    8    7    6    5    4    3    2    1

# Contents

# Acknowledgments

Fieldwork with a family of five has both advantages and disadvantages, but it can't in any case be done without a great deal of help from a community of support. For their intellectual, moral, and practical support, we thank Janet, Alan, Jamie, and Ruth Baldwin; Jenny Owen, Graham Burkin, Jack, and Ruth; and Debby Glass, Matthew Toulmin, and Eleanor. Our project could not have progressed very far without continued contact with organizations and individuals in the labor movement and working class, for which we thank especially Ken and Lillian Randell and Ken Curran. Similarly, we needed the support of program officers and community contacts and access to academic resources; our thanks to Michael Barratt Brown, John Darwin, Mike Fitter, Bob Fryer, John Grayson, John Halstead and Margaret Gent, Bob and Jill Heath, and Bill Hampton.

In the conventions of anthropology, it is not appropriate to identify by name each informant whose comments we quote or whose perspective we relate in some way, though it is appropriate to name those who publish or speak publicly. The former convention exists to protect those who might be harmed and is of some value as a means of soliciting cooperation. However, there are problems with the anonymous discourse that follows from these conventions, including the creation of an aura of generality that is not warranted. Moreover, the practice inevitably implies that the really valuable information and analysis comes from named "experts." Most field-workers would readily acknowledge that this is simply not so.

To protect those whose participation was given freely, we have generally employed pseudonyms in our text, using real names only in relation to the public speeches of public figures or the written works of scholars or local journalists. Nonetheless, we wish to acknowledge here those who consented to be interviewed, allowed us to participate in activities, and in some other concrete way participated in our research. In addition to those mentioned above, they include:

- In the Sheffield business community, Mary Collinson, Neal Goodenough, John Hambridge, John Handscome, and Dave Smith.
- At and through the Sheffield District Council, Daryl Agnew, Phil Asquith, Ted Baldwin, Alan Beaver, Clive Betts, Jean Bickerstaff, David Blunkett, M.P., Steve Bond, Geoff Green, Ed Guyton, Joan Harrison, Jo Henderson, Ann Howard, Bruce Hughes, Helen Jackson, Steve Jackson, Rob Jones, Alan McGauley, Joel Miskin, Emma Morgan, Brigitte Pemberton, Gordon Reid,

Brian Salisbury, Dan Sequerra, Allison Spencer, and Ann Stewart.

- In our Greystones neighborhood, Kate Green, Terry Howard, Paul, Chris, and Allison Tildsley, Mrs. Gibson, and Mrs. Armstrong.
- At Northern College of Adult Education, Pam Cole, Ed Ellis, Ray Hearn, Keith Jackson, Ian Linn, Colin Thunhurst, Jill Venard, and Ruth Winterton.
- At Sheffield Polytechnic, Ruth Aylett, Doug Bell, Malcolm Brewer, Kath Corfield, Barry Hines, Fergus Murray, and Den Paine.
- At Sheffield University, Harry Barnes, M.P., Marie Brazil, Pam Briggs, Bernard Burns, Cath Cassell, Phil Healey, Jill and Bob Heath, Nick Howard, Clive Opie, Alan Wellington, and Phil Wright.
- In the trade union and political movement, Martin Ashworth, Roger and Joan Barton, Rap Bird, Alan Burrows, Richard Caborn, M.P., Brian Clarke, Ken Curran, Jr., Dave Feikart, Vi Gill, Roy Harrison, Pam Holmes, Jean Miller, Derek Simpson, Seb Smoller, Julia Stallibras, Jesse Taylor, and Nans Thompson.
- In the South Yorkshire women's movement, Val Binney, Ruth Blunkett, Mandy Bryce, Betty Heathfield, Fran Holmwood, Angela Kalish, Ruth Midgeley, Wendy Miller, Jean in Thurnscoe, and Pam Stubbs.
- Outside of South Yorkshire in Britain, Sue Berger, Carlos Dabezies, John Field, Jane Humphries, Rog Smith, Robin Williams, Jonathan Winterton, and Jane Woddis.
- In Europe, Susanne Bødker, Titje Bos, Tone Bratteterg, Ellen de Ru, Pelle Ehn, Hakon Finne, Noor Greahard, Toon Jansen, Hugo Levie, Anker Brink Lund, Bente Rassmussen, Kea Tijdens, Marya Visser, and Margaret Weggelar.

At SUNY Institute of Technology, Lori Munger coded, and deans Ted Hanley and Bill Harrell supported this research and its write-up in a number of ways, including equipment, sabbatical support, release time, and funds for travel. The Joint Labor Management program of the State University of New York and United University Professions, Inc., provided a small grant for travel to plan research. Major funding for the fieldwork came from the U.S. National Science Foundation Anthropology Program. The NSF Program on Ethics and Value Studies in Science, Technology, and Society and the New York State Science and Technology Foundation have supported subsequent related research. Our first fieldwork in Sheffield, during 1976–1977, was supported by the U.S. Social Science Research Council.

Major thanks to Reed Couglan of SUNY Empire State College for reading and discussing the first draft of this manuscript at great length. Helpful readings and comments were also provided by Doug Caulkins, Eve Hochwald, and Kellie Masterson of Westview Press. Kellie has supported completion of the text in several other ways as well. Thanks also to Sabina Vanish for diligent copyediting.

Although we made several attempts to write the book in a completely joint manner, the pressures of survival and careers in the late twentieth century made this impossible. Nonetheless, the text could never have been completed without the help that each of us has tried to give to the other, in this as well as in a range of other endeavors.

Perhaps the most important acknowledgment is to Nathan, Karl, and Luke, for whom the year in Sheffield was not "research" or a job but their life. Their willingness to try new things and to let their parents in on how they felt about their experiences was as important as anything else to our sense of understanding what it was like to be a real participant in the reproduction of Sheffield culture.

*David Hakken*
*Barbara Andrews*

# Introduction

*Computing Myths, Class Realities* is about the extensive change—on the job, where people live, in social relations—taking place in contemporary societies. The book examines whether this social change is caused by the introduction of computer-based new technology or "computerization." To answer this question, computerization is examined culturally, through the holistic approach of anthropology.

The conclusions presented in the book were reached through ethnographic fieldwork, an activity that we believe is a valid way of knowing in its own right. Once having settled upon a problem that they wish to investigate, ethnographers next identify a sociogeographic space in which events relevant to the problem are likely to be manifest; then they use participant observation to uncover the interpretations, structures, and processes that constitute the context within which these events take place.

Our sociogeographic space was occupied by working-class people in Sheffield, South Yorkshire—an industrial area in the North of England experiencing extensive computerization. In order to analyze the relationship of computing in Sheffield to the social change associated with it, we draw attention to two kinds of contexts: what was happening with computerization in other places, and other, nontechnological changes taking place in the lives of Sheffield workers and their families. In presenting our ethnography, we draw attention to not only what happens when computers appear in production but also to their correlates in basic relationships among people, the language and other cultural constructs people use, and so on. Our rigorous examination of the social correlates of computerization in one specific place constitutes an elaborated approximation of the set of general factors that interact with and influence most strongly the changes accompanying computing as it becomes integrated into daily life elsewhere.

## Theoretical Issues Addressed by the Book

Can the bulk of the social change *associated with* computing be said to have been *caused by* computer technology, developing as a largely independent force

*1*

having an internally generated direction? Conversely, should the changes be viewed as more fundamentally determined by other, nontechnological, social forces?

In the 1980s, much social commentary presumed the era to be one of technology-induced transformation and that the age was traumatic, especially for ordinary people (Friedrichs and Schaff 1982; Bjorn-Andersen, Mumford, and Novotney 1982; Jones 1982; Gorz 1985). Throughout the world, industries, workers and their organizations, national and local governments, and other groups struggled to cope with computerization's effects. New technology-related terms— "postindustrial" (Bell 1973), "technotronic" (Levitan and Johnson 1982), and "information society" (Lenk 1982)—were invented to describe the era. A new American Anthropological Association Panel on Disorder and Its Development in Industrial and Postindustrial Societies, for example, was based on these presumptions.[1]

Such apparently self-evident presumptions are not valid. One must examine computing in context, in broad, processual terms, not narrowly, conceived of merely as a set of machines and techniques. Other technology has not had simple "impacts," their character determined immediately and straightforwardly (Bijker, Hughes, and Pinch 1987). Because technology is constructed socially, within the context of broader social formations, the experience of new information technology takes different forms in different situations.

Still, the dynamics of social formations themselves change as they are reproduced, and in human cultural evolution, technologies have often placed substantial limits on what is possible. If we wish to understand what computing does in society, we have to find a way to analyze the interactions between a technology and its broader contexts, a framework that is predisposed neither to understate nor overstate their relative autonomy from each other. Only a broad research approach can hope to capture such complex interdependencies, and the question of computerization is unanswerable without a complex theory of the dynamics of social change.

### Technicism

Such breadth of approach is not characteristic of many extant studies of computerization. Rather, these tend to assume the "computerization hypothesis"—the widely held view articulated above that adoption of new information technology is the central cause of current sociocultural change (e.g., Toffler 1980; Servan-Schriber 1981). The presumption of massive, computer-induced social change is less a consequence of convincing evidence than of social myth. David Noble (1979) argues that those living in employment-based or "industrial" social formations tend to view social change in technicist terms—that is, they presume that what happens in society is generally determined by the nature of technology; therefore, any new change is assumed, rather than demonstrated, to be the consequence of technological change. A corollary myth (explored by Noble 1984) is that technological development is largely independent of social influences other than the internal dialectic of science-based practice; thus, social policy to influence technology is futile and likely to make things worse.

Technicism is mythic in the anthropological sense: It is taken for granted in popular discourse, and its presumptions are seldom examined critically in their own right. Indeed, popular authors are not the only ones who have difficulty expressing themselves consistently when they talk about computerization. Ambiguities traceable to technicism remain a major presence in the academic and political literatures about computerization.[2]

## The Scientific Technical Revolution Perspective

In order to develop a proper sense of the social consequences of computing, we must operate outside of technicism's presumptions. The necessary critical distance can grow out of identifying the conditions in which technicist discourse emerged. Benson and Lloyd (1983) trace several technicist presumptions to the 1930s, when the modern period became viewed as the era of the scientific technical revolution (STR). The STR view—that we are living through a science and technology-induced major social revolution—was articulated in Britain by a group of influential scientists.

These people developed a strategy for hastening the transition to the socialism that they saw as inherent in the STR. Central to their strategy was an intellectual machinery, an abstract technology, to speed the changes in production, economy, and government necessitated by scientific practice. Jonathan Rosenhead (1986), chairman of the British Operations Research Society, traces several influential technologies to this left academic STR culture, including operations research, cybernetics, general systems theory, and the modeling of modern economies in the manner of, for example, Leontiev Input-Output matrices. Computer science itself can be described as an STR-based abstract technology. All these ways of thought tend to analyze complex problems—whether material, organizational, or social—by reducing them to technical questions.

This 1930s STR perspective tended to dualize technology and society along Cartesian lines. That is, STR intellectuals rigorously discussed issues held tractable within a technical frame, but rigor was often abandoned when attention was turned to the social processes in which technical acts take place. The contradiction between technology and society was typically displaced through affirmation of technology as a transcendent force: Technology must be transcendent if, as presumed, society is being revolutionized by science and technology despite social difficulties.

Within the academic STR literature (e.g., Bernal 1965), a "scientific utopian" view, optimistic about technological and social progress in spite of existing tendencies toward social disintegration, came to dominate. A belief in the capacity of technology to solve almost any problem is a consistent STR theme. STR technological determinism, along with generally hubristic, technologistic thought, was manifest in many of the "social engineering" schemes of the time. The problems of capitalist social formations came to be conceived as soluble through the intervention of an exogenous force, technology based on a priori science.

The STR perspective has more recent political counterparts, as in Labour Prime Minister Harold Wilson's 1960s enthusiastic promotion of "the white hot heat of the technological revolution." Advocates of private utilities in the U.S. continue to present technology as a cornucopia of good, negative results being labeled "by-products," consequences of the irrationalities of pretechnological society (Starr 1983). A similar utopianism is common in the "computers and society" textbooks used in contemporary college curricula (e.g., Frates and Molderup 1983). There, a positive view of the power of technology contrasts sharply with a negative view of less tractable processes, especially social power.

STR thought was by no means restricted to the West. The "forces of production" optimism of "Third International period" communism was another form of STR thought; it was recently still influential in computer policy in Bulgaria, for example (Dobrianov 1986). Nor are its presumptions limited to those on the left. The critique of technology articulated by Jacques Ellul (1964), for example, is generally viewed as humanist-conservative, opposed to liberal STR thought. However, though Ellulian views are pessimistic about the social impacts of technology, they share the most general STR presumption: that of massive, technologically based social change.

### Computopia

It seems logical that to grasp the consequences of widespread computing, one would focus separately on (1) the technology itself, (2) the social changes that happen at the same time, and (3) the social forces which shape them both. Yet the electronic computer, developed during World War II, is the most powerful contemporary symbol of the STR perspective, so powerful that it is very difficult to separate conceptions about computing from the STR presumptions within which it was created and that are characteristic of modernist, mid-twentieth century thought. Reflecting the dualities in STR thought referred to above, the social correlates and contexts of computing are largely presumed to follow from technology and are not themselves made the object of study. In effect, social contexts and correlates are either deduced from a machine-centered orientation, ignored, or wished away as ultimately irrelevant "by-products."

The popular literature on computerization that developed especially after the mid-1970s manifests the simplistics of STR. Primarily, this meant a confidence that what was technically feasible would surely become implemented. The rhetorical question asked by a Xerox promotional film—"If the technology is here, can the system be far behind?"—encapsulates the view nicely. Rapid technical progress was presumed to be the best general way to insure that any social difficulties following from computerization would be overcome quickly. We call views of computerization that reflect this mythology "computopian."

The computopian view of computer society has several manifestations. Many of them build on Daniel Bell's positive characterization of "post-industrial society" (1973). A number of social forces, including the incessant need in a capitalist political economy to develop and promote consumption of new commodities— for example, home computers—as well as the powerful ideologies of both conservative and liberal/social democratic political movements, encourage the computopian vision. Essentially a celebration of a computer culture presumed to be developing according to its own dynamic, computopianism marginalizes the role of social policy, reducing it to finding ways to ease adaptation to the inevitable.

## Compputropia

The dominant view of the computerization process is surely computopian. However, the explosion of computer use in the 1970s was associated with a series of worrying hesitations in the Western economies. This conjunction was one source of a persistent minority view, that computing is socially degenerative or "putrefying." After Raymond Williams (1989), we label such analyses of computerization "compputropian." (The label "computer Luddite," also in use, perpetuates a historical misrepresentation; see e.g., Clawson 1980.)

Social critics who identified with a trade union or broad working-class perspective developed a vigorous compputropian critique of computerization (e.g., Cooley 1982; CSE Microelectronics Group 1980; Shaiken 1985). Like the nineteenth-century publicists and activists to whom the Luddite label was first applied, compputropians direct their attention first to the degradations of workers' conditions, skills, and collective power that happened in conjunction with computerization. They also address broader social implications, such as the massive unemployment and disruption implicated in technologies promoted as "worker proof" and "labor saving." Compputropian critiques of technology share much with Ellulism, but they also draw on the developing ecology movement and general new left scholarship.

In Britain, the clash between computopians and compputropians became public in 1978, identified by many (e.g., Huws 1982) with the controversy surrounding a specific BBC "Horizon" television program, "Now the Chips Are Down." This program contained a debate over alternative social futures, positive views of *The Third Wave* (Toffler 1980) being confronted by such clarion calls to resistance as *Sleepers, Wake!* (Jones 1982). Seldom given an empirical cast, this debate was based instead on conflicting, ideologically derived hunches about the most likely course for future society. One's view on the quality of the social change was directly related to one's allegiance to the various groups and interests within society. Despite real differences, this computopian/compputropian discourse shared one presumption, the basic STR view: that computers were at the root of the displacement of much current human activity and the cause of substantial social change.

### Computing Studies

A third perspective on computerization began to develop in the 1980s. Found largely in social science, the "computing studies" approach is critical of both STR assumptions: that current social change is profound and that it is technology-induced. In the computing studies view, the STR is yet to be demonstrated. Its existence is an open, empirical question, as is the idea that the social correlates of computerization are predetermined by a technological trajectory. At least theoretically, such correlates may be influenced by human activity as groups constitute and reconstitute themselves in the process of reproducing social life.

The computing studies perspective had several sources. One was earlier studies of the effects of centralized data processing systems on management or on personal privacy (e.g., Rule 1974). In opposition to earlier technical models, revisionist studies of the labor market (e.g., Gordon, Edwards, and Reich 1982; Wright 1979) stressed segmentation theories holding that the present has more continuity with the past than presumed by STR. Another source was the study of the social politics of technology, reinvigorated by Harry Braverman (1974). Especially in England, computing studies has also drawn energy from the critiques of Braverman (e.g., Wood 1982) and segmented labor market theory (e.g., Wilkinson 1981). These academics took an empirical approach to computing, seeing it as a process against which to test historically derived theories about social change.[3]

### Computing Studies, Ethics, and Computer Science

Some contemporary philosophers have turned their attention to the ethical and value difficulties that accompany computerization (Hoffman and Mills 1982; Johnson 1985; Johnson and Snapper 1985). Projects with thorough cross-disciplinary content require a higher than usual degree of articulation of the underlying presumptions and value commitments of their diverse participants. For this reason, the study of these kinds of projects offers a good opportunity for the identification and analysis of real-life examples of dilemmas in computer ethics. Still, the concern with computer ethics tends to be framed within the STR computerization hypothesis—for example, if the spread of computers inevitably means massive social change, by what criteria will social choices be made in the future society? What concepts will determine how we cope with dislocation? Is it possible to determine a computer-based ethics in embryo form?

A variant of the computing studies perspective developed within computer science itself (e.g., Kling 1974). Earlier simplistic assumptions—for instance, that computer system development is a strictly technical process—are slowly being replaced by the recognition that computing practice involves social development as well as technical design, and failure is increasingly recognized as more frequently a consequence of organizational rather than technical factors (Lucas 1975). A few, such as the lecturers in computer studies at Sheffield Polytechnic, look increasingly to collaboration with social scientists. They seek knowledge with which to build computer systems fully cognizant of human social process. Yet, although not oblivious to the broader implications of computerization, professionals within the computer field still tend to address social development only *after* technological/engineering problems are seen to be solved (e.g., Shackel 1986).

Nonetheless, one can identify an increasing convergence among some computer professionals, social scientists, and philosophers in promoting an empirical approach to computerization. This approach aims to integrate sociocultural perspectives into computer system development. In computing studies, the dualism in the discussion over the social consequences of technology—a dualism that meant that one was either optimistic or pessimistic about both the technological and the social sides of computerization—has begun to recede. Attewell and Rule (1984), for example, hypothesize that the prospects for both new information technology and its social correlates are highly contingent, dependent for their outcome on a variety of social factors. Consequently, understanding the role of computerization in inducing change in any existing social formation depends upon sensitization to the many different forms such interactions take.

We aim to present and explicate a theory of computerization by identifying empirically the social factors most relevant to the development of new information technology in a specific social context, that of South Yorkshire in England, and then by generalizing these factors into a comprehensive analytic framework. The goal is to provoke computing studies to a more general level of analysis, complementing empirical studies with explicit theory.

### Social Policy Research

Our book is based on the premise that there is much of general value to be gained by studying what has happened in a well-chosen particular place, like Sheffield. However, the actual course of computerization has varied substantially from society to society. It is precisely this variability that is the best prima facie evidence for seeing computerization as a more social than technological process.

Moreover, as a social process, computerization is at least potentially open to the influence of coherent social policy. However, the ability of human groups to influence a technological process consciously—to control computerization through social policy, rather than to be controlled by computers—depends strongly on how accurately people perceive their situations and how effectively they organize themselves.

An additional contribution of the book to computing studies is our discussion of the successes and failures of public policies that apply a social perspective on computerization. Through our study of what happens when peoples and their governments apply social knowledge of computerization, we wish to increase humans' collective abilities to influence its outcome ethically. Thus we aim not only to understand computerization but also to indicate how such understanding can be used to improve both the technology and the lives of the people affected by it.

Our work in Sheffield led us to believe that a proactive approach toward computerization is not only desirable but is also a practical possibility. In order to demonstrate the applicability of what we learned about computerization, this volume includes several illustrations of projects that attempt to exercise a social influence over computerization. In the tradition of anthropological humanism, we also include suggestions about the way in which we feel the knowledge gained by the study of computing can be best applied.

## Computerization and Working-Class People in South Yorkshire

Most comments on technology and change presume that new forms of information technology have particularly strong implications for those who work—that is, the social groups who produce most of the physical subsistence consumed by society.

When Sheffielder workers say that what you experience with computers depends on your class, they are pointing out that technology is not an independent force but is affected by other social forces. Class language is less often used in Utica, New York, yet in all such employment-based societies people talk, think, and write extensively about new technology and its relationship to the rapid social changes they are experiencing. What happens "when the computers come" to the Upper Mohawk Valley is as much influenced by the nature of cultural constructs and social relationships as it is in Sheffield.

Unlike many other regions, however, Sheffield has had a large, organized, and quite powerful working class for a long time, and this is partly why Sheffield is one of the few regions to meet computerization with social policy. Moreover, our analysis of what happens when Sheffielders use policy to influence the social correlates of computing should also illuminate the general question of what forms the technology/social change relationship can take. South Yorkshire has attempted to control or at least to exert a conscious, collective social influence on the course of computerization and its social consequences for working-class people.

Our thorough examination of the spread of computing and the accompanying social changes in a place where policy is well developed should help us to specify the central elements of the general relationship of new technology and social change. Placing the Sheffield experience in relationship to that of other regions will ultimately allow us to identify both possibilities for intervention and limits to public influence over the process of computer-related social change.

## An Ethnographic/Ethnological Record

Like any rigorous ethnography—"a picture of a people"—this book takes as its first goal the presentation of an accurate description of its subject, computerization in Sheffield. Modern ethnography is particularly concerned to insure that interpretation is grounded in the lived reality of real people and places. Consequently, much of our book is composed of vignettes, brief descriptions of events experienced in the field. These vignettes include a great deal of the speech of those in Sheffield whom anthropologists call "informants." This speech, whether obtained by tape recorder, records of observations and interviews, field notes compiled the next morning, or speeches delivered and articles written, is necessarily edited by our understanding of Sheffield. The speech and the vignettes are of course also contextualized by the chapter within which they are placed.

Besides their listening carefully, researchers' accuracy in ethnography depends upon good ethnology, the analytical theories and methods developed by cross-cultural anthropological research. Ethnology is the result of the comparative study of the similarities and differences among all peoples' lived experience. The discourse of ethnology aims to find concepts that, because they are applicable in different sociocultural contexts, allow students of culture to *illuminate* as well as to describe social processes. Since the ethnology of computerization has only a short history, there are few agreed-upon ethnological constructs on which we can draw. As a result, rather more of our book than we would have liked is given over to explaining and justifying concepts used. This conceptual preoccupation allows us, however, to use the speech of informants to label and illustrate our points. The cultural practices of informants, including unemployed or "labor-free" young people from Barnsley in South Yorkshire as well as the "computer literate" nurse from Clinton in the Upper Mohawk Valley of New York State, become part of the ethnology we are creating.

## Structure of the Book

Part One, "Studying Computerization," addresses the why, where, and how of our ethnography. In Chapter 1 we offer a humanistic answer to the question, "Why study computerization?" The chapter presents examples of how various people in South Yorkshire talk about computers. We argue that studying this discourse grounds our ethnography of computing in the lived experience of real people.

In Chapter 2 we explain why we feel that ethnography through extended fieldwork is an essential part of the systematic study of computing and social change. The chapter begins with a discussion of what ethnography is and how it is done, and a case is made for studying such processes at the regional level. In the bulk of the chapter, we show why South Yorkshire, because of its social history, politics, computing, and computing policy, is a desirable place for such a study. We pay particular attention to the vibrant working-class culture characteristic of the region, as well as to the advantages of building on our previous field research in the area.

Chapter 3 contains a detailed account of the field experiences on which the descriptions and analyses contained in the book are based. To demystify, at least partially, the field anthropology process, the chapter contains two illustrations of the kinds of difficulties encountered during fieldwork. We also address our research problem, the research design, what we actually did in the field, and our social role as action researchers. The chapter concludes with a discussion of action research and activism.

Part Two, "Describing Computerization" details the forms of computerization in Sheffield. In Chapter 4 we discuss the issues that one confronts when one attempts to describe complex relationships ethnographically and we also explain the descriptive strategy we employ. We then describe the computerization of work as conceived anthropologically; that is, changes in the ways working-class people in Sheffield produce and obtain food, clothing, shelter, energy, and health or well-being. We show how the physical act of production has changed (but not evenly) with the introduction of computers over the last ten years.

Chapter 5 takes up the impact of computing on the job, the basic relationship in employment social formations. We begin the chapter with a discussion of the jobs of two "computerized" Sheffield workers, a "data shop" worker and a programmer. We then turn to activities more directly involved with making money than with providing necessary human subsistence: manufacturing and newer business-related services. Service computerization is more extensive than manufacturing, and there is variety in the impact of computing on skill. In manufacturing, computerization takes place incrementally, substantive skill remains roughly the same, and women lose more than men.

In Chapter 6 we examine computing and the cultural constructs through which Sheffielders perceive and communicate. We address the way in which changes in the reproduction of culture affect the patterns of working-class collective behavior that are so distinctive of South Yorkshire. In the chapter we relate how computerization mediates working-class people's experiences at school, in their communities, in the mass media, in their organizations, and in their politics.

Part Three, "Analyzing Computing Structurally," focuses on the large-scale structures that constitute much of the context for computing and social change, especially those that place substantial limits on what is possible. Many of the developments described in this section are relatively independent from computer technology, but they have important mediating effects on the British national economy and in South Yorkshire.

In Chapter 7 we reflect on the intellectual conceptions from which our analysis is constructed. Despite some recent controversies over the nature of ethnography, we argue for the necessity of a theoretical discourse if one is to connect descriptions of particular cases to general issues. Particular theoretical issues addressed include: the ethnographic argument for ethnology; the choice of an ethnographically valid label for our current era; the nature of the different types of technology; technology and ethnology; the types of social formations; social formation reproduction; cultural approaches to class; and philosophical realism. The chapter outlines the model of general social processes, social formation reproduction, and other parts of the Marxist philosophy on which our book is based.

In Chapter 8 we describe the national state, the first of three specific social structures that strongly influence the nature of computerization. After we have identified the British national state's policies on computing and then placed these specific policies in the context of more general state policies, we examine several particular areas, including the state media, civil rights, and centralization of state services. We include vignettes that focus on the role of the police and computing during the miners' strike. We then illustrate and account for contradictions in state policy in terms of a "state-for-itself" analysis.

In Chapter 9, production managers and trade unionists look at the impact of developments in world economic relationships on the computerization of South Yorkshire. We summarize these developments in terms of the notion of "disorganizing capitalism," the tendencies of which include: increasing resistance to public policy; a new international division of labor; instability; unevenness of economic growth and contraction; and corroding existing social relations, semiotic structures, and investment.

Chapter 10 takes up the South Yorkshire region as a context. We look particularly at the labor market structures through which most Sheffield workers interact with employment institutions. Following a statistical profile of contemporary South Yorkshire, we focus on skill, building a distinction between the formal and the substantive. Even though the level of substantive skill associated with particular jobs may not be changing that much, computerization is affecting the level of recognized or formal skill. Placing skill in such broad contexts illuminates the differential gender impacts of computing and the forms of collective action that remain possible in the future.

Part Four, "Making Computerization," focuses on the ways that direct human action, as opposed to structures, shapes computerization and social reproduction—especially the actions of working-class people, both conscious and unconscious, collective and individual. In Chapter 11 we explore the relationship between the local state and "culture-centered" computing, the term we use for the new approach to computerization that is manifest in Sheffield projects. Culture-centered computing is an approach that actively involves users in the design of information systems that they will operate. Further, these systems are developed in a manner that incorporates an understanding of the social dimensions of computing. The chapter contains a vignette about a worker cooperative in which computers are used positively, in a manner quite distinct from their use in many other private organizations. The bulk of the chapter deals with the attempt of labor activists to use the local state in Sheffield to influence computerization. We place this policy in the context of recent local political history, especially efforts to construct a politics of new municipal socialism (NMS). We identify factors that have kept Sheffield's new technology policy from being as influential as it might have been.

In Chapter 12 we explore a theme found frequently in several previous chapters, computing and the process by which male/female differentiations are created, perpetuated, and changed in society. We describe controversial events regarding both computing classes for women and a performance in which contradictions in working-class conceptions of gender were evident. Issues of gender change and computing are often commingled, and the actions of women and men in the current conjunction imply new conceptions of what gender means. "Gendering" refers to the process by which extraphysical female and male differentiations are produced and reproduced. Computing is important as a terrain on which the reformulation of gendering is taking place.

In Chapter 13 we summarize our ideas regarding a cultural analysis of the computing/social change nexus. We present an "insiders'" view of the lives of the "labor-free" (people in South Yorkshire whose cultural milieu lies largely outside the boundaries of employment institutions) and their role in the creation of both computer culture and the more general culture of the future. Our discussion introduces an analysis of South Yorkshire discourse on culture. Through some examples of working-class artistic activity, we show how to combine expressive, semiotic, and situational views of culture into a single, holistic frame, and we contrast our cultural approach with the views of the "vanishing worker" theory of computerization. Through their collaboration on a cultural approach to computerizing or "informating" (Zuboff 1988) human life, the computer scientist, the anthropologist, and the organizer can make positive contributions to the lives of working-class people in such cities as Sheffield.

## The Authors

"We" are David Hakken and Barbara Andrews. The first person plural voice in which the book is written is appropriate because of our shared experience. The text before you was written primarily by David, with a great deal of input from Barbara; it is thus oriented more to his concerns as a politically active anthropologist than to hers as a politically active writer. David is an American anthropologist and worker educator. He teaches applied social and computer science at the SUNY Institute of Technology at Utica/Rome, a technological campus of the State University of New York. His knowledge of Sheffield is based primarily on two year-long anthropological field studies there, one in 1976–1977, supported by the U.S. Social Science Research Council, and one in 1986–1987 supported by the U.S. National Science Foundation Anthropology Program. He has made several shorter visits to Sheffield as well, supported by the SUNY Institute of Technology and the SUNY/United University Professions joint labor management program. David's most recent Sheffield research is part of a comparative study of computerization that includes fieldwork in the Upper Mohawk Valley region of New York State in the United States as well as other study trips to Western, Northern, and Eastern Europe. He has recently worked with a team to develop a computer system based on the eye movements of severely disabled people so that they may access a wide range of assistive technologies, he has organized a conference on disability technology policy, and he has established a technology policy center. His current research focuses on scientific management and the history of disability technology and how to use social policy to increase access to disability technology.

Coauthor Barbara Andrews shared several of these Sheffield research experiences. She was a formal consultant in the 1986–1987 research supported by the U.S. National Science Foundation. Her role in the writing of this book has been primarily in the generation of vignettes and ideas and the critiquing of perspectives. After having taught literature, film, and writing for eight years at the Institute of Technology, she brought her interest in women and cultural process to the issues of computerization. Her interests in computing now inform her work as an administrator in an arts in education program.

## Notes

1. *Anthropology Newsletter* 1987; the "and Postindustrial" was subsequently dropped from the panel title.

2. This is true despite the recent development of a more sophisticated sociology of technology (e.g., Bijker, Hughes, and Pinch 1987). Russell and Williams (1987) argue that even this work is flawed by an overly narrow conception of the relationship between technology and society.

3. A branch of this empirical literature grew out of attempts to service trade unions. Williams and Moseley (1982), for example, evaluate the attempts of several British trade unions, following the leadership of the national Trade Union Congress, to develop a technology strategy. The preferred mechanism was the technology agreement, through which the normal apparatus of collective bargaining was to be extended to insure that workers were protected against whatever deskilling and unemployment followed from computerization. They conclude that the technology agreements have not worked well as a tactic to control computerization. Instead, the hope lies in the development of strategies that shape the nature and uses of the technology itself.

PART ONE

# Studying Computerization

# 1

# Why Study Computerization?

Northern College is a residential adult education facility housed in an old stately home in South Yorkshire. In what was once a small parlor, Barbara sat at one corner of the tables arranged in a rectangle. The ten adult students described how they had been made redundant (unemployed) and related their own particular pleasures at being able to participate in this one-week "Understanding Unemployment" course. As the guest speaker, David had just indicated that if anyone had questions during his presentation on unemployment and new information technology, he or she should feel free to speak up.

**"I've just got one question," said an unemployed miner. "Will computers make people redundant?"**

The cover of the pamphlet for the Women's Technology Training Workshop (WTTW) in Sheffield has a drawing of a woman bent over the washing up (dishes), being nagged by a small child: "What can I do now? I'm still hungry! My bike's broken." The woman is thinking, "There must be more to life…"

The pamphlet goes on to describe the one year WTTW program:

> WTTW is a centre providing high quality training in micro-electronics and computing for women over 25. The Workshop has a wide range of micro-electronic and computing equipment and a highly qualified staff. It has been set up by Sheffield City Council Department of Employment and Economic Development (DEED) to provide women in Sheffield with a comprehensive overview of new technology and its applications and increased opportunities to enter the rapidly developing field of new technology.

Women who attend the workshop are provided money for child care and a weekly expenses payment. In addition to finding employment, many former trainees go on to further education. Mike, leader of the training team at DEED, contrasts the WTTW program to those run by the national government's Manpower Services Commission (MSC), which uses training to soak up unemployment. MSC programmes have a narrow focus, away from the broader approach to life. Our DEED programs try to communicate both a liberal education attitude and vocational skills. We try to raise issues about the politics of new technology at the same time as we maintain a good record on employment placement and quality. The most important way we do this is through positive action, reaching out to the disadvantaged— women, the unemployed, and minorities—because these seem to be suffering the most. Because we only have a small amount of funds, we try to run a limited number of quality programmes of our own, like the WTTW, as models for the future.

Jenny, a member of the Human-Centered Office Systems Group at Sheffield Polytechnic, and Barbara have been invited to the WTTW as part of the social education curriculum. Their goals are to help the trainees think about women and new technology and to ask the women why they applied for a place at the WTTW. Many were quite positive:

I feel this way about the course including new technology, something like that, at the end of the course, you'd be more likely to have a job.

What brought me on this course is like what this other woman said, you could get into "modern." You'd been at home, your kids were growing up, and you start feeling you'd been left behind. It felt like an opportunity to get into the twentieth century.

Well, you can't get left behind, can you, when everything is updating. I used to work in an office before, where if you had an electric typewriter, then you were, Oh! …

That's how it is with technology. I think that any change for the better is going to improve life. Computers are a relatively new thing, and there's an opportunity there for women. We're getting in at the beginning of something, and hopefully there might be a chance for us.

Others were more guarded:

I know there's opportunity, but I'm not sure I can make it. I thought computers had got brains, like the moon was a made of cheese. I thought you just gave them a problem and they did it. I didn't realize you've got to tell them what to do. I'd seen them on television, falling in love with the operator.

To teach computing, that's my dream. But I can't really take it all in. You've got a computer that's no bigger than that, and it's taking numbers into files, and files into directories, and you can't see it doing any of those things. If only I could see t'bus going to there, and picking it up, and moving it. If you're younger, you accept things.

These women think about the social dimensions of computing:

So often you're made to feel that way, like you're daft—that's why I think having this course for women only is good. Men, for some reason, regardless of whether they know anything about new technology, make out they do, and I think it would be a bit inhibiting to have men here as well.

Right, 'cause if you go around the shops where the computers are, who do you see playing on the computers? It's mainly all boys. Earlier, nobody would have thought about women and technology. It's still not as it should be. You can go on a course, and learn about technology, but you go out for a job, a man'll get preference. You've got to excel at whatever, rather than do it on a par with a man.

How is it that men get into computers, even without typing skills? Simply because they're a man. You don't need to be able to type to use a computer if you're a man. With a woman, you're expected to be able to type. If you can't, it's a disadvantage.

Determined to press ahead, they were still anxious about whether their experience with computers would be fair to them:

Even if we are at a disadvantage, we've got to do computers. You read it, that these are the jobs of the future. The only jobs are going to be for people that know the technology, to work with the equipment. A lot of the people have left jobs—there aren't going to be jobs for them. Well, there aren't any jobs for them now, they have to move away. New technology is making Sheffield a ghost town, there's hardly any jobs. All we've got is the shops. That could happen to us. You either keep abreast or get left behind.

Progress in one way is very good, but in another, not very nice when people don't have a job. We're progressing so much, with computers and all that, and in the end, there is no job for the people. In a backward country, they earn very little, but at least they've got the satisfaction that they're getting out of the house and they've got a job. It makes you wonder sometime who's better off.

The first get-together of our "support group" for computerization researchers was beginning. Jenny was talking about the difficulties of developing "human-centered" office systems:

My project involves setting up study groups, to give largely female clerical employees an active role in the information system development process. We have trouble getting the groups off the ground, and we sometimes wonder if it will ever really work. Perhaps the situation of women workers really is the way it's described on the back cover of Cynthia Cockburn's book *[Machinery of Dominance: Women, Men and Technical Know-How]*:

Why are there so few women engineers, technicians and craftworkers? Not because women aren't interested and capable, says Cynthia Cockburn, but because men as a sex strive to retain the power that comes from controlling technology. Hierarchies and subdivisions at work, and the gendering process, enable men to keep themselves separate from and superior to women in a world of "men's jobs" and "women's jobs."

Each of these vignettes—from the unemployment class, the language from the brochure, the training session, and the discussion group—communicates something about how and why working-class people in South Yorkshire pay attention to new technology, especially the kind of technology based on computers.[1] They perceive the new technologies to have profound implications for their lives; they have already experienced frequent and significant change. Consequently, the most basic humanistic reason for studying computerization is perceptual or "emic"; that is, people affected by it think it's important.[2]

## Computerization's Perceived Connection to Social Change

Sheffielders don't only believe that the new technology affects people individually; it is also perceived to be changing the society in which they live. Because of the historical importance of explicit class notions in Sheffield, perceptions of basic social arrangements have a dominant place in conceptions of personal identity. It is thus quite predictable that social change will be conceived of in terms of new arrangements of groups in society—for example, men and women, workers and bosses.

Sheffielders' comments reflect diverse positions on a broad continuum of the possible relations between computing and social change (Hakken 1989). This continuum is illustrated in Figure 1.1.

By means of a pun on the word "redundant," the unemployed miner in the first vignette places himself at the extreme right end of this continuum. In Britain, to be "made redundant" means to lose one's job, as well as to be made unnecessary. The question "Will computers make people redundant?" links a personal fate to the potential passage of the human species from the biosphere—Will machines developed by humans render human activity itself as pointless as he feels his pursuit of a decent job to be?

In contrast, one of the WTTW women compares the difference between today's and the future society to that between "developed" and "backward" societies. She suggests that computers may mean a very different kind of society, one as different from contemporary employment-based societies as these are from previous ones. In her view, by its intensification of preexisting forms of social inequality, its creation of new ones, and its disruption of access to essential social assets such as energy and food, computerization may force people to find completely new social roles, not just new jobs.

FIGURE 1.1    Possible Degrees of Social Change Related to Computing

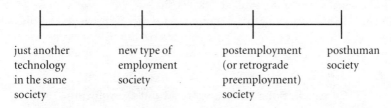

| just another technology in the same society | new type of employment society | postemployment (or retrograde preemployment) society | posthuman society |

Other comments suggest substantial changes, but ones that result in societies still based primarily on the sale of human labor power. The WTTW women, like most of the Sheffielders we talked to, are willing to "have a go" at technology. They see it as holding out promise as a means to improve their lives and to protect their futures in a new but still employment-based "industrial" society.[3] Yet they are skeptical about whether the new technology will mean any substantive difference in regard to such things as labor market discrimination; in reinforcing existing social arrangements computers may be "just another technology."

Such diverse conceptions of the society associated with computing are as characteristic of the academic literature on computerization discussed in our introduction as they are of "ordinary" people. Another important reason for sorting out its social correlates is to identify just what kind of change computing leads to; this is a second motive for studying computerization.

### *Influencing Computing-Related Social Change*

Like the trainees, our colleague Jenny was afraid that existing social forces would undermine efforts to influence the social effects of computing. Nonetheless, her goal was to integrate an analysis of such social forces into the development of information systems so that they would be of more social benefit, particularly to women.

Interventionist approaches for dealing with computing were not restricted to academics like Jenny, however. Several working-class people saw computing as leading to a redefinition of what it means to be a human being. This redefinition is seen as an opportunity to shape and use the new technology rather than just to adapt to it. For example, a group of disabled activists developed a data base to help run their organization. A union activist argued for a political strategy that takes advantage of the forms of industrial power available to workers in new technology-based industries. Some younger working-class males sought out identities as "computer people."

Some politically cognizant computer users spoke enthusiastically about using computer technology to reinforce and broaden worker skills rather than to eliminate them. Expressing a proactive attitude, speaking of computing as tractable, something whose shape and functioning is malleable, one user was eager to master computerization socially: "I see technological development allowing a break up of the working-class demoralization. The scene is being set right now, for only socialism is capable of dealing with the silicon chip."

In Sheffield, interest in how to use computers for socially progressive goals was palpable, so a third reason for studying computerization is to help people find more effective ways to influence how their lives change with computerization.

## Contradictions in Discourse About Computing

During our study we also encountered organizations reluctant to confront the implications of the spread of information technology, as well as people who had difficulty discussing the issue directly. A trade union studies tutor suggested, for example, that it was too bad we weren't doing our study in the early 1980s, when new information technology was the "flavour of the month for trade unions. Now, we've gone beyond that issue to other things, like workplace flexibility schemes."

"Of course unionists don't want to talk about new information technology," remarked a Sheffield Employment Department officer to whom we related this comment. "They've been decimated by it and have no idea how to deal with it." A lecturer at the Polytechnic bemoaned the return of a decline, after some growth, in the number of women choosing to enroll in computer studies. He was convinced that it wasn't just because they had trouble finding jobs: "It had something to do with how they feel about technology itself."

In other words, despite Sheffielders' consciousness of a high stake in the social correlates of new information technology and the will to do "summat" (something) about these correlates, it was not clear exactly what. Sheffielders hold conflicting views about computers and their relationship to social change. At times, they expressed an almost sociological conceptualization of a "computer revolution" in society, selecting forms of speech that presume technology to be a profound, largely autonomous, independent force, as in this comment in a political discussion group: "The silicon chip has caused a revolution in the mode of production, leading to a demise in manufacturing industry, the destruction of unions, which are on their knees, and a change in industrial relations." We found that working-class people in Sheffield tended to speak pessimistically when addressing broad social issues, though they were positive when speaking of their personal *experience* of computerization. It was also common for people to assert that new information technology had little impact in Sheffield and to identify it, on a more abstract level, as the major force for change in society. The contradictions were not so much *between* individuals as *within* them; the same person often expressed conflicting views.

Early in our research, it was not uncommon for people to respond to a brief description of our project with a quizzical comment, perhaps including the view that there wasn't that much for us to study, because "there really aren't that many computers in South Yorkshire." Yet even if they didn't work with computers themselves, there was plenty of computing going on in South Yorkshire.

As the above vignettes and comments illustrate, at the base of Sheffield computing discourse was the issue of whether computerization forces change in human culture, or whether the cumulative effect of human action drives computerization (or can at least influence the course of its development). Difficulty in assessing the extent and nature of computerization's role in provoking social change virtually insures contradictions in Sheffielders' attitudes toward computerization.

### Accounting for These Contradictions

How can one account for such contradictory speech and the disparity between it and the actual course of computerization in the region? There are several possible explanations. Initially, we attributed the ambiguity in discourse on computing to, for example, our difficulty in understanding the meanings people were trying to convey. Another explanation was the cultivated Yorkshire tendency for regional self-deprecation, a common counter to the "puffery" of social pretense. Further, some forms of computerization—such as general systems of production like flexible manufacturing—are more developed in the southeast of England than in South Yorkshire, where computing in production tends to be more piecemeal. Nor is there a significant computer or computer component manufacturing sector in the local economy, only a stagnating software sector. Finally, some of the discourse contradictions may be a manifestation of a common language "game" of compputropian expressions and their counters. Some older women said such things as, "They can bring the computers in here—we just won't use 'em." But younger women would counter with comments such as, "I won't work in an office unless they have a computer."

Gradually, however, we became aware of another discourse feature: silences and the contradictions in talking about computers paralleled doubts about political strategy. Hesitation had eclipsed the confidence so evident among working-class Sheffield activists in the mid-1970s. At that time, a highly elaborated, self-conscious working class culture, one that depended on effective working class political activity, was characteristic of South Yorkshire. In the 1980s, the general Northern English political disenchantment was reflected in a working-class preoccupation with nonpolitical activities like their families and homes. In contrast to the 1970s, for example, Sheffield workers were more interested in what was happening in other places—for instance, in the impact of Swedish legislation on computing.

Indeed, computerization had become an important symbol, both of political doubt and of the kinds of change processes that must be dealt with for the doubt to be overcome. Politically as well as linguistically, the working class in Sheffield is of two minds about computerization. One mind-set sees it primarily as a threat, to be avoided where possible, if only by structuring personal consciousnesses. The other mind-set approaches computerization positively, as a new means to accomplish accepted goals. Often both mind-sets were held by the same person.

The Sheffield region changed profoundly between 1976 and 1986. From a pleasant, if somewhat stodgy, "workers' capital," Sheffield became a high unemployment, capital poor, physically transforming region. These changes took place within the context of radical policy emanating from the national state led by Margaret Thatcher. They also occurred during major social and technological transformations taking place simultaneously in several regions of the world, transformations referred to with such phrases as, "the computer revolution."

For working-class people, as for other social groups in contemporary society, the culture of computerized society is in the process of being created. The sorting out of the ambivalences described above is a prerequisite to the development of consistent policies and politics as well as a fourth reason for studying computerization.

## Notes

1. The term "working class" is used to refer to those in an employment social formation who subsist primarily through their work, that is, through their participation in the social production of social subsistence use-values (Hakken 1987a). These are the material items necessary for the day-to-day physical reproduction of the human life form, including food, clothing, shelter, and energy, and for health and well-being. Operationally, to be in the working class means that one obtains more than half of one's means of survival through income from a job or from other subsistence work, rather than from ownership of a substantial portion of the social surplus, such as capital or real property.

The phrase "working-class people" is preferable to, for example, "working people." In Sheffield, "working people" refers first to those "in work," with paid jobs. Especially in Sheffield, where unemployment has quadrupled since the 1970s, one is made acutely aware of the numbers of long-term unemployed working-class people. Although they are not "working people," they are still very much "working-class people"; they do not have jobs, but the major proportion of their time is devoted to obtaining the means of physical subsistence. We believe it important to include the "labor-free" within the working class.

2. The term "emic" is used by American anthropologists to refer to that aspect of events that involves perceptions and images shared by large groups of people, the learned cultural constructs through which individuals make sense out of their existence. "Etic" is used to refer to other, less cultural construct-dependent, aspects of events.

Language is a good example of emics, but other behavior is cultural construct-dependent as well. "Emic" is also used to characterize explanatory theories that give substantial weight to such cultural constructs in accounting for particular phenomena. In this latter sense, the term has much in common with "semiotics," a term that refers to "the study of signifying."

3. A frequent label for computerized society is "postindustrial," but this term obfuscates the relationship between computing and social change (Hakken 1988a), often because the user articulates no clear concept of what an industrial social formation is. We prefer "employment social formation," a society in which most human relationships are mediated by market and contract relations, a market in labor being especially important. In such societies, the primary mechanism for accumulating a social surplus is the large-scale production and sale of commodities. Capitalistic social formations accumulate surplus in the form of privately appropriated profit that, when reinvested, becomes capital.

# 2

## Studying Computing Ethnographically in South Yorkshire

In the Introduction, we argued that much thinking about computing is limited by technicist assumptions and that a more empirical approach to computing is desirable. Chapter 1 made a more positive, essentially humanistic, case for studying computerization empirically—because people think computers are important to changes taking place in their lives and because sorting out what to do about these changes is essential to working out strategies for the future. The humanistic approach also implies something about how to study computing—the use of methods that give meaningful attention to the cultural constructs through which real people apprehend their experience. An ethnographic approach can complement the preoccupations of structuralisms with attention to the "emic" dimension of technological change—that is, how the change is experienced by people and what cultural categories they use.

### What Is Ethnography?

However they might identify the purpose of ethnography, most anthropologists would agree that it gives substantial attention to the way a group of people *experience* their lives. To accomplish this, ethnographers often focus on the way words and other cultural constructs with which people conceive of and talk about their world affect their experiences.[1] Ethnography is the traditional methodology of cultural or social anthropology, that branch of anthropology that studies in context the culture of contemporary human groups. Ethnography involves fieldwork or long-term participant observation among a particular group of people, with the aim of understanding in detail both their situation and their perceptions of their situation.[2] It is through field study, the anthropologist believes, that one is best able to develop a holistic understanding of both the physical, material contexts of human existence and the shared perceptions and collective and individual actions through which humans, intentionally or unintentionally, influence what happens to them.[3]

The term "ethnography" is also applied to the books, articles, or films through which cultural anthropologists present their information. Such media are often characterized by the close and systematic attention given to the specific speech and experiences of particular peoples. This is what anthropologist Clifford Geertz (1973) aptly calls "thick description."

In anthropology, holistic contextualization of human events is held to be a necessary antidote to the ethnocentric biases that are inevitable when humans try to use themselves as scientific instruments of observation. Field study is useful to avoid two forms of objectification: abstract material approaches (e.g., technicism, political economism), which tend to minimize the role of human agency, and equally abstract idealist approaches, which romanticize individual action at the expense of context. Through their concentration on the in-depth study of a single situation in context, ethnographers believe they decrease the likelihood of such misunderstandings.

### Doing Ethnography

Endemic to ethnography is a basic dilemma regarding selection of the site for fieldwork: The ethnographer normally can't know if a proposed field site is representative of the phenomenon he or she wishes to study until something substantial about the phenomenon is known. However, one can't possess such knowledge without first studying the phenomenon.

The ethnographer's response to this dilemma is normally to forsake representativeness in favor of some form of optimization. He or she looks for a "strong case" field site, one that maximizes the likelihood that the problem of interest is accessible to study. To choose a strong case, one first needs a good sense of the problem, a clear notion of the question one wishes to answer and the kind of information that will allow one to answer it. Second, the ethnographer searches out sites where there is good reason to believe that the phenomenon of interest is manifest, its dynamics lying close to the surface of social life and thus accessible to observation. Third, it is helpful if the phenomenon is also of concern to the people who live there—that they talk about it. It is particularly desirable if the phenomenon is felt to be so important that potential informants are trying to do something about it, collectively as well as individually. Finally, the ethnographer chooses a site where there is good reason to believe that informants will be cooperative.

## Computerization in South Yorkshire

We begin with a thumbnail sketch of computing in Sheffield during 1986 and 1987. During this period, computerization was already of importance to daily life in the region.

When we returned to Sheffield in 1986 for a second period of extended fieldwork, we found that computerization was already extensive. For example, paid work was mediated by computers in a number of ways. The remaining large steel

and engineering firms had generally introduced computer controls into their production process, and small- and medium-sized manufacturing firms were quite
likely to have computerized milling machines and stock control systems. A few
large plants, generally those controlled by multinational corporations, had moved
further in the direction of fully integrated computerized manufacturing, but it
was much more typical to see computerization in relatively small, more or less
self-contained aspects of the manufacturing process.

Computerization had extended even further in service sectors of the paid work
economy. Word processing equipment was a common feature of many offices, as
were electronic filing systems. A major bank had recently introduced a system for
counter entry of transaction data; this was deeply implicated in major changes in
organizational structure. A proportion of local service industry—software production, data processing, and computerized business services—was directly involved in computing.

As more and more Sheffielders used supermarkets rather than corner shops,
they were increasingly likely to have their purchases checked by workers using
computer-based bar code readers; if they stopped for a meal at one of the fast food
restaurants, such as MacDonald's (by then the largest restaurant chain in Britain)
or Wimpy's, their purchases were calculated and recorded electronically. Although
the local newsagent may not yet have had his or her own microcomputer, chances
were that the large corporation that provided the inventory was keeping close control on that inventory by computer. Chemist shops (drugstores), music shops, and
stationers were very likely to have a stock of computer games available on cassette
tapes and disks; along with some shops that dealt exclusively with computer components and equipment, these catered to the extensive market in home computers.
(However, the number of businesses designed to serve this "lower end" of the
computer market had actually contracted in the early 1980s.)

Two major national government programs had aimed to make sure there was at
least one computer, and some educational software, in every school. Creative
teachers in first and middle schools used them to teach skills like writing, and
most secondary computer instruction revolved around simple programming in
BASIC. Computer literacy was a prominent component of the extensive range of
adult education courses available in the cities and towns of South Yorkshire. General awareness of computers was high, an outgrowth of visible programs to promote computerization sponsored by local and national governments as well as the
prominence given to computerization on television and in the national press. (The
*Guardian,* for example, continues to run a computer section every week.)

There were several other aspects of living in South Yorkshire for which computerization had significant, if less visible, effects. Major changes in the administration of the National Health Service (NHS) were intimately connected with new
management-oriented information systems; further changes, known as the
Fowler reforms, were introduced into the administration of social welfare programs in 1988. Designed and justified as cost-cutting measures, these changes

were met in the North of England by public anxiety about the availability of public services and a decline in the social wage.

Several of the major differences we observed between 1976 and 1986 in Sheffield had to do with the changed nature of the national state. Computers were an important part of these changes. For example, during the miners' strike of 1984 and 1985, the national police cordoned off major areas of Yorkshire and neighboring Nottinghamshire as "no go" areas, in order to impede miners' "flying pickets." This kind of state action would have been impossible without the communications capability provided by the national police computer. The miners were unable to win their demands through tactics that were, by and large, successful in the 1970s.

The failure of the miners' strike contributed substantially to the sense of a change in the fundamental power relations between labor and capital in the British social formation. The national state under Margaret Thatcher promoted change in basic cultural constructs, including notions of what it meant to be a person. For the Thatcherite, to know about computers was to promote an image of a Britain changing with the times, one distant from the anachronistic "traditional working class."

Much of what we have said about computerization in South Yorkshire could also be said about other regions of Britain at that time. What was distinctive about the Sheffield region was the extent to which people there had pushed for local policies to influence computing. These policies aimed to channel computerization into "socially useful production." That is, they aimed to promote computer uses that built on rather than replaced existing worker skills and local economic structures. In part as a consequence of strong worker education institutions, the policies encouraged "community computing" in opposition to "administrative computing."

### The Social and Historical Context

By 1986 computerization was deeply implicated in several important dimensions of the lives of working people in the Sheffield region: It not only was of material importance and perceived to be problematic but it had also become the focus of public policy. What features of the region led to this distinctive course with regard to computing? Were these features accessible to observation? To answer such questions satisfactorily, one must first grasp the social history of South Yorkshire.

Employment social formations like that in Sheffield create a social surplus through the production and sale of commodities. England is generally acknowledged by social historians to be the place in which such social formations first came into existence.

The southern part of Yorkshire, about 200 miles north of London, had a central role in the development of employment society or the "Industrial Revolution." Each period since the Norman invasion has seen important commodity developments in the region, including the establishment of ironworks by religious orders in the Norman period; the development of the world's first commercially viable processes for steel making and silver plating; some of the earliest factories (the Arkwright mills) in the eighteenth century; the adoption of first the crucible method and then the world's first commercial Bessemer converter for mass steel production in the eighteenth and nineteenth centuries; and, in the twentieth, the expansion of the Yorkshire coalfield, still the largest in Britain. By the fourteenth century, Sheffield metalworking already had a national market—Chaucer refers to a "Sheffield thwittle," a small knife, in the *Canterbury Tales*. In the eighteenth century, Sheffield metal goods began to be traded in bulk around the world; by the end of the nineteenth century, according to local folklore, approximately half of Europe's steel production was concentrated in the Lower Don Valley of South Yorkshire. Metalworking and coal mining were still the main forms of material production in the South Yorkshire region during the 1970s, and Sheffield, a city of approximately 500,000 people, still enjoyed an international reputation as the world's premier producer of cutlery.

In the 1970s the Sheffield region was strongly identified with heavy industry. The rest of the South Yorkshire region was equally "heavy," with steel making in Rotherham and coal mining in the Barnsley and Doncaster areas. Secure in a manufacturing identity, Sheffielders frequently referred to their region (inaccurately, but deliberately) as "the dirty picture in the golden frame." They repeated the Yorkshire saying, "Where there's muck, there's brass" (that is, where there's dirty, heavy industry, there's money to be made). Social images of the region constantly reflected this vision of heavy technology. Train drivers whom David accompanied on a tour of Parliament in 1976 referred to London as "a different world" and to the North around Sheffield as "the workers' capital." For them, life in Sheffield prefigured life in a Britain where the whole society was being run by, or at least for, the working class.

## Working-Class Culture

There are several reasons for using the label "working-class culture" to refer to the distinctive way of life experienced by the bulk of the Sheffield population in the 1970s. Working-class people shared a common situation, since they depended on the job as the primary means of obtaining survival necessities. They shared a repertoire of collective and individual patterns of behavior for dealing with their situations. These patterns included self-identities, languages, and forms of organization as well as action. These are the patterns that E.P. Thompson had in mind when he described the English working class as being "present at its own creation" (1963:6), or what Pierre Bourdieu (1978) called a class habitus. To an uncommon degree, Sheffield workers created a culture based on class awareness.

In the 1970s the distinctively working-class aspects of Sheffield culture were perhaps most obvious in ordinary people's work—how they obtained shelter, food, clothing, energy, and health—and in other relations to their material environment. In the late nineteenth century, Liberal councilors had initiated one of the earliest programs for the construction of public housing. By the 1970s the local council provided more than half the city's housing stock (over 90,000 units), most of which had been built by public labor. During this time, the extensive public transport system was expanded and fares were cut. Workers used this system heavily, to travel to jobs in material production—steel, metalworking, and coal— and in service provision. A preponderance of these jobs, in manufacturing as well as service, were in the public sector, either in nationalized industries such as steel or in services, such as home helps or recreation work, managed primarily by the region's local states. Many working-class people shopped in municipal markets and at cooperative stores; gas and electricity, as well as water, were provided by public enterprises. Health needs were mostly taken care of within a national health service.

In short, the physical existence of many working-class people was heavily de-pendent on expanding local and national state provision. These material relations were closely paralleled by similarly organized social relationships. Sons sought work similar to their father's, and daughters placed emphasis on finding housing on the same "housing estate" as other family members. Nonfamily social relation-ships tended to cluster around work or housing estate living groups. Trade union branches, organized around either residence or work site, provided important so-cial connections. Leisure time was often spent at workingmen's clubs or at such worker-oriented seaside resorts as Skegness or Blackpool. Even amateur sports clubs tended to have a work site or neighborhood identity rather than, say, a school one.

The institutions of the local state had a substantial influence on the reproduc-tion of the identity of working-class people. Institutions, such as public council housing, met material needs and established an important basis for social rela-tionships. Such institutions often incorporated an explicit cultural construction of "the working class." The Sheffield Educational Authority (LEA) had been among the first in the nation to switch to a comprehensive model for secondary educa-tion, thus doing away with the invidious distinction between grammar (middle-class) and secondary modern (working-class) schools. This and other similar practices were justified as "giving the working class the culture it desires." An ex-tensive program of evening classes oriented toward working-class people was also provided by the LEA, the Workers' Educational Association, and the Sheffield University Department of Extramural Studies.

The symbols of working-class culture were actively reproduced through mili-tant trade unionism. In the 1970s the center of local working-class politics was the District Trades Council (DTC). In this organization, as in similar ones, the terrain of political debate was divided among several areas of thought, but all were working-class identified. On one side were supporters of the Labour Party in power, while on the other were critics of that party, generally from the left. Some of the latter were Labour Party members, but others had relocated to the workers' capital because of the "workerist" orientation of 1960s left political groups. DTC meetings were the ultimate forum for the extensive political debate that went on in the region's trade union branches, shop stewards' committees, and in various other class-identified political organizations, including the Sheffield District Communist Party.

In many respects, working-class culture was male oriented and male dominated. The District Trades Council, the local Labour Party, and the left political groups all were organized and run primarily by men. Union structures were heavily male dominated; even in unions in which the membership was largely female the full-time officials and leadership were primarily male. By the mid-1970s this male orientation was criticized by feminist groups that were pressing issues of particular concern to women—equal pay, child care, reproductive rights, and so on,

The primary presence in the electronic mass media was the state-run British Broadcasting Corporation (BBC). Local public artistic and other cultural institutions, such as Sheffield's Crucible Theatre, promoted programs designed to be of interest to a working-class audience. Extensive efforts to influence working-class people were made by various campaigning groups, such as the Campaign for Nuclear Disarmament (CND).

Research reporting on the region in this period (Hakken 1978, 1980, 1983) documents the impact of these activities on the reproduction of public material provision and social relationships. The working people we got to know in the mid-1970s acknowledged the importance of educational and cultural activities to the maintenance and extension of their life-styles. They recognized that discussion of such central symbols as "the working class" and "socialism" created the conditions for unified action and the continued viability of the dominant working-class social strategy, "Labourism" (Barratt Brown 1972). Even those critical of Labourism held it largely responsible for the creation and reproduction of the distinctive life-style of the region.

Sheffield holds a unique place politically as the leading workers' city. The initiatives described above (e.g., to promote forms of computerization that build on existing skills rather than replace them) are a recent manifestation of a tradition of class-oriented policy, what local Labour politician Tony Benn calls "the proud history of the working class in the city." This history includes substantial roles in the development of nineteenth-century craft unionism and municipal reform as well as the initiation of the British shop steward's movement during World War I. Shortly after the General Strike of 1926, Sheffield's became the first substantial British city government with a Labour majority; Labour has been in office almost continuously since then. In 1974 the new South Yorkshire Metropolitan County Council justified its policies—cheap fares on public transport, for example—as "socialism in action." South Yorkshire local governments have led in the innovative provision of public services, from the first council housing to the unique community-based services of the 1980s for people with severe disabilities. Even the skyline of the city is dominated by public structures, particularly the huge housing blocks built during the 1960s. Municipal markets for shopping, workingmen's clubs, rambling in nearby Derbyshire for leisure, Yorkshire dialect, and a developed Yorkshire "regional character"—all of these are elements of a distinct regional culture of which Sheffield workers are understandably proud.

## Class in Sheffield

Cultural self-awareness is something of a preoccupation in Britain. South Yorkshire has become a preferred location for journalistic descriptions of the underside of Thatcherism. An award-winning 1988 national television drama, Chris Mullin's "A Very British Coup," captures this sense of Sheffield as an "anticapital." In the film, the head of the British security state comments, "Those whom the Gods wish to destroy they first send to Sheffield."

Such associations are not always negative. The leader of Sheffield's Employment Committee described at length the difficulties she experienced within the Centre for Local Economic Strategies (CLES) when trying to develop a critical analysis of the Sheffield situation. Other left local governments held Sheffield in virtual reverence.Whether positively or negatively, Sheffield is identified nationally with the realities of class.

Class is manifest starkly in numerous aspects of social life in the city. On the west side is the affluent Hallam region, by demographic criteria the most uniformly middle-class parliamentary constituency in the country. Industry and council housing dominate areas to the east. It is culturally quite appropriate that the headquarters of the National Union of Mineworkers (NUM) was moved to Sheffield in preparation for the mid-1980s strike, and it is equally appropriate that the most important battle of that struggle took place at Orgreave in Sheffield.

During the 1970s, the painful policy choices made by the national Labour government, in the face of pressure from the International Monetary Fund, were experienced as an affront by the working-class movement of South Yorkshire. *How* to fight Labour-imposed cuts in public spending, not *whether* to do so, was the dominant topic of the District Trades Council debate. Miners spoke openly of their desire to "get the Tories back in so we can have another go at them and do them again like we did in '74," when a miners' strike contributed to Tory electoral defeats. Frustration with national Labour policy contributed to the sense of a need to develop a new politics.

### The Character of Working-Class Culture

In our recognition of the existence of a distinct working-class culture in 1970s Sheffield, we should be careful to stress that this culture was not dominant or "hegemonic" in Gramsci's (1971) term. Difficulties in the political economy were already being used to justify extensive cuts, as opposed to expansions, in national state provision. Labour politicians like Prime Minister James Callaghan were among those who loudly condemned the "excessive" influence of trade unions. Many of the working-class activists we met in the 1970s were skeptical about Labourism's long-term prospects. They doubted its ability to control the national state sufficiently to pursue a distinctively working-class and adequately independent, foreign and economic policy.

Nonetheless, orienting the South Yorkshire regional social formation to the working class seemed to be effective. The social relationships associated with this working-class culture even gave support to the generation of profit in the capitalist political economy. The extensive availability of publicly provided goods and services helped profit, for example, in that high wages were less necessary to the maintenance of a decent standard of living. Similarly, strong local communities mitigated against the centralization and suburbanization of consumption into nationally owned shops. This resulted in a large and relatively healthy small shop and "self-employed" economic sector. People often spoke with pride about "what the working class have been able to accomplish in Sheffield."[4] Although the discourse of class has been long recognized as an important feature of the British symbolic landscape, this discourse in 1970s South Yorkshire was particularly positive and strong: In the words of a plaque on the wall at "Labour's home," Wortley Hall in South Yorkshire: "Knowledge Is Power, and Knowledge in the Hands of Working Men and Women Is Power That Will Change the World."

Thus in South Yorkshire, class, culture, and technology had been forged together to an unusual degree, even for an industrial case. It follows that the nature of the relationship of technological to cultural change should be more easily grasped here than in a location where the relationship is historically more muted. The extensive new information technology outlined in the beginning of this chapter was introduced into the reproduction of this particular regional social formation. Is there culture change that might be related to the new technology?

### Culture Change in Sheffield: 1987

Substantial sociocultural change has taken place in Sheffield. The presence of change does not mean that computing is the cause of change. Still, as many informants remarked on their own, the lives we shared with Sheffielders in 1986 were very different from those we shared in the earlier period. Among the important changes for working people in this period in the region of South Yorkshire is the movement from low unemployment (less than 4 percent in 1976) to high unemployment (about 16 percent in 1986). These figures understate the actual difference; intervening changes in the way unemployment statistics were calculated reduced the figures substantially. Rising unemployment was related to a major contraction of the main manufacturing industries (steel, heavy engineering, cutlery and coal mining). These industries have contracted to perhaps one-quarter of their previous size in terms of employment.

Change affected people at every social level in the region. At a conference on "the growing divide" between social strata in contemporary Britain, one participant suggested that "there is no more local ruling class in Sheffield; there used to be industrialists, but they've all either closed up or sold out."

The decline in "traditional" industries has meant a relative increase in the importance of other economic sectors. One member of the Sheffield Rotary Club described the new social relations this way:

> Ten years ago, there was just one Rotary in Sheffield, and its members were the commercial elite. This was a very small group. Wherever you were, at a party or whatever, you knew everybody there, because there just wasn't that much commerce—in Sheffield, you were either an industrialist or a worker. Now there are five Rotary Clubs; commerce and the service industries in general have taken off.

The decline of manufacturing, the growth of service, and shifts in economic control meant great differences in employment patterns. These included a growth in the proportion of women looking for work and an increase in part-time labor. Whereas ten years before it was typical for young males to leave school at fifteen and to find an apprenticeship in a skilled manufacturing trade, in 1986 Sheffield was one of the most difficult places in Britain for a young person to find a job. These changes were linked to major strains in family life. The subsistence pattern of male waged employment and female domestic labor had been disrupted by the rapid arrival of substantial unemployment just as family dependence on female wages was increasing.

In political terms, there was a strong decline in the influence of the District Trades Council and an increase in the power of the Labour Party in local government; a turn to the left on the local Council was remarked upon frequently. The building of state-sector housing had ceased, and control of what existed was passing out of local/public hands, as was municipal transport. A large proportion of the holdings of public sector enterprises had been privatized.

Access to many benefits of the social wage contracted significantly under the Thatcher national government, the level of support also being cut. Cuts in the provision of social services were justified in terms of encouraging the private sector by increasing the incentive to find paid employment. Continuing low wages for those lucky enough to "be in employment," high unemployment, and fewer public services meant change and diversity in family patterns, including a substantial increase in the number of multigeneration and multiincome households. They also meant the increased dependence of families on female income, part-time employment, and public benefits, even though benefit levels had been cut. Over 40 percent of Sheffielders under twenty-five couldn't find work. Young males seldom thought of following their father's employment path because there wasn't a similar job to be had. Despite the high unemployment, young females were much more likely to assume that paid labor would be a regular part of their future.

The stable intra–working-class social patterns described as characteristic of the 1970s, patterns based on publicly supported subsistence and associated trade unionism and Labour Party membership, had been disrupted. Occupational status relationships and income levels were more changeable; job and geographic mobility increased. The various programs of the national Manpower Services Commission occupied substantial portions of most young people's lives, enough so that "being on YTS" (Youth Training Scheme) had become a recognized social status, an alternative to either "stopping at school" beyond the statutory leaving age or to having a job. Nonetheless, Labour votes continued to increase.

Social identities within the working class became differently, and perhaps more extensively, stratified. Youths were split into groups of "punks" and "trendies," that is, those with "no future" and those "pursuing a career," probably in the new service industries. This split among youth paralleled a new division among older people, between families "on the dole" and those with sufficient family members "in work." Like social services under Thatcher, working-class people's leisure became more privatized, increasingly channeled into television and "decorating" the home.

Even the ecology of public houses changed, with more pubs aiming for distinct social strata from a regionwide clientele, rather than the surrounding neighborhood. Trade unions attracted the active interest of fewer workers; activists, especially in the private sector, were fired with impunity, and worker organizations had less obvious impact on terms and conditions at particular work sites, let alone on the reproduction of the regional social formation. Trades Council meetings were less well attended and traveling political theater groups less present in community halls and miners' welfare clubs.

Patterns of semiotic reproduction were also altered. Leisure in workingmen's clubs and community centers, supplemented by occasional evening classes, allotments, pubs, bingo, rambles in Derbyshire, and visits to traditional seaside resorts, were all less popular than they once were. The particular institutions of worker education had lost influence nationally, although innovative programs continued in the Sheffield region. The students at the Women's Technology Training Workshop in Sheffield all stressed the profound changes they had experienced and perceived in men's and women's activity. None of the people we talked to were sanguine about such changes being easily incorporated into "traditional" working-class life. (Perhaps equally major changes involve a substantial increase in the proportion of non-"English," nonwhites in the South Yorkshire population. The minority population has expanded rapidly, including Yemenis, South Asians, Traveler/Gypsies, and Afro-Caribbeans.)[5]

In South Yorkshire, change in the reproduction of working-class culture was most vivid in pit villages—mining communities. South Yorkshire miners are still among the most militant of miners, who, in turn, have been among the most militant of British workers. For example, Yorkshire miners traveling around the country as flying pickets played an important role in the 1974 industrial actions. The miners and their perceived industrial strength were the key component of what is now called "traditional" working-class culture; in the 1970s it was merely called working-class culture.

Shortly after its election in 1979, the Thatcher government took several steps that enabled it to take a stronger path of resistance to miners than the one taken by the Heath government in 1974. The radical Thatcher government's winning of the miners' strike of 1984–1985 accomplished some of its important industrial relations and political objectives. In 1987 the influence of the National Union of Mineworkers was much reduced, partly as a consequence of the formation of a breakaway union in some of the coalfields where participation in the 1984–1985 strike was lower.

There were some results of the strike that appeared positive to those hoping for the retention of a viable working-class culture. One was the formation of the Women Against Pit Closures (WAPC) and the Miners' Wives Support Group, organizations that brought previously inactive women into political activity. Yet these movements, born of an effort to preserve pit communities that had traditionally been male identified and male dominated, also manifest the contradictions often associated with a developing feminism. In 1987 the remnants of these organizations were helping women to cope with massive changes in the pit community that were due to the acceleration of pit closures after the strike. Numerous coalfield communities were becoming like ghost towns as Coal Board houses were sold to estate agents and developers in London. A whole way of life, based on the solidarity of the pit village, was disappearing. The miners' failure to win the strike had a chilling effect on militancy in other sections of the working-class movement. It would be difficult to think of a more momentous event in the nations's history over the ten-year period.

## Summary

The selection of a field site for ethnography inevitably has an element of the arbitrary, particularly the way one decides to optimize the presence of desired phenomena, access to informants, degree of informant awareness, and so on. The particular factors that make Sheffield unique have a direct relationship to its value as a research site. By the mid-1980s, the Sheffield region had changed profoundly. Sheffield, a low unemployment, pleasant, if somewhat stodgy, "workers' capital" in the 1970s, by the mid-1980s had become a high unemployment, capital poor, physically transforming region. These changes took place within the context of the radical policy emanating from the national state of Margaret Thatcher.

Of course, these local changes also paralleled more general social and technological transformations taking place in the world. Yet, at least in part because of social history, people in Sheffield responded proactively to these changes, by developing policies to influence computerization. These unique conditions, plus our previous familiarity with the region, warranted its selection for an ethnographic study of computing and social change.

## Notes

1. However, one can't *argue for* the relevance of words and how experience is perceived while *assuming* their relevance, precisely the humanistic assumption underlying Chapter 1. To do so would be to presume the relevance of what we wish to demonstrate. We don't begin Chapter 2 with vignettes; instead, we argue more formally for the analytic relevance of listening to such talk and perceptions.

2. Extended fieldwork or "participant observation" was championed by B. Malinowski (e.g., 1932) as the essential method of British social anthropology; his argument was accepted in U.S. cultural anthropology as well. There is much variation in the way anthropologists implement ethnographic methodology, and even more variation among those non-anthropologists who attempt to use forms of it (e.g., sociologist Harold Garfinkel's "ethnomethodology"[1984]).

We feel it is important to state our differences with one notion of participant observation—the "semiotic" or semioticist ethnography of such anthropologists as Schneider (1968), Geertz (1973), and Sahlins (1976). For various reasons, these "culturalist" (in the lexicon of dialectical materialism, "abstract idealist") anthropologists equate ethnography with the study of emics, the shared perceptions/cultural constructs of their "people." In a trenchant critique of similar trends in radical feminism, also described by its proponents as ethnography/participant observation, Lynne Segal (1987) describes an equally one-sided attention to perceptions.

In our view, participant observation should not be conceived of as limited to the perceptual, interpretive aspects of human life. More holistic understandings of particular ethnographic contexts can be developed by paying attention to etic phenomena, such as people's actual behavior and the historically derived structures that constrain both behavior and perception. In short, a narrow culturalist interpretation of fieldwork is not the only possible one.

3. This holistic view of the nature of ethnography conflicts with the "literary" perspective fashionable in anthropology at the moment. Essentially an extension of the semioticist approach discussed in note 2, the literary view equates ethnography with narrative. Because of semiotic incommensurability, the ethnographer cannot really understand the experience of another people; epistemologically, all he or she can legitimately strive for is an effective reflexive moment, the construction of a narrative that reflects compellingly his or her own experience of the other.

We agree that anthropologists need to reflect more on the conditions under which anthropological knowledge is created, especially those things that influence their perceptions. To make this moment the sole focus of anthropology is a form of solipsism. We believe that cross-cultural understanding is difficult but not impossible. The ultimate goal of social science must be the development of the best possible understanding of general social process. This volume is our attempt to push ethnography as far in this direction as we can.

4. It is grammatical in British English to use a plural verb with a singular collective noun which in American English would be accompanied by a singular noun—for example, "what the working class *have* accomplished," versus "what the working class *has* accomplished."

This difference in usage may relate to a higher level of British comfort with the notion of individual autonomy within a collectivity. One of the major difficulties of doing field research in Britain for an American is the frequency with which one is forced to realize that because of such hidden differences in speech one often overestimates one's understanding. The "shared" language is often used differently. As a popular phrase expresses it, Britain and the United States are "two nations divided by a common language."

5. Although we deal somewhat with the relationship of computerization to the ethnic/racial dimension of the Sheffield experience—e.g., as with SADACA, one of the SPRITE community computing sites—attention to it was not a part of our systematic research design.

# 3

## The Methods Used to Study
## Computing in Sheffield

Implicitly, ethnographies ask the reader to accept the accuracy of at least the general description of the field situation and to believe that the field-worker is a credible witness. In this chapter we describe how we got the information we present in later sections, so that readers have information on which to base their own judgments as to the validity of our data and our reliability as researchers. In two vignettes, we present some of the problems with which we had to contend. We conclude the chapter with an explanation of the "action research" orientation that we adopted in the course of resolving such difficulties.[1]

### The Research Problem

The essential prerequisite of good ethnographic research is a strong *sense of problem*; without it, one cannot identify the kind of information one needs, whether any particular datum is relevant, or which of the myriad options for research are to be pursued. One manifestation of a good sense of problem is a clear problem statement: as precise an articulation as possible of the issue to be addressed.

A clear statement of the problem often only emerges after a sometimes difficult and long process of problem identification. Problem identification typically begins with an anomaly, something unusual in social life that attracts one's attention. Once identified as a potential research topic, this anomaly becomes the reference point of diffuse reading and attempts to express how the topic might be investigated rigorously. Consideration of the thoughts of other people relevant to the topic leads to restatement of the topic in the form of a question, then more talk, reading, and investigation, and so forth. If one goes back and forth among topics, possible methods of investigation, and various statements of the problem, one becomes increasingly able to state what is already known and to specify what is knowable, what part of this one wishes to know, and how one is most likely to find it out.[2]

The sense of problem that guided us in Sheffield had its roots in our 1970s research on new educational technology. We had become interested in computerized teaching machines and the associated notion of "teacher proof" materials while working for a U.S. new left political organization, the New University Conference. David's research interest in computerization was rekindled in the early 1980s while teaching a class in "computers and society" at the SUNY Institute of Technology in Utica, a medium-sized manufacturing town about 250 miles north of New York City. While reading through various texts on the subject, most of which were written by people with more knowledge of computer science than sociology, he was struck by the difference between the discussion they contained about computers and about society. Authors were very precise when discussing technological issues, but they were maddeningly imprecise when discussing social changes. Most presumed that social change was "brought about by technology," as if such a sociological proposition was self-evidently true.

After he had railed against such imprecision at some length in classes, students challenged David to show how technically good research on computerization could be done. He constructed a simple questionnaire for discussion with managers and workers in local work sites where computerization had taken place; he felt that as long as entrée to both sides was legitimated, studying "both sides" should increase the chances that good data could be collected without the effort involved in, for example, studies over a long period of time. His previous experience in studying work culture in New York's Upper Mohawk region and his activities as the Education Committee chairman of the Central New York Labor Council provided entrée to labor, whereas his position as a college professor gave entrée to management.

When David analyzed the results of initial interviews based on this approach, the picture of computing that emerged was more complex than he had anticipated. To his surprise, the results partly confirmed the visions of the computopians. For example, in some work sites, computerization was beneficial and relatively painless for both labor and management, especially when direct results were abstracted from those due to other causes, such as changing markets. Compputropian views were also partly supported: Computerization was clearly a disaster in some labor sites. Interestingly, the best predictor of the course of computerization was not the state of preexisting technology so much as the quality of the relations between workers and managers (Hakken 1986). Trying to make sense out of these results drove David to look elsewhere for ideas on computing. Eventually, he encountered the "computing studies" trend described in the Introduction, which prompted him to think about a more ambitious research project.

## Choosing an Alternative Ethnographic Site

During this period, we returned to Sheffield, visiting friends we had gotten to know during our previous stay. We had initially come to Sheffield in 1976 to observe the attempts of working-class people to influence and control their own culture. In 1983 several previous informants speculated that the obvious changes had to do with computerization. Although similar concerns about computerization were articulated occasionally in the Utica area, unlike Sheffield there was little interest in local policy to address them.

During this visit, Barbara was struck by the contradictory feelings associated with the increased number of women entering the labor market. The desires of these women did not fit easily with the "traditional" programs of the trade unions trying to recruit them nor the politicians who claimed to represent the working class. Some men felt that the issues of top priority to women—for example, for child care—were "diverting" the labor movement, and some women felt these issues were being ignored. If the labor movement was going to include them, it had to also put their needs on the priority list.

In Sheffield during 1985, David met with Computers for People (CfP), an organizational spin-off of the "Science for People" group in which he had been active ten years earlier. CfP had been organized originally to warn working-class people about the dangers of computerization. As their work developed, its members had found themselves involved more and more with helping working-class people find a way to have a positive and humane impact on computerization.

As we tried to talk our way through all these anomalies, we came to think of extending the Utica research to include a comparison with South Yorkshire, in order to sketch out main lines of variation. A comparison between the two regions made sense because of both the very different worker histories and the current profiles of working peoples' political activity, with much more activism in Sheffield. If the character of both computerization and social change is essentially the same in two such different regions, it would be more reasonable to speak of social change as being in some important sense *caused* by the technology. Conversely, substantial differences in the nature of either computerization or social change (or both) in the two regions would tend to suggest that the connection between computing and social change was less direct.

### The Research Design Developed

First, we wanted to design research that would extend computing studies by adding ethnography to its available methodologies. Our research would address the cultural dimension of computerization, the ways different social groups—for instance, men and women, workers and bosses—experienced computerization. We gradually developed another design goal, to bridge the frequently encountered gap between microlevel and macrolevel studies. Analyses of computing tended to be either detailed studies of particular work sites or aggregate studies, usually based on national or international statistics. The relationship between these levels is not clear. With regard to the employment implications of computing, for example, compputropians point to case studies of labor processes in which computerization leads to substantial job loss or deskilling. In contrast, computopians point to the growth of jobs in "the information sector" of the national economy.

We began to see that the study of computerization at the regional level might be an effective way to bridge such local to national gaps. One wishes to know not just whether some workers lose their jobs when the computers come, but what happens to these workers next? Do they enter the ranks of the long-term unemployed, or do they enter new "information sector" positions? Equally important, what happens to the households of such workers? Do displaced workers or other family members find jobs? Are deskilled jobs complemented by reskilled positions?

With the support of the State University of New York/United University Professionals Joint Labor/Management Committee on Professional Development, David was able to return to Sheffield for two weeks in 1985 in order to focus our field study proposals. The research design was narrowed to focus on the role of computerization in the reproduction of working-class culture as manifest in three areas: the labor process, working-class activism, and working-class symboling—that is, worker knowledge, self-identities, norms, and key symbols, and how these together fit into specifically working-class systems of meaning and categorization.[3]

### The Research Actually Executed in Sheffield

Fieldwork in Sheffield was completed between August 1986 and August 1987. In broad outline, the Sheffield research used participant observation techniques to gather information about the nature and extent of computerization in Sheffield, changes in the lives of working people over the last ten years, and the nature of the relationship between these two developments. Among the methods we used were case studies of work site computerization; extensive interviews with computer specialists, management, and workforce representatives, and program specialists with responsibility for computerization projects; participant observation in numerous projects and organizations oriented toward working people; and the review of statistical and analytic data already gathered by others. In approximately the middle of the field study, we decided to concentrate participant observation more narrowly on programs and projects oriented toward what we started calling culture-centered computing. Personal funds were used to extend the stay in Sheffield from the end of April through July, to support travel on the Continent to establish contact with other computerization scholars, and to explore potential future research sites.

In both the 1970s and the 1980s studies, the basic method of research was participant observation. During 1976–1977 we had pursued a two-track ethnographic research strategy. One track was the use of various techniques—interviews with practitioners, classroom ethnography, and participation as teaching staff—to develop a sense of the various forms of worker education. The second track was to use similar techniques to observe and, where possible, participate actively in trade union and other working-class activities, such as the District Trades Council's Trade Union Safety Committee and tenants' organizations.

During the 1986–1987 period, three somewhat different tracks were followed: execution of a number of case studies of work site and organizational computerization; interviews about and observation of the same kinds of working-class-oriented activities in which we had participated in the 1970s; and active participation in, as well as observation of, the various programs trying to support intelligent uses of computers.

## Developing a Social Role

An important goal of any ethnographer is to develop an "insider's" understanding of the cultural constructs used by informants. To do this, the ethnographer has to negotiate a social position that will allow appropriate access to the cultural system to be studied, some social role meaningful to one's "people." The choice is *which* role, not *whether* to chose one. Even if it isn't necessary to develop a full social role, ethnographers still need to develop a way to communicate their intentions to potential informants. Indeed, one must be able to do this quickly and easily, so that informants do not deny cooperation because it appears onerous, but it must be done accurately as well.

Though the ethnographer entering a gathering and hunting society can only gain entrée by inventing a new social role, one who studies in a "modern" city has perhaps the opposite problem. In Sheffield there were numerous roles into which we could "naturally" fit, but they tended to carry associations for informants that complicated research. For example, informants had preconceptions about the society from which we came; David's position as an associate professor from a U.S. state university doing research carried (inappropriate) "high status" implications for how people related to us and therefore for the information we were likely to get. Although "American professor" is a role whose characteristics are translatable into the English cultural frame, subtle differences in the content of the cultural categories meant miscommunication as often as easier communication. English mass media carry a great deal of information about the United States, and Sheffield informants were intensely curious about events in the States and often had detailed preformed notions about "Yanks" that got in the way.

In Sheffield we selected from the array of identities available locally. The vignettes that follow illustrate our strategy though which, as well as conditions within which, we constructed social identities. The first vignette communicates both how role construction leads to data and how it creates its own problems.

On a cold Saturday morning in late February 1987, David climbed the grand staircase of the Sheffield Town Hall. The town hall is a large sandstone building whose pillared facade is one of the few examples of city center Victorian architecture that survived the blitz in World War II. Ornate stairs, marble balustrades, and paneled walls reflect the sober self-importance of the local manufacturing elite whose marble busts line the stair and hallways.

In the 1970s working-class political meetings were likely to be held at the local branch of the Transport and General Worker's Union, but by 1986 the town hall had become the preferred location. The change of location was a reflection of the new local Labour Party leaders' desire to be seen as aggressively and publicly pursuing new policies.

David was at the town hall to attend the Inaugural Conference of the Yorkshire, Humberside, and North Derbyshire Region of the British Peace Assembly, a new affiliate of the World Peace Council. As he walked into the ballroom's foyer, David tried to "suss out" or identify the political coloration of the meeting. We had found out about it only the day before and were not clear about where it fit into the Sheffield political ecology. The assembly was being sponsored by a number of trade union groups but did not seem to involve the Campaign for Nuclear Disarmament or other "single issue" peace-oriented groups.

The foyer was lined with long tables, about half of them covered with books and pamphlets, some from trade unions, a bit from the Labour Party, but the bulk reflected the range of views current in the British Communist Party (CP). Many of the trade union groups listed on the program as sponsoring the meeting included active CP members whom we knew. As we looked around the room, where about fifty people had already gathered, we saw several faces that were familiar from a local CP branch that David had addressed a few weeks before. Among them David noticed Ron, a middle-aged former shopkeeper who now ran an unemployed center. Ron was carrying an armload of copies of one CP publication, the *Morning Star*. This was significant data; at the previous meeting, David had not been able to identify the allegiance of the group—were they traditionalist, *Morning Star* readers, or did they side with the readers of the more "Eurocommunist" *Marxism Today?* The readers of this latter publication tended to be those in the party actively trying to develop distinctly new approaches to politics.

David's first impulse was to say hello to Ron, but to do so might mean that he became identified by others in the room as a *Morning Star* sympathizer; in the future, some might be less willing to talk to him. So instead, David struck up a conversation with Tony, an organizer for Sheffield Woodcraft Folk. "The Folk" are an organization for young people, begun early in the century by leftists who wanted an alternative to the militaristic Boy Scouts and Girl Guides. A brief conversation with Tony confirmed David's sense of a large CP presence, as well as his impression of Tony's politics: "While I don't identify meself personally with t'CP, I do support them, because they work hard for peace. I'll support any group that represents working people and works for peace."

David congratulated himself on being able to confirm his reading of the politics of the situation without becoming identified with any particular political faction. However, Ron shortly approached David, offering to sell him a copy of the *Morning Star*. Perhaps David's enthusiastic assent was a bit overdone, because Ron narrowed his eyes and remarked, "Ya know, I saw you at the Trades' Council meeting the other night, writin' feverishly. When you finish, you're going to have a powerful lot of information in them notebooks." David laughed, but as he looked for a place to sit in the ballroom, he wondered how to interpret the tone of suspicion in Ron's voice. Was Ron wary of David as an academic, part of the "talking classes" who never act? Was he just uncomfortable because David was a "foreigner"? Had David not been sufficiently "workerist" in his remarks to Ron's branch? David recognized that once again he was frustrated by the class and ideological typecasting that was so much a part of Sheffield politics.

David's ethnographic model of Sheffield working-class politics was about to receive another shock. Instead of a casually dressed Yorkshire trade unionist, an official in frock coat and white gloves intoned, "Hear Ye, Hear Ye, Be Upstanding for His Honor, the Lord mayor of Sheffield." Everyone in the room rose solemnly while the Mayor, dressed in a black business suit and carrying around his neck a heavy gold medallion (one slightly bigger than that worn by the president of the Sheffield Rotary Club), walked to the front of the room and faced forward. "You may be seated."

The mayor explained to the assembled group that, despite his great interest in peace and support for the new organization, he wouldn't be able to stay through the whole conference, since it conflicted with a Sheffield Wednesday football fixture (soccer match). He then introduced the meeting "chairman," a sturdy woman in her fifties. She described the meeting as a major event in turning the attention of the local labor movement to the cause of peace. The speeches, given by a Labour Party member of Parliament and an American professor, legitimated a somewhat formal, traditional CP approach to the peace issue, but David wondered if the form of the legitimacy weren't anachronistic, more relevant to the 1950s than the 1980s.

This vignette shows some of the "tactical" difficulties of managing one's "field identity" performance. It also communicates something about the relationship between the model of social process that the ethnographer develops and the way in which this model, as well as his or her personality, is constantly tested in action. Fieldwork often involves a long-term commitment to a relationship that is somewhat like a friendship, one in which dissembling can destroy the necessary trust. Earlier anthropology defined itself as the study of the imponderabilia of everyday life—what people did, where they went, what they ate, and so on. When one's topic moves toward matters with overt political implications, the chances increase that research relationships might turn sour. Our approach to this problem was to present ourselves as doing "action research," a more involved form of participant observation than is typical of traditional ethnography. The second vignette introduces both this approach and some of the problems with it.

We rushed into the bar at the Leadmill before the applause for the first group had faded completely. The Leadmill prides itself on being "the best attended Fringe Theatre outside London," and "the North's premiere Jazz Venue." Sponsored by the District Council, it was the major addition to the Sheffield cultural scene since our last field trip in 1976–1977. As we fought the crush to get a drink, we tried to decide which of the ten varieties of real ale "on offer" we should try. It was easier to decide what had been the best line in the antisexist satirical revue that had just been completed—the one about how "real men don't change their underwear." As we turned from the bar, trying not to spill our drinks, we faced Malcolm, someone we had known in the seventies. He looked at us, remarked disdainfully, "So you're back in Sheffield," and walked away.

We talked later about the time ten years earlier when Malcolm and some others from a worker education group were in our sitting room. We were all very uncomfortable that evening, as Malcolm slowly revealed what was on his mind. Initially, he had worked enthusiastically with us on several projects. Later, he had grown distrustful of our showing up in Sheffield, a place where it was unusual for Americans to come. We had gotten to know so many people so quickly, but we didn't seem to fit into any particular political location. Finally, one day he had been reading the paper about the deportation from Britain of an American, Phillip Agee. A former CIA agent who had written a book about covert activity, Agee was being forced to leave Britain at the request of the United States. It had struck Malcolm that if the CIA was powerful enough to get a Labour government to deport a well-known but politically embarrassing author, it had surely occurred to them that someone posing as an anthropologist could infiltrate the British left in a northern city and obtain useful information. Having articulated this suspicion to himself, he had chosen to confront us with it.

What was uppermost in our minds ten years earlier was how vulnerable our research was, a vulnerability that we tended to see primarily in political terms. Ten years later at the Leadmill, we saw more clearly that the distrust had social as well as political sources: Because as "political Yanks" we couldn't easily be fit into the complex set of social relations the English call the class system, our very existence was "an acute and unseemly embarrassment," as they say in the House of Commons.

The personal problems that can arise when negotiating a field identity are particularly acute in the more active, even activist, forms of participation that we chose to take on. Not only do we ask people to accept the legitimacy of anthropology and us as field-workers but we also ask them to accept us as political people, at least in a broad sense. As the vignettes further suggest, our very success became grounds for suspicion.

As in any research, there are reasons to be concerned about "Hawthorne Effect" problems, including the creation of situations in which the researchers become the focus of attention. At least for a time, this happened in the second vignette; we had indeed had an effect on the behavior that we wished to observe. Like many—perhaps most—anthropological colleagues, we managed to complete the project by persevering in the face of such difficulties. The vignette also indicates that the form our participation took had certain unique characteristics, grounded in how we responded to the previous experience.

## The 1970s: Research on Workers' Education

Though Sheffield working-class people are quite warm and friendly, it is not easy for an outsider to enter their organizations and networks. As Americans, and as individuals with means of support but doing no obvious labor, it was almost inevitable that we would be treated as "middle class" when we arrived in Sheffield in the 1970s. One of the most important mechanisms available to English people to influence others' perceptions of them is their use of subtly different class and regional accents. Although Barbara in particular possessed detailed knowledge of these processes from her reading of English literature, it is not at all easy to translate this into practice; we were as individuals quite inept at the speech "fencing" that went on between people as they attempted to manage others' impressions of them.[4] Moreover, as suggested by our first vignette, working-class activists for a long time have had to deal with those perceived as outsiders who wish to influence their movements, and they have developed an extensive array of social mechanisms by which they screen out those privileged by education or class who attempt to enter and influence their organizations and activities.

In this situation, our only hope of gaining the "insider's" view that every ethnographer aims for was to locate opportunities to practice our politics and thereby show that trusting us was warranted. The role that made research acceptable to and therefore possible with working-class people was that of "worker educator." The institutions of worker education provided a point of social entry for outsiders, whatever their class, into the working-class community through an institutionalized demonstration of an understanding of and concern for the situation of working-class people. Because of its subordinate position, working-class culture must be actively recreated in order to be reproduced. Cultural activists are necessary; therefore, potentially helpful outsiders are tolerated, especially those who demonstrate that they deserve to be taken seriously because of the quality of their understanding. To be effective, educator/activists must have a fairly useful model of the forces affecting those whom they would teach or organize. (It was also of not inconsiderable benefit that both the educator and activist roles require development of models of social process similar to those that are the objective of ethnography.)

In addition to doing worker education, we became as actively involved as possible in the organizations we wished to observe. Initially, we established working relationships through political as much as scholarly contacts. Among other things, this meant we, too, put forward our own ideas about "what is to be done." We doubt that our personal projects had much impact on the working-class movement in South Yorkshire; like anthropologists everywhere, we learned that a slightly bemused toleration was enough. On the whole, however, our research was taken seriously because we took others' causes seriously.

## The 1980s: Action Research in Computing Studies

In the field again in 1986, we described our activity as "action research on new information technology" (NIT). The latter was a term used to refer to a broad range of activities in which computing was involved, including telecommunication and administration, as well as computing itself; it corresponds roughly to the broad range of computer-based activities that the computerization literature implicated in social change.

"Action research" was a good label for what we were doing. A term frequently used by Sheffielders, it refers both to social science research that locates itself self-consciously within ongoing social process and to research directed to meeting the immediate needs of organizations. This in both its referents corresponds to what we were trying to do: relevant research on a topic of contemporary importance, research on a scientifically conceived object that both explores peoples' lived experience and is helpful to them. As participants in 1960s social movements, we had come to be suspicious of many claims of so-called scientific objectivity, especially those based on "neutrality." We had by and large accepted the critique that the pose "scientist as neutral observer" often masked unexamined presumptions favorable to the preservation of the class, race, and gender privilege of the researcher. Many of our friends and informants shared this view in the 1970s, and they still felt this way in the 1980s.

This meant that we had both to demonstrate the quality of our research design and to show how our research, or at least our presence, was actually of use to those whose cooperation we desired. People like Ron and Malcolm came to tolerate us, whatever their personal feelings, because they recognized that their movements were, at least to some extent, dependent on the involvement of people like us, as long as we knew our place. Besides, they had their own problems finding a place "in t'new working-class movement." Indeed, our difficulties should not be overdramatized. For example, as "political Yanks" we were able to draw on the strong, if not always reliable, commitment to internationalism on the British left. Perhaps equally important was the interest of British political activists in the social workings of our home country, although we sometimes felt more like informants than researchers when quizzed at length about "life in the States."

In any case, we found it both necessary and helpful to present ourseves as what we were: political activists attempting to do research of potential value to an international movement comprised of working-class people, women, antiracists, and other progressives. It was as "activist action researchers" that we gained the rapport that enabled us to do the project.

In the 1980s we were essentially able to reenter roles similar to those occupied previously. Of course, our contacts had gotten older and the political scene had changed greatly. One consequence of the political discouragement was that political disagreement seemed to be nastier than in the 1970s, but, with a few exceptions, we were able to establish the contacts, study the work processes, and participate in the activities that we desired to study. Indeed, a main difference in the 1980s was a greater appreciation of what good research could contribute to deciding "what is to be done."

## Summary

On the face of it, the dialectic of field research is not particularly complex. Once in the field, one searches out ways to observe and participate in activities that theory suggests are likely to be relevant to the problem to be investigated. On the basis of such experience, one develops mental models of relevant cultural structures and processes. Models of discrete activities are then related to each other in a search for more generally encompassing models. Through further participation, one tests the validity of these more general models, and so on. The methodological assumption underlying this dialectic is the idea that, given sufficient time, intelligent field-workers will be able to identify those aspects of their models that are valid and abandon those that are not. Once they have left the field, colleagues' critiques supplement informants' responses.

The particular problem that we attempted to study and the conditions of our work in Sheffield meant that our understandings were subject to an additional test, what Marxists used to refer to as "the course of history." In the course of our research we were driven to search out ways to apply our understanding of the dynamics to affect the course of computerization. This desire to have an effect as well as to observe takes us to the edge of our roles as field-workers. To effect change meant we had to work closely with informants who themselves were already involved in change processes, what in the 1960s we used to call organizing. As Braverman argued (1974), organizers can be particularly good informants, because in order to be effective at inducing change they have to have more or less accurate models of the reproductive dynamics of the situation that they wish to alter.

We are of course aware that there are limitations that follow from being dependent on activism for access to the field. Our desire here has been to explain why we made these choices in our project rather than to argue that they were infallibly correct. Such judgments depend on the quality of the data actually collected.

## Notes

1. In the previous chapter's notes, we discussed some aspects of contemporary ethnography with which we disagree. As we illustrate in this chapter, however, we concur with the call for greater reflexivity in ethnography. We believe that a good way to avoid the mystification implicit in much social science research is to present as explicitly as possible the methodological assumptions that underpin a particular piece of research.

The activities described in this chapter were constrained in several ways. First, our research was conceived of as social science and therefore developed in terms of explicit conceptions of social process; here we illustrate how these social scientific constructs were translated into a research design. Second, choices forced on us by scarcity meant that we had to concentrate more exclusively on traditional ethnography than we had first intended. Third, we took additional steps to deal with the epistemological perils of field work on this topic in this place as well as with the reduced resources.

2. Without a strong sense of problem, the complexity of social process can engulf the ethnographer doing basic research in complex social formations. Such a sense allows one to separate, for example, what one really needs to know from closely related but distinct problems. Without a clear sense of problem, it is difficult to decide which methods to use; one is tempted merely to "collect data" passively or to slavishly follow the initial research design. In such moments, the ethnographer is particularly vulnerable to the "fetishism of method" so rightly criticized by C. Wright Mills (1959).

3. To gather information on computerization in these three areas we originally proposed five basic research activities:

1) a stratified set of some forty work site case studies of computerization, the data from which were to be transformed into computer models of work site changes;
2) collection and analysis of all available statistical data on computerization and social changes in the South Yorkshire region in the period between 1976 and 1986; these data were also to be computer modeled and compared/contrasted with work site models;
3) participant observation in several working-class organizations and networks;
4) an attitude/conceptualization study of a sample of working-class activists;
5) an "activity" or time budget study of two matched samples of working-class individuals; the only difference between the samples being that one group would use computers extensively and the other would not.

We argued that a staff of four and a budget of slightly over $92,000 were necessary to execute this project; David's field-planning trip had identified potential field staff. As it turns out, we were only able to obtain $25,000, so the project had to be scaled down.

4. In the 1970s, one of David's techniques for learning about the dynamics of class was to introduce two people he already knew but who didn't know each other. He then listened carefully to the changing inflections of speech as the two sought out mutually acceptable locations on the inverted accent-cum-class hierarchy of the British left.

# PART TWO

# Describing Computerization

# 4

# Computerization of Work

The factory makes extrahard tips for cutting tools used in mining. When we visited it in 1977 there were over 1,100 employees; in 1986 there were barely 100. Mike, the convener of trade unions at the works, pointed out the empty lot where the machining had been done.

We went to meet with the managing director, whom the workers refer to as "our Emelyn," after an effusive Sheffield footballer-turned-television personality. "Emelyn" was certainly upbeat about the impact of computers, which he portrayed as central to his positive view of the works' future. An established Yorkshire mineral mining firm had recently bought the works to secure their supply of specialized mining equipment, "to avoid being held for ransom" by dependence on outside economic forces. Cutting tools for other buyers are made here as well. (Mike pointed out, however, that the firm had not purchased the plant that makes the compounds out of which the tips are formed, an odd flaw in their plan.)

Our first stop on the production floor was the area where metal powders are sifted and mixed by hand. Paraffin is added to form the mixture into beads to avoid "packing" by subsequent machines. A woman—one of the few left in the plant—was running a machine that pressed the powder beads into the shape desired for a cutting blade.

In the plant's shop area, where the dies used to form the powder were produced, much of work was done on four or five computerized numerically controlled (CNC) lathes and milling machines. The goals of the shop foreman, who clearly controlled the work flow in his area, were to assign "his men" to jobs they could see through to completion, to give them an opportunity to work on a variety of machines, and to move workers from one area of the shop to another. Consequently, most knew how to operate all of the machines, as did he. One man was operating an electrolytic cutting machine that took a very long time to complete its task. This operator, responsible at the same time for a CNC lathe that could be programmed to do in a few minutes what a skilled operator could only do in several hours, was allowed to read while the machines ran.

In the large production area we visited next, tips were fired and then cut to give them the desired point. A number of high-speed, noncomputerized mass production machines were on the floor but not in use. Mike said that most of them were used at one point or another, but some for only a few hours per year. The most recent purchase, an automated finisher, which was being used for a nine-hour job, had only thirty hours of use since being purchased several months before.

Many of the older machines in the plant had been retrofitted with microprocessor sensors to provide digital measures of the work being done. The microprocessors, which compensate for the old, unreliable manual settings, extend machine life. Mike disparagingly described another man's task, the making of a "button," as unskilled, "throw-away" work. As often as three times per piece, the operator had to stop to measure with a micrometer the accuracy of what was being done. Unlike most of the others in the plant, these operators were paid by the piece; their machines had no digitized microprocessors.

Computer technology was clearly an aid in the production process, but was not the "revolution" we had been led to expect by "Emelyn's" comments. Mike expressed sympathy with the manager's dilemma, which he attributed to "outside" factors—such as "the consumer being in the ascendancy," "the poor economy," and "the government's anti-industry position." Although he described a number of "management cockups," the combined effect was "to shove people in manufacturing industry to the wall." To survive, the company had to be ready to serve 2,000 customers, each of whom demanded an increasingly more customized product at a lower price.

Mike also talked prescriptively: "The whole infrastructure of manufacturing industry needs to be revitalized. What [Neil] Kinnock [leader of the Labour Party] does not talk about in his speeches is the need to put money into manufacturing. He talks about creating jobs, but those jobs are in the service sector. What manufacturing needs is low cost loans to buy new machinery. Even though the new system might replace one which had employed fifty workers before, it would still save twenty-five jobs.

"At many times in the past ten years, I've been frightened by the new technology, but not now. If it's used properly, it can save works like these and protect jobs. If it's not used properly, this is usually because of bad management, which anyroad [in any case] would probably destroy the firm."

Mike, "Emelyn," and the other people who work in this plant have experience with a variety of computer-based new technologies. The capacities (and lack thereof) of computer-based equipment are relevant to what happens in this plant, but so are the characteristics of previous equipment and patterns of work organization. Employees' experience of computing is mediated by several other social relationships as well—the character of markets, the "ownership of physical means of production," the strategic actions and mutual assessments of management and labor, and the history of their interactions.

In the vignette, we see numerous, often contradictory correlates of computerization. In some cases, computers mean an increase in the skill range of workers, and microprocessors have extended the useful age of machines. In other instances, production is sped up through use of piece rates, and the purchase of new information technology is avoided. Finally, computing is associated with a disproportionate decline in the number of female employees. At a general level, the computerization evident on the shop floor in this works is important but not massive, replacing or supporting individual machines rather than radically transforming production.

## How Should Computerization Be Described?

The complexity of the phenomenon of computerization is not merely a function of the developed nature of computing technology; it is a characteristic of how humans everywhere experience their reality. Humans' reality is not experienced directly and independently; it is mediated by the dynamics of social formation reproduction. Working-class people in the Sheffield region do not experience computerization solely as a material technology but *within* the social relationships and *through* the semiotic categories that mediate many other activities.

The vignette is an example of how computerization is experienced in a subsistence workplace, a place where people make equipment for coal, an important source of energy. The contradictory effects of computer technology in the works—as likely to reinforce older patterns as to impose new ones—are fairly typical of computerization in South Yorkshire. In the works described, people are also laboring for a wage, but this clearly cannot be necessary to qualify as "work" in an anthropological sense. People's subsistence (work) experience is computerized in other sites, too—in their homes, in organizations and shops, and in their relations with the state. And, in regard to these other subsistence "moments"—that is, similar instances abstracted for analysis from the flow of life—just how do we decide how much attention they deserve? Moreover, people experience computerization in a more totalizing way, not just as the sum of discrete experiences. How can we insure that appropriate attention is given to the cumulating aspects of computerization?

An ethnography of computerization—a picture of people "being computerized"—must aim to communicate this complexity. The descriptive strategy cannot be simply a matter of listing how many computers there are or which work processes have them. We must employ a sophisticated strategy for describing computing if we are to achieve our ultimate goal: to assess the extent to which computers cause social change or, conversely, the extent to which computers' impacts are determined by the broader social reproduction dynamics within which computerization takes place. To enable this assessment, we need a discourse that communicates about both the technology and its social contexts without prejudging the causal importance of either.

Ultimate answers to these questions depend on developing a satisfactory theory of computerization. Our descriptive strategy is to separate out three distinguishable aspects of computing, to "deconstruct" this phenomenon in a way that makes it more comprehensible. The discourse that follows is unorthodox for computing studies, but it begins where anthropologists regularly begin—with a people's material relations to their environment. Humans, like other life forms, must find an adequate adaptation to their environment if they are to survive. Consequently, we focus in this chapter on *computing in primary productive activities, or "work"*—that is, the way computers mediate the basic subsistence patterns on which Sheffielders physically depend.

In the next chapter we will focus on the role of computers in those activities that have to do most directly with the creation and dissolution of the central social relationships within which humans in such social formations experience their lives. We go on in Chapter 6 to discuss *computers and symboling,* activities with which computerization is most directly implicated in the reproduction of semiotics.[1]

## Computers in Primary Productive Activity

"Work" or primary productive activity includes the things done by groups of humans to provide themselves and others with the physical means for day-to-day reproduction—food, shelter, clothing, energy, and well-being. "Day-to-day reproduction" contrasts with longer term aspects of social formation reproduction, such as the reproduction of the species (still accomplished through sexual reproduction), the reproduction of the relationships among groups of people, or the general perpetuation of semiotic forms. These other aspects of reproduction are of course important to general social formation reproduction; their relationship to computing is discussed in subsequent chapters.

Thinking of "work" as day-to-day reproduction gives us a clear starting point for the description of computerization. (It also avoids much of the confusion currently marring the discussion of work in social science [Hakken 1987a].[2]) After describing the forms of primary productive activity in South Yorkshire we will assess the patterns of computer technology integral to them. What emerges from the ethnography is an important difference in the pattern of public sector and private sector computerization.

### Food

Most of the food eaten by Sheffielders is produced for markets within large institutions, such as the international agribusinesses, which provide most fresh fruits and vegetables. The topographic and climatic premises of modern food production technology mean that most food is grown far from where it is consumed.

The home gardens and allotments—small gardens on "surplus" land scattered about the urban and rural landscapes—are of course an exception, but what they produce constitutes only a small portion of total caloric intake.[3]

Food is normally procured at small neighborhood butchers, greengrocers, and so on, or it is purchased at the large supermarkets, which have spread recently across the city, or at the large municipal markets downtown, where stalls are rented to shopkeepers. Cooking takes place largely in the domestic sphere. With the exception of their continuing patronage of the numerous fish and chips shops and public houses with their "snacks" and "pub lunches," people in South Yorkshire buy less food in restaurants than people elsewhere in England and certainly less than people do in the United States.

In 1986 food activities—growth, initial preparation, transport, procurement, and cooking—were only slightly to moderately mediated by computer technology. In agribusinesses, computers were an increasing presence in planning and record keeping, but not so much in the physical acts of actual production. Computerization may have accelerated the relative advantage of producing food elsewhere, but the dependence of Yorkshire on other regions for food has a very long history.

In the region itself, there were really only a few physically present forms of computerization relevant to food. For example, in a local meat pie production facility, the only use of computers was for office work. Also, the large regional food wholesalers used computers to keep track of storage and distribution to retailers, a use particularly evident at "Macro," a cavernous building that is to the small shopkeeper what a supermarket is to the individual consumer. Another form was the computerized universal bar code readers that had appeared in one of the leading area supermarkets, Sainsbury's. There were also some greengrocers, off-licenses, and even some corner shops that had installed microcomputers to help keep track of stock and automate bookkeeping. The uptake here, as in other sectors of small business, had slowed considerably, probably due to the large number of small computers purchased but never successfully integrated into the labor process.

A few microprocessors had made it into individual kitchens, as in microwave ovens, but they had done little to transform cooking. Indeed, part of the increasingly health-conscious population preferred to cook in what is held to be the "natural" way, by using older technologies. The only growing arena of public food consumption was the "American" style fast-food franchises of the restaurant sector. MacDonald's had large new restaurants in the main up-market shopping precincts of Sheffield and Barnsley, where computerized point-of-sale cash machines were conspicuous.

### Shelter

In complex social formations, among the most obvious forms of social inequality are the differences in the social geography of people's domiciles. The social geography of Sheffield is extreme in its segregation of the affluent "middle-class" neighborhoods of the southwest and the "working-class" housing estates of the rest of the city. The southwest section is distinguished by a number of quite extraordinary examples of nineteenth-century suburban planned housing, built largely for the emerging steel and engineering factory owners and their functionaries. During the end of the century, the Liberal-controlled District (city) Council began experimenting with the construction of housing for working-class people; by 1976 roughly half of the people in a city of over 500,000 lived in council housing.

As a consequence of policies implemented by the Conservative national government, the building of council housing had virtually ceased by 1986. Something of a boomlet was evident in the construction of private single-family dwellings for the middle class. A small amount of more moderately priced housing was also under construction through housing associations, a not-for-profit form more or less acceptable to the Tory ideology of anticollectivism. The materials from which this new noncouncil housing continues to be built (basically brick and mortar), South Yorkshire's hilly geography, and its frequency of inclement weather inhibit the computerization of shelter building other than in general planning and inventory.

In the Sheffield District Council Housing Department, which administers those units still owned by the council, extensive computerization has taken place. For example, the decentralization of housing into numerous area offices was contingent on development of an accessible central data base. The computerization of housing was the occasion of a sharp confrontation between the District Council and its workforce. Indeed, this battle was the major crisis in local municipal socialism.

In addition to keeping track of tenancies, repairs, and housing benefits, computers were used by the Sheffield Council to coordinate the ambitious refurbishing program undertaken by the Council's Direct Works Department. Although it was one of the largest construction enterprises in the country, employing over three thousand people, this department was no longer allowed by the national government to build significant new housing. Finally, on at least a few of the council's housing estates, tenants' organizations had begun to develop computerized data bases on the housing stock and residents. The activity of these organizations, which have an important place in at least the ideology of popular mobilization within the Sheffield Council, is an example of culture-centered computing.

A final comment about the considerable energy put into home improvement: That there was increased attention to the domestic sphere was suggested by the numerous publications devoted to "improving the home," as well as a rapid growth of large U.S.-style "D.I.Y." (Do-It-Yourself) shops. Like the similar retail warehouses for purchasing furniture, these D.I.Y. shops depended on computers for stock control and, often, for delivery of goods to the consumer. These developments are a part of the privatization of social life promoted by various national government policies, such as the sale of council houses.

### Clothing

Working-class people in Sheffield have long produced some of their own clothing through weaving, sewing, and, especially, knitting at home. In the 1980s these domestic activities spilled over into the small commercial sector, as in the craft production of jumpers (sweaters) and even shoes. An apparently brisk business was done in the large number of secondhand clothing shops (many of which are run by charities like Oxfam) and at the weekly "unemployed market" in the city center. The "Trendies" and "Yuppies" of the southwest of the city purchased designer clothes in small shops. If not imported from Italy, these clothes were often made on commission in people's homes, a minor resurgence of the "putting out" of clothing production. This resurgence, as well as being due to the rise in Sheffield unemployment, may have had something to do with the brief period in the early 1980s when there was an attempt to reestablish London as a center of world fashion design. This small market for exotic designer clothes seemed to be one of the few remaining niches for the British clothing industry nationwide, never a large part of the South Yorkshire economy.

Most clothing was purchased ready-to-wear in the large chain shops and department stores in the city center. In a year of traveling around Britain, we were struck by the extent to which consumer choice had become standardized, with the same shops dominant in virtually every city of any size. This process seemed to have accelerated rapidly in the last ten years and was reflected in the growing importance of retail distribution companies in the "league table" of profitable corporations. These large stores, like the supermarkets, were becoming increasingly computerized in terms of stock control and cash management. Perhaps the apotheosis of this process was the establishment of the Sheffield "Benetton" shop, part of the worldwide chain. As in all the shops in the chain, computers were used to keep strict control over marketing as well as stock. Though there was increasing use of computers in clothing design and some computerization of certain functions, such as cutting with computer-directed lasers, the primary economic advantage enjoyed by such large firms is their international sourcing. This allows them to take advantage of cheap Third World labor. Thus, computer technology has played a role in the shift toward the dominance of the clothing marketplace by large firms.

## Energy

One of the most obvious features of employment social formations is their heavy dependence on nonliving forms of energy for well-being, food, and shelter, as well as on the production and sale of commodities. Of all of the forms of basic productive activity, it was with regard to energy that computerization had been most important in South Yorkshire. Computerization had spread gradually, somewhat passively, into various areas of power generation; computers made possible, for example, the operation of the kind of complex technology used in nuclear generation of electrical energy.

The crucial role of computerization in South Yorkshire energy, however, was in the extraction of raw materials. It is difficult to overemphasize the importance of the recent changes in the coal industry, or the role of computers in making these changes possible, to the lives of working-class people in South Yorkshire. The South Yorkshire coalfield is the largest in Britain; indeed, prior to the creation of South Yorkshire County Council in 1974, "South Yorkshire" was a phrase only heard in relation to the coalfield and the miners, whose perceived industrial strength was an essential component of the regional working-class culture.

In a confidential memo circulated within management in 1973, member of the National Coal Board Wilfred Miron analyzed the problems of the coal industry as basically political. He specifically cited the influence of leftists, committed to "overthrow of the present 'system'" within the National Union of Mineworkers (Miron 1973:1). Miron argued that this influence was too heavily entrenched ever to be eliminated within the miners' union and that, therefore, the only way to solve the industry's problems was to reduce radically its dependence on human labor power. The way to accomplish this, according to Miron, was through the implementation of computer-based mining technology. Much experimentation with computerized mining had taken place in the industry in the 1960s, but computerized mining had been abandoned as impractical. In spite of this, Miron urged that the new technology be implemented whatever the cost in order to solve the industry's problems.

In 1979 a Conservative national government came to power on a manifesto that argued similarly that union power was a primary cause of the economic and social problems of Britain. The new government made extensive preparations for a confrontation with the miners: They converted a number of electrical power stations to gas or oil from coal; ran up coal stocks at those stations still requiring coal; switched coal transport from British Rail to road transport, which was at that time being privatized; and developed a national police information technology network. The new government, as Miron advocated, directed the National Coal Board to implement computerized mining technology very rapidly. Through the use of essentially the same premicrocomputer, Direct Numerical Control (DNC) technology that had once been abandoned, the new mining systems centralized information in management hands. In 1984, after five years of preparation, an accelerated program of pit closures was announced, in certain knowledge that this would provoke a coal strike. The ensuing strike, described as the bitterest industrial relations conflict in the postwar era, lasted over a year, but the miners went back to work without winning any of their pit closure demands. Since the strike ended numerous pits have been closed, the labor force has been drastically cut, and even more DNC computerization has been introduced.

In 1986 National Union of Mineworkers staffers argued that it might have been possible to maintain unity and win the strike had the focus been more on technology as opposed strictly to pit closures. They cited the fact that technology-related issues of work practice and organization, such as the six-day working week that the National Coal Board argues is necessary for economic operation of the new information technology-based pits, continued to be the focus of industrial conflict. At pit level, disruption continued, especially over introduction of the new technology, in both NUM and non-NUM areas. Still, the political and economic influence of the NUM was much reduced, partly as a consequence of the formation of a breakaway union in some of the coalfields, such as neighboring Nottinghamshire, which did not participate as actively in the strike. Militancy had also declined in other working-class organizations, and numerous coalfield communities were becoming like ghost towns as council housing was sold to London speculators.

It would be difficult to think of an event with more momentous implications for the reproduction of working-class culture in South Yorkshire than the coal strike. Prior to the strike, the NUM had moved its national headquarters from London to Sheffield, and it is culturally appropriate that the most important battle of the strike took place at Orgreave in Sheffield. What we have tried to indicate here is the particular role of new information technology (or NIT) in these events. On the one hand, the role is central, in that the transformations in production sought by management could not have been attained without NIT. On the other hand, the specific role taken by the technology was much more a consequence of political objectives than of any internally dictated technological imperative. If we wish to understand the role of NIT, then we must look beyond the narrow scope within which technology is usually considered.

Harry Scarborough's account of NIT developments at British Leyland, a national state enterprise that experienced a "shakedown" comparable to the Coal Board, reaches similar conclusions: "Although new technology was per se far from being the primary instrument in the reshaping of work practices—this being performed by the Draft [Industrial Relations] Agreement—it certainly played a useful role in both promulgating and legitimating the re-structuring of production and in the process unsettling even the most secure union job controls" (1986:113).

Thus, although it is true that NIT has no internally dictated dynamic, we cannot treat it as simply neutral in its implementation. This is because NIT is always implemented within social situations with preexisting human dynamics and because it is implemented to accomplish particular goals. In 1987 NIT provoked continuing resistance among workers in mining in spite of the weakened condition of the union.

The events in the coalfield demonstrate that the implemented form of technology is not politically neutral. A 1984 report (Best) emphasizes continuing difficulties with the computer-based British mining technology. The report traces several production problems to the extreme centralization of information control, unlike the systems adopted in Germany. There, union bargaining over technology led to more productive computer-based systems in which information is generally fed to production workers rather than to managers. For all of these reasons, it appears that centralization is less a consequence of technological imperatives than of industrial relations considerations. The fact that both the National Coal Board and

British Leyland were state enterprises when NIT was introduced in these ways suggests that political considerations are particularly pertinent in public sector computerization of work.

### Well-Being

Humans' ability to engage in most activity depends on being well, having a positive physical state as a life form. To a great extent, wellness is a function of access to food, clothing, shelter, and energy, but it is also a result of how well a culture heals the sick and avoids degrading its ecology. Within health anthropology, it is argued that a population's health status is a good indicator of the quality of ecological adaptation or social reproduction.

The development of social formations based on employment institutions has meant great wealth for humans as a group, but it has also meant increased health vulnerability for direct producers. The vulnerability is due in part to the more powerful and therefore more dangerous processes and forces of production integrated into larger-scale production and a detailed division of labor. Health vulnerability is increased by wide fluctuations in income from employment, which hampers the ability of individuals to deal with threats to their well-being.

In employment societies, promotion of health tends to become institutionalized. In Britain, wellness is promoted in part through the welfare state, a complex array of means tested and entitlement programs and directly provided services. Some of these are administered locally, but almost all access is monitored by national bureaucracies such as the Department of Health and Social Services (DHSS).

Within the Sheffield Council, rapid spread of computerization in social services was put forward as an important component of the new municipal socialism program adopted in 1980. The idea was to use NIT as a means to insure that each individual received maximum information on all the benefits to which they were entitled. By 1986, however, only limited record-keeping functions in the provision of cash benefits and the administration of services had been computerized. At least in part because of the difficulties over new technology in the Council Housing Department, computerization of client records had made little progress, for example, in the Department of Family and Community Services. The development of a councilwide public access integrated benefits system remained a distant goal.

On the national level, recent legislation had resulted in both massive change in DHSS procedures and a marked increase in computerization. Staff discretion in benefit administration was greatly reduced. Critics of these changes pointed out that they also reduced the number of individuals eligible for benefits. Government ministers countered that simplification of procedures, which would substantially reduce operating staff requirements, was required by computerization. Since the same ministers also argued that computerization could allow more manipulation of greater amounts of data in other areas, this justification struck us as disingenuous.

Interestingly, experience up to 1987 suggested that no substantial staff savings had yet occurred. The more rigid procedures apparently meant that staff time had been shifted to dealing with a mountain of appeals, admittedly aggravated by the increasing complexity of welfare problems that follow from high levels of long-term unemployment.

Social formations based on employment and profit have a tendency to place more emphasis on after-the-fact curative rather than preventative approaches to health. The primary curing institution in Britain is the National Health Service, or NHS. One of the two major forms of computerization within the NHS in South Yorkshire was the purchase of computer-based acute care medical machinery. Given the government's predilection for virtually steady state funding and the promotion of private health insurance, this "high-tech" orientation was one factor contributing to the decreasing availability of "before-the-fact" primary health care. The other major role of computers in health care was administrative, a major change in work organization implemented as part of the Griffith's management revisions. These revisions replaced a system of collective regional responsibility with a line management system. To implement Griffith's, management information systems (MISs) multiplied. These systems primarily provide data, such as labor force and throughput numbers, for management concerns in the narrow sense.

Local pressure in Sheffield had sped implementation of at least one nonmanagement, prevention-oriented computerization system, however. This system used available information to remind women to have periodic cervical cancer tests. This and other interesting pilot projects outside of Griffith's were implemented in a manner that contrasted with the centralizing forms of computerization noted above. Another project promoted the use of computers by general practitioners (family doctors), both to increase the effectiveness and profitability of practice management and to promote a more preventative approach. Of even greater potential interest was a council campaign to help eliminate major geographic inequities in health outcomes. Cross-referencing health and census data bases led to the identification of inequities in health outcomes, and this knowledge was used to encourage redistribution of services to the areas of the city where they were most needed. Despite these interesting counterexamples, wellness computerization to 1987 was oriented more to administrative goals than to direct promotion of health.

## Summary

By 1986 computerization of basic productive activity or "work" in South Yorkshire was clearly extensive, but the pattern of computerization was uneven. There was an important and unanticipated difference between the course of computerization in private and state institutions, and there were some differences when it was implemented by the national state as opposed to the local state.

In predominantly private sector activities—such as food provision, the making of mining machinery, and new housing construction—computerization was ancillary, introduced primarily for separable tasks like accounting or for a particular productive task. By and large, computers had here been fit into existing patterns, perhaps moderately accelerating trends already present, like centralization or labor reduction, but not altering the general character of basic production itself.

In contrast, computerization had been much more extensive and had been associated with greater degrees of transformation in primary production mediated by the state. In mining, computerization was essential to government policy. In aiming to reduce drastically both the numbers and the scope of discretion of humans in the labor process, British mining computerization transformed the nature of production. This transformation had profound effects on local communities and a major impact on the contours of British industry and social life in general. Although the results were less visible than in mining, computerization was important in national health care and social service delivery initiatives.

It was also in these public sector mediated primary productive activities that worker resistance to new technology was most manifest. Computerization provoked worker action in the local state, as in the Sheffield housing strike, although it can be argued that computer technology was more the occasion than the fundamental cause of such action. More frequently, the local state in South Yorkshire tried to project different notions of appropriate policy in its uses of NIT, as in the project on health inequity described briefly above.

In sum, it would appear that in primary productive activity there is a close relationship between politics and the extent and correlates of computerization. Politics is a more important determinant of the course of computerization than the "computerizability" of an activity from a purely physical or technical point of view. This conclusion about the nature of computerization in basic productive activity prefigures a more general conclusion, that computerization has more to do with human than with machine priorities. In the following two chapters, we describe similar computerization patterns in other moments of life in South Yorkshire.

### Notes

1. The basic justification for such an anthropological descriptive structure is comparative: This framework can be used to structure discussion of any cultural practice in any social formation. Structuring description in this way reduces the inadvertent use of ethnocentric concepts in subsequent analyses.

2. Such nonanthropological definitions of work often manifest one of two problems. The first is a tendency to equate production with human activity in general, which by definition rules out the assignment of any causal priority to human's characteristics as a life form. The second is a tendency to confuse "work" with activities that result in an income, an approach that minimizes the possibility of cross-cultural comparisons of work as well as

unfairly downgrades work done in the domestic spheres and in the community within employment-based social formations.

3. Allotments are of increasing importance for the "labor-free," who are forced into increasing their involvement in the community and domestic productive spheres that supplement the industrial capitalist and small-scale "self-employment" sectors of regional basic production.

# 5

# Computing and Jobs

In this chapter we examine the connection between computing and the reproduction of the job, the predominant social relationship in Sheffield as in all other employment social formations. That computing changes jobs is a central notion in most arguments for the computerization hypothesis (that computing is responsible for fundamental social change). Adam Schaff (1982), for example, contends that computing will cause major psychological difficulties, because it will decrease both the number of jobs and the role of the job in the individual's life. Shoshona Zuboff (1988) argues that "informating" (computerizing) jobs is intrinsically positive.

If computing is transforming society, the characteristics of the new world should be prefigured in computered jobs. Although the jobs described in the following two vignettes are ostensibly quite different, there are underlying similarities. These similarities and differences provide an appropriate point at which to start an analysis of computing and jobs.

Mavis, a student at Sheffield's Women's Technology Training Workshop, is talking about her last job:

It was in one of those data agencies, you know, takes data in. The pay has finally gone up from a pound sixty an hour (in 1986, about $2.50, or two-thirds U.S. minimum wage) to two pound. That's basic, but to turn your bonus, you've got to get over 12,000 key strokes an hour. For every 1,000 more you get an extra fifteen pence! I know if you do numerics they like you to get between 12–13,000 key strokes an hour. Some of them who've been doing it for years can get up to 20,000 an hour, for eight hours a day. Fifteen minutes morning and afternoon break, half an hour for lunch, and you're at it all day! I did the job full time and part time, but I packed it in after four or five weeks. It's soul-destroying. It's all right if you're getting somewhere, but you don't.

And they expect a hell of a lot for what actually they give you. And the conditions are not what you would call perfect. They usually have the draftiest offices you can find, there's twenty women doing it, there's building going on at the same time, poor lighting, no facilities, especially for part-timers at night, and

66

twenty-one hours a week minimum that you've got to work. No sick pay, no nothing. No union rights because there isn't enough of you together, because they've got to have 75 percent or something. You're all right with the part-timers and unions, but the full timers don't want to know, because they'll be chucked out and they need the work. Eye strain, headaches,—it's not just that, it's boring. Bad backs and bad necks.

And then there's the blokes. One comes in on me during my break and treats me like I'm a typist, but I tell him, 'If you think I'm sitting here doing this for you for my ten minutes break you can chuck it.' And he slungers out—I think he went to work for Trent Regional Health Authority as a programmer, yet we can't get higher than the office manager as such. The bloke that operates the actual data programming won't allow women in; he says they're not good enough. But we're good enough to train the bloody blokes!

Mavis's job—entry of information from several organizations into a data base at a location that is physically separated from any of them—only makes economic sense because of computers. The conditions in which she works have much continuity with those of precomputer offices, especially those encountered by many women in manufacturing: gendering, poor physical conditions, the speed-up, encouragement of self-exploitation through piece rates, poor pay, antiunion environments, and so on. Several studies of computerized word processing pools (e.g., Glenn and Feldberg 1979) equate computerization of office work with proletarianization, arguing essentially that computerized jobs are simply a new territory in which old employment dynamics are manifest. The following vignette, though illustrating some similar dynamics, also suggests more about what might be new.

Albert, who was born in a pit village in South Yorkshire, had started work at the face of the coal seam deep underground. He then spent time on the Coal Board staff until he was blacklisted in the early 1970s because of his communist politics. While at the Coal Board, he wrote a program to automate coal pricing; he speaks highly of the boss who gave him the project as well as an open door whenever Albert needed to talk to him. Albert went back to night school to get a degree in biology, and then he did postgraduate work in math at Sheffield Polytechnic. He is still angry at the Poly, which closed a program when he was the only student, so he never got his certificate.

During this time, Albert began to work at Sheffield University as a technician, analyzing data with skills that he picked up, never taking formal courses in programming. He was made redundant when the grant that employed him was eliminated in 1983 as a consequence of cuts in government funds to the research councils, even though all that remained of the project was the analysis of data already collected. He spoke bitterly of the impact of the Thatcher government on science, how departments were being disbanded and how the only ones left to teach were those who had been trained long ago.

At fifty-five, Albert had gone three months without a job. He was finally hired at a large local branch of a transnational manufacturing firm. Albert is convinced that the only reason he got the job was because he was hired immediately after being interviewed on a day when the personnel manager was away. He has had two heart attacks, suffers from a bowel disorder, and has had polio. Albert refers to himself as handicapped but has never registered for benefits, fearing that this might lead to discrimination. In 1987 he was being paid £10,000 a year (about $17,500) for programming on a kind of troubleshooting basis. He has complained about his salary, given how essential his work is to the firm, but feels he is in a weak position. His physical condition, the high rate of unemployment, and his political activism mean that, at his age, he could probably never get another job.

Mostly, Albert writes programs for use on the company's Prime computer system, "which is badly overworked and consequently very slow. I've written bookkeeping programs, queue programs for production planning, inventory programs, and electronic mail programs. They ask me to take on jobs from all over the plant, even though my job is formally in production automation. The programs I write seem to work very well, and they cost nothing to the company, since they run on existing machinery."

"The way I program is to identify a potential use, suggest it indirectly to the workers involved, and wait for the idea to germinate. I write it so as not to eliminate their job, but I point out how, as things develop, jobs will inevitably be lost, since the role of the computer is to automate activities currently being done by people. I think office automation will develop this same way, with little bits being automated here and there; only eventually does a whole system come into being. The way to protect your job is to join the union and protect the access to work; the work will inevitably change."

As with Mavis, there is much continuity between Albert's computered and noncomputered job experiences: the individual insecurity, the relevance of politics, the irrationality, and so on. Albert is indispensable to the firm, but indispensability does not lead to security. Like the proverbial executive secretary, Albert is not an important person in the command structure, yet his work is central to the completion of productive tasks.

Still, we can see in his work a potentially new role for computing in organizations. Albert is responsible for creating programs that shape the direction of growth. His approach to programming—indirect rather than direct, growing "organically" rather than based on strategic information plans and procedures—could eventually foster fundamental change in the way the corporation works.

In an important sense, our task in Sheffield came down to this: Which kind of experience, Mavis's or Albert's, is most characteristic of computed jobs? Jobs exist within particular social arrangements, which we call the employment or wage labor relationship. At least in the private sector, employers hire labor in order to

make a profit, and all employment social formations depend on a disparity between costs of production and income to produce a social surplus, which when
privately appropriated becomes capital. Thus the key to determining which experience is most characteristic of computered jobs is to grasp the connection between computerization and the job as a social relationship: Does computerization
change the nature of the employment relationship, or does the nature of the preexisting employment relationship determine the course of computerization? Does
computing change the way capital is accumulated, or does the reproduction of
capital determine computing?

## Computing and Labor

A focus on employment is easier to maintain when we look at labor in a more
pure form, jobs which less directly involve the subsistence work described in the
previous chapter. Though work and labor are often conflated by persons living in
employment-based social formations, much production of food, clothing, shelter,
well-being, and energy often takes place outside the labor form. It is confusing analytically to consider some forms of labor as "work" in that they produce commodities that have little use—for example, pet rocks.[1]

However, separating the dynamic of "work" from that of "labor" is not simple.
Not an either-or distinction, there are many human activities in a place like Sheffield that involve both. Although some subsistence materials are produced outside
the wage relationship (in the home, for example), most are produced by people
within a "labor" social relationship. Even nonwaged subsistence activities depend
greatly on income generated through employment: You can't cook food that you
haven't bought.

What we aim at here is to tease out the "labor" moment of computerization—
that is, the activity that takes place within the commodity form—just as in the last
chapter we looked at computerization from a "work" perspective. We accomplish
this by focusing on nonwork forms of labor, because by definition they are more
reproductive of social relationships than they are of physical subsistence.[2]

Distinguishing between work labor and nonwork labor makes sense theoretically. In a capitalistic, employment-based social formation like Sheffield, production often takes place within both state and private corporations. In the former,
production is a means to achieve state policy objectives, and in the latter, the intended outcome is to make a profit to be appropriated privately. Either type of objective can conflict with the dynamic of material production, especially the production of subsistence. There may be discernible differences between the
computerization dynamics of work and nonwork labor: Because their result is less
necessary to the physical existence of humans as a life form, nonwork forms of
production are generally more closely connected to reproduction of capital, less
mediated by the requirements of the physical reproduction of humans as a life
form. Indeed, many "labor site" (as opposed to work site) activities, such as servic-

ing the system that makes instantaneous exchange of international currency possible, are only remotely connected to basic production, having much more to do with surplus realization.

## Manufacturing

Both capital and employment in manufacturing industry in Sheffield have contracted sharply over the last ten years—by as much as one-half, according to the Sheffield Employment Department. The computerization situation in manufacturing is different in different labor sites. The kind of computerization present in the metalworks described in the previous chapter is fairly typical of medium-sized South Yorkshire manufacturing facilities, especially those with a strong history of trade union organization. In most works, a small number of computerized machines, purchased used if possible, have been placed on the shop floor. After much trial and error, good uses have been found for some of them, especially in comparison with less flexible "hard" or "Detroit" automation machinery. It is of course an irony that microelectronic-based digital sensors or "computers" (to use the term broadly) have actually extended the life of some old machinery. Interestingly, the system of work relations that has evolved for operating the machinery has led to a "hybrid" workforce, with those who program the machines tending to also be setters, proofers, and even operators, and with those who may have started as operators becoming involved in the more skilled aspects of using the machines as a consequence of computerization.

There is an interesting similarity between the metalworking firm and another engineering firm, one with perhaps the strongest trade union organization in the region. This latter organization has been able to keep workforce levels relatively higher through supreme efforts such as short-time working; at one point, rather than lay people off, nobody in the factory worked for over seven weeks. Here, the union has chosen to attempt to contain the impacts of new technology on the quality of work life, bargaining for reduced work time for the operators of new information-based technology, for example, as a way to maintain wage-level comparability in the firm. The union has also refused to be involved in computer system development; in the words of the trade union convener, "I would feel I was in the wrong place" to be doing such things, which are seen as management responsibilities.

A somewhat different picture of the effects of computerization emerges from Bernard Burns's longitudinal study of Computer Numerically Controlled (CNC) machine tools in ten Sheffield engineering firms (1985). Some of Burns's most interesting data concern management's approach to computerization. Burns was unable to find a single case in which, prior to purchase, the relative merits of CNC technology were systematically compared to those of noncomputerized equipment, despite the fact that in several cases alternative technology plausibly made as much production sense. Managers seemed to be more motivated by the "dazzle" factor when buying computers than by any concrete understanding of their capabilities. (This motivation may also explain why poor training was almost universal.) Managers themselves claimed to buy computer-based equipment either to maintain or extend management control over the work process. Despite a wide variety in worker organizational strength, in none of Burns's cases were workers involved in computerization planning, nor did they fight collectively against it.

Burns's longitudinal perspective allows him to address the results of computerization after extended periods of time. In several of the cases, no stable system for using the equipment had developed, even after several years. In those where stability was developed, despite management's intentions, the "hybrid" role—a sharing of programming, setting, proofing, and operating roles, rather than rigid role differentiation—was characteristic of eventual work organization. Fewer men lost jobs than women. (Before computerization, women were in less formally recognized skill categories than men.) In Burns's cases, efficiency was not generally improved by computers; though skills were changed, they were not necessarily lowered in level.

When the imperatives of a political economic system conflict with production objectives, there is room for disparity between perceptions and actual behavior. We referred to examples of such disparity in Chapter 4 work sites; they are even more evident in labor sites. The managers of firms often justify computer technology to decrease costs rather than to improve the quality of production, but we saw the latter more than the former. The hybrid system of work relations predominates. Although it is true that labor is lost, this is more frequently attributed, by both labor and management, to nontechnological factors (primarily market change and contraction) than to technological ones. When technology was implicated, it was generally in the form of poor machine purchases and faulty planning rather than direct disemployment due to computing.

It is very likely that managers' perceptions, like those of Burns's informants, were subject to the computer "dazzle" effect. The overselling of computers and other high-tech equipment means that managers buy computer technology as much in order to be perceived as "modern, up-to-date" as on the basis of well worked out production or profit plans. In the mining equipment plant, the result was costly errors in the purchase of equipment. The dynamic of capitalism has led many managers to equate "modernness on the shop floor" with "the elimination of substantively skilled labor," and consequently computers are sold as if this were their primary impact on production. By encouraging technologically inappropriate computer implementations, the ideology of capitalism actually interferes with its own reproduction.

The metalworking plant mentioned in Chapter 4 produces, in addition to mining tips, a large variety of cutting tools for other producers. In that vignette, we saw how the dynamics of the secondary productive activity of making tools for mining coal was affected by the imperative of the capitalist social relationship to amass surplus in the form of capital. Most of the decisions taken within the firm with regard to production, certainly many of those having to do with computerization, are made with primary reference to the dynamics of British and world capitalism.

In general, the following patterns are manifest in Sheffield manufacturing computerization:

- a gradual, tentative approach, often after negative early experience with systems that failed to live up to expectations;
- a piecemeal approach, with computerized machinery purchased primarily to replace an existing piece of equipment; the few firms that have moved more in the direction of computer-based integrated manufacturing systems tend to be branch plants of transnational corporations;
- an evolution of computer systems, for example, when discrete tasks are linked through shared data bases. Albert is unique in his articulation of the value of this gradualist approach; others knowledgeable about computerization in South Yorkshire manufacturing tend to bemoan it;
- comparatively small investment in computer-based equipment, probably in many cases due to the poor resource position of firms that perceive themselves as "pushed to the wall";
- introduction of computer-based machinery that exacerbates existing problems in jobs and decisionmaking processes; few organizations risked the kinds of change in structure required if computer-based systems were to have been utilized to what their proponents saw as the fullest capacity.

### Organizational Service

Around the turn of the century, factory owners attempted to limit the influence of workers on the labor process through the introduction of complex machines (machinofacture) and work reorganization schemes like Taylorization. Essential to such schemes was the marginalization of skilled workers in decisions about production and the development of alternative structures for circulating information and creating knowledge, such as technical departments for design and data processing; management to make decisions; clerical armies to gather, store, and communicate data; and elaborate hierarchies of production supervisors. Because some of these activities are spun out of production facilities themselves, organizational services are created as essentially derivative profit-making activities.

Computerization has spread more fully into services such as banking and accounting than it has in manufacturing. This is partly due to the lower cost of computer technology in these areas, the relative economic health of such enterprises, and their smallness and newness. In the field, we encountered two very different approaches to computerization in organizational services. One, like Mavis's, demeaned the labor experience of human beings, using machinery to undermine the sense of control. The other enhanced labor through increasing control. The difference between these two approaches to computerization can be illustrated by comparing the data service described by Mavis to a traffic signal repair service. Both enterprises service organizations, they both encourage extensive computer application, and both are computerized to roughly the same extent. In the data service, however, computer systems are imposed on the workers from the outside, but in the traffic signal repair facility workers are actively involved in developing systems.

This difference in the character of computerization in the two services is related to several factors. The data processing provided by the "Data Shop" follows no necessary productive imperative; it could be applied to data on share (stock) dividends as easily as to a productive activity. In contrast, traffic signal repair does follow such an imperative. First, although it does not produce subsistence items directly, it clearly contributes to the smooth operation of a transport system, itself a necessary prerequisite to the distribution of food, provision of medical care, and so forth, in a complex social formation. Second, there is a likely connection between the fact that the traffic signal service, the site of the more humane approach to computing, is organized as a cooperative. Like the other worker co-ops supported by Sheffield District Council, the signal service is dedicated to reproducing a collective approach to human social relations and to encouraging the breakdown of distinctions among types of work and workers. The deskilling approach is being developed within an organization more strongly oriented toward the realization of profit. This approach reinforces invidious hierarchical distinctions and results in sexist discrimination.

The way computers are used appears related to two factors: the extent to which the activity is oriented to subsistence production as opposed to the reproduction of capital and the character of the social relations that the organization reproduces. Unfortunately for those optimistic about the social consequences of computers, we found relatively few examples among organizational services of the very positive kind of computerization manifest at Traffic Systems Co-op. Yet the extremely negative computerization of the Data Shop was not modal either. Rather, we encountered a range of computerization in organizational services.

For example, in a new business services bureau oriented toward the developing cooperative sector, workers were making significant attempts to use computers to share office skills. According to the work of Sheffielder Brigitte Pemberton (1986) on computers in building societies (comparable to U.S. savings and loan associations), computerization has not on average deskilled clerical personnel. Because computerization took place within a context of a general organizational change, one which broadened the range of services offered by the societies, skills in new areas were replacing skills disappearing in old areas. Pemberton sees these relatively benign correlates of computerization as related to the history of the building societies, many of which emerged from the nineteenth-century cooperative movement and were therefore less oriented to immediate profit.

The results of Pemberton's work contrast strongly with those of Fergus Murray (1987), who studied new information technology in local clearing ("full service") banks, where computerization appears to have had a more adverse impact on skills. Murray points out, however, that computerization has made more obvious the dependence of the banks on the substantive but not formally recognized "human relations" skills of its female workforce. Several difficulties in new system implementation can be traced to the banks' tendency to ignore these skills in the system design process, and the latest systems take these factors more into account.

### Computer Services

One final area in which computerization should not be ignored is computer services. (Computer production, like electronics in general, has not been and is not now a major part of the South Yorkshire economy.) There was a regional software industry—a source of considerable pride to the 1986 Chamber of Commerce president—even though the industry was stagnating. An early 1980s network of home computer service centers had collapsed, both because large retail houses now sell computers at a discounted price and because faulty home computers are either fixed at home or thrown away and replaced by newer machines. Those computer-oriented services that survived did so because they found a particular niche based on nontechnological areas of expertise. One example of this was a computer games company located in an incubator enterprise workshop near Rotherham. Here a group of young males (some in their midteens) made a living by reprogramming popular computer games for national software vendors so that the games could be played on different hardware. A second example was CODUS, a computerized data base service to the electronic industry that assisted manufacturers in selecting appropriate electronic components. The culmination of several years work by electronic engineering lecturers at the University of Sheffield, CODUS was a recently spun-off private company, 75 percent of whose capital was owned by the university. Its procedures were becoming standard in similar data base ventures worldwide. A final example was Microsystems, a Sheffield cooperative developing an Urdu word processor for education markets; it was also working on foreign language spread sheets. In the short run, Microsystems had survived by selling computer hardware to educational and community computing agencies in the region.

### Patterns of Labor Computerization

The patterns of computerization characteristic of manufacturing—a gradual approach, piecemeal purchase of equipment, the evolution of systems to accomplish discrete tasks, and small investment—paralleled those characteristics of the nonstate sector work organizations described in Chapter 4. Even on a relatively small scale, however, computer-based machinery had highlighted serious problems in management and general organizational structure in both manufacturing labor sites and nonstate sector work sites. There was more diversity in the character of computerization in services than in manufacturing, services being more like the state-owned organizations described in the preceding chapter. Although some computerization—for instance, in cooperatives—enhanced skills, much also deskilled. The modal cases—for example, building societies—were ones in which the process had only moderate impacts with regard to skill and employment levels. Even in cases such as clearing banks where it appeared to have had a more adverse impact on skills, computerization has highlighted certain social features of the labor process, such as the "human interaction" skills of employees.

With regard to how computing changes the employment relationship, our results are highly conditional, suggesting a complex interdeterminancy. We found as many jobs like Mavis's as like Albert's. How jobs change with computerization depends on the extent to which their content is connected to basic production, on the one hand, and social reproductive dynamics, on the other. When a job is part of an organization involved in a material, subsistence commodity or service, the impacts of computerization tend to be less extreme, more "piecemeal." When a job with an organization whose goals involve the creation of new social relationships is computerized, the results also deviate substantially from the deskilling and disemployment predicted by compputropians. Conversely, like the state sector subsistence producers described in the previous chapter, private sector organizations whose commodities are not material or subsistence tend to introduce the most radical forms of computerization. Extensive and radical computerization, however, appears to reinforce rather than fundamentally alter the job dynamics characteristic of previous forms of capital accumulation—for example, deskilling, Taylorization.

The results of computerization are particularly difficult to predict when the dynamics of, say, capital accumulation conflict with those inherent in subsistence or the productive process. When introduced into nonsubsistence, wage-labor related activities, computers often seem caught between contradictory imperatives—the logic of production, on the one hand, and the logic of profit, on the other. Though the labor sites described in this chapter are relatively autonomous from the activities necessary to day-to-day reproduction, some connection between their basic productive dynamics and social reproductive activities is maintained. In order for a futures market in agricultural commodities to function for any extended period of time, some grain must be grown somewhere. Moreover, basic productive activities are clearly affected by the dynamic of the reproduction of social relations—the computerization of the mining industry discussed in the previous chapter is a good example of this. Nonetheless, the connections to the processes of physical life are most direct in work, although the connections to social reproduction are more direct in what we have called labor.

The mining tip manufacturing vignette of Chapter 4 helps us to understand why the shape of job computerization is not reducible to the dynamic of capital reproduction alone. Humans *create* as well as replicate the social groups of which they are a part; laborers begin, transform, and end entities like unions and tenants' associations—indeed, all the aspects of Sheffield working-class culture described in Chapter 2. As both labor and management in the mining tip plant agree, the creation of the union and a politically conscious leadership increased the ability of the works to survive in adverse economic conditions. In this plant, computers have generally been implemented in a fashion that makes work more flexible. To some extent, this is a consequence of workers' demands that those jobs left after computerization be eu- or "up-"skilled rather than deskilled.

To some degree also, increased flexibility is due to inherent characteristics of computers as a technology: To an important extent, "increasing flexibility" is what computers are for. Microcomputer technology is a good way to increase flexibility, but to produce or "put out the work" effectively, it generally needs to be operated by competent, actively engaged humans. In the following chapter, we describe the ways in which computerization relates to change in the kinds of entities that mediate the degree of human engagement, the cultural constructs—the words, values, beliefs, and so on—of working-class Sheffielders.

## Notes

1. A "commodity" is something that one gets through a market; whether a physical object or a human activity for an individual or group, commodities are "made" to be exchanged. Capital is accumulated through the production and sale of commodities, and, in general, the more widespread the commodity form, the more easily capital is reproduced, irrespective of the use value of the commodities available.

2. People in Sheffield are not in the habit of distinguishing between work and nonwork as we are here. They are less aware of the distinctions between mining coal (energy) and manufacturing a pet rock or between working for the health service or working in a private office than they are of that between "working"—that is, laboring, or "being in employment"—and being "on the dole." The lives of most working-class people—their individual, group, and class identities—revolve around past, present, or future jobs.

Further, activities such as the maintenance of a transport system, though not, strictly speaking, subsistence work, have a strong functional relationship to basic production. One could argue that they belong more in a discussion of producing subsistence than one about reproducing society. Since much subsistence production shares the commodity connection, since the "natives" don't normally separate subsistence and nonsubsistence commodities, and since there are difficulties in operationalizing the distinction, why bother making it?

Such a distinction is important on ethnological grounds. All human social formations must solve the problems of physical reproduction, but all human social formations also develop social relations whose dynamic is not reducible to the imperatives of physical reproduction. We must be able to distinguish between these two moments in the reproduction of social formations if we are to analyze the relationships among them.

Further, the distinction between the dynamics of work and the dynamics of labor is necessary for a comparative study of computing. If our aim is to specify how widespread the changes brought about by computerization are, we must be able to differentiate among social formations. This is especially necessary if we are to evaluate the claim that computerization is implicated in the creation of some new social formation. Since our aim here is to use this framework to organize a description of computerization rather than to demonstrate the validity of a general theory of social reproduction, some lack of specificity regarding where to draw the line between work and nonwork labor is of less importance than the attempt to do so.

# 6

## Computerization and the Reproduction of Symbols

The characteristics of a culture reflect work and on social relations, but they also depend on symbols. Unlike other species, for humans, symbols and the culturally constructed meanings on which they are based are the vehicles through which culture is perpetuated over generations. Because they are not organic, symbols can only be reproduced through human action. Our interaction with our environment is mediated by the symbols that give particular meanings to physical items, as are our determinations regarding the validity of what we think—how perceptions come to be treated as knowledge.

Symbols are also particularly subject to change during the complex process of cultural reproduction. This is because their recreation almost of necessity involves their elaboration if they are to be of continued relevance to changed material and social circumstances. During cultural reproduction, the specific subsistence strategies or work patterns, dominant social relationships, and symbols of any culture articulate with and have an influence on each other as the culture is perpetuated through time. For a subordinate social group, one that controls neither subsistence patterns (work) nor basic social relations (e.g., capital), the symbolic moment is particularly important to class cultural reproduction (Hakken 1978).

In this chapter we describe the relationship of computerization to symboling in working-class Sheffield, what happened when computing came to social processes important to the way working-class people think about themselves, how they perceive their world, and therefore the reproduction of their culture. To focus specifically on the symbolic, we examine forms of computerization that are somewhat distanced from the material reproduction of work or the social reproduction of the employment nexus. The following vignette introduces a number of the issues that we wish to consider.

We left the dining room of the ramshackle manor house at Northern College, on our way to the newer classroom block where the software demonstration was being held. We were participating in a weekend school for SPRITE (Sheffield People's Resource in Information TEchnology). Our movement was slowed by the poorly articulated architecture that impeded a member of one of the SPRITE groups, the Forum for People with Disabilities. The Forum people were full of ideas about how computers could assist people with disabilities, but inaccessible buildings reminded us of the continuing relevance of "low tech" to the realization of "high-tech" dreams.

SPRITE is a project that encourages computing within existing community organizations. The groups involved in SPRITE have different needs and histories; the weekend school was intended to sort out difficulties that arose from these differences as well as to share information and resources. We mounted yet another set of stairs in the newer classroom block and squeezed into a hot and crowded room. Computers recently purchased by the college from a U.S. company were distributed around the room, as were the "users" from SPRITE. Several of them had changed from the casual jeans and shirts of afternoon workshops to dressier clothes for the disco, clearly the high point of the school.

Above the crowd we heard the unmistakable voice of a computer salesperson rattling on and on about the advantages of the machines that the college had purchased. Dressed in a moderately trendy grey wool double-breasted suit, he paused occasionally for support from his software colleague seated at a side table. One could hardly miss this one's costume—shining red patent leather shoes and bright trousers (one leg green, the other white). The audience was already profoundly bored and restless.

Barbara busied herself with seven-year-old Luke, helping him find space for his pad and colored pencils. David lapsed into "fieldwork" mode, a mental state in which one distances oneself from unpleasant situations by acting like an invisible piece of research technology. As the presentation dragged on, David developed a certain sympathy for the salesperson's predicament. He was in trouble because the desktop publishing package he was supposed to be demonstrating hadn't arrived, and he had to "skive" or fake his way. The problem was compounded because he only knew two ways to present his material, one for business people and another for academics. This group was impressed neither by spreadsheet size nor number-crunching speed.

His journey through bits and bytes, interfaces and peripherals, was interrupted by a member of the Forum. "You've got incredible nerve doing a presentation like this here. I think of myself as more or less as bright as the average working-class person, but I can't understand a thing you're saying. This is no help to me at all. What are you trying to do here? What does it have to do with community computing?" Though we were taken aback by the abrasive tone, others in the group asked similar questions. The salesperson stammered in response, "Maybe you'd like to know about the desktop publishing system we had hoped to demonstrate. It has double the number of pixels per inch of any comparable product on the market ... ," his compubabble supplemented by the occasional comment from the software "boffin" (wizard).

A young man from The Space, a computer club on a housing estate that had been one of the first recruits into the SPRITE network, interrupted. "The problem I have with desktop publishing is that no matter how smart you can make it look, you still have to get it reproduced by photocopying. We can't afford that for our newsletter. And while I'm impressed with the capabilities of your machine, I wonder if we can run any of the software we've got for our old Commodore or BBC on it?" The salesman said no, and the young man asked if the company was developing a program to allow easy conversion to the new machine's environment. Again the answer was no. "This is just another example of how the computer industry is of little use to those of us in the community. We've put a lot of energy into learning about computers, and have even developed some of our own software, in use by the Sheffield Libraries, but you want us to forget about all that work and throw our lot in with your flash new machine. You've got to spend some time thinking about our needs and capabilities before we'll be impressed by all your wonderful talk." After a long silence, the salesman suggested that some people might like to see an action demonstration of the local area network purchased by the college with the machines. Most of the group left for the disco.

This vignette regarding nonwork, nonwaged computerization concerns is about how some working-class people are computerizing in a deliberate, unique way, as a group. For them, information technology is not so much an issue as a tool for living, a means to achieve a desired sense of self-identity and self-worth, irrespective of what it has to do with labor.

In the vignette, SPRITE people react to a common source of compumyths—hucksterism (noted by, e.g., John von Neuman). The reactions depicted are informed by experience, which has given people a concrete sense of what computers can do and therefore what it makes sense to want from them. The ability of SPRITE members to act together in relation to computers suggest a broader possibility, that working-class people can bend computing to their own social purposes and thereby participate actively in the creation of computing culture. This approach to "computer literacy" constitutes something of an end point on the spectrum of possible relationships between computing and the reproduction of symboling in Sheffield.

## Arenas of Semiotic Reproduction

In employment social formations, symbolic or semiotic reproduction takes place in formal institutions, including research and development organizations, schools for education and training, the mass media, and political and community organizations. In such locales, computerization is both a technology and an important symbol in its own right. In all societies, no matter how complex, the dynamics of intimate social networks—the people with whom one interacts on a daily basis, such as family and neighbors—have much to do with how symbols are reproduced. In this chapter, we examine computerization in relation both to such formal symboling creating institutions and to the more intimate social interactions of community in which symbols are communicated and incorporated.

## Research and Development

Mature employment societies generally develop separate institutions to produce new knowledge, to convert knowledge into technology, and to transfer technology to businesses for profit creation. Historically, Sheffield has had a number of such research and development (R & D) institutions, some connected to higher education and others to the early industries, especially mineral and metal. Because much early computerization had to do with armaments and because of the long-term involvement of Sheffield region engineering concerns in the production of shell casings, some of the earliest regional applications of computer technology were in metalurgical R & D. Recently, R & D computerization has been a small source of new industries, such as the software houses described in the previous chapter. Despite massive cuts in funding, some R & D projects continue in computer studies and other departments at Sheffield University; CODUS the computer-based system for identifying engineering components, was a spin-off of one of these projects. Computer-related R & D activity, such as with the various transputer (computer network on a chip) and Human-Centered Office Systems Group projects, continues at Sheffield Polytechnic as well.

Many new initiatives in computerization R & D involve the local government; for example, the new data base on regional employers being assembled by the District Council's Department of Employment and Economic Development. The DEED, locus of the council's attempt to develop progressive computerization policy, also put considerable effort into the European Poly-Office System Environment (EPOSE). This was to be a cooperative venture of Sheffield Council, the European Economic Community (EEC), and several transnational computer corporations. Envisioned as a model computerized office system that integrated social and technological factors, EPOSE was to be housed in the Business and Technology Innovation Centre at Sheffield's new Science Park. In addition, the DEED sponsored a project to increase coordination among scholars doing research relevant to new technology and local economic development.

These initiatives took place in the context of the general discouragement among academic R & D workers such as Albert. Much of this discouragement is related to the reorganization of the national system of institutions of higher education. Many academics, who actively pursued research ten years ago, had abandoned their work in the face of hostility and financial pressure. National government reorganization of research funding agencies in the 1980s, for example, isolated decisions on structure and priorities from collegial academic judgment. A "profit orientation" was to operate in place of academic conclusions, but it was often difficult to decide what was "profitable." The national government's 1983 Alvey program attempted to concentrate Britain's computerization efforts by introducing a narrow set of priorities, but even these were undercut by the pursuit of other privatization objectives. European funds for the EPOSE were blocked by another national policy, an unwillingness to release any Eurofunds for new technology research until the British agenda for EEC economic reforms had been adopted.

There are, of course, factors other than national government policy that have contributed to the pessimism among R & D workers. Within the DEED, for example, the internal development of computerized research applications was hampered by early disagreements over the goals of research: Should research have a long-term orientation, as in the development of data bases for popular economic planning, or a short-term orientation to serving the immediate needs of political agitation, as in campaigns to keep steel plants open? The result of conflicting pressures is that computerization as an object of local R & D has stagnated in the Sheffield area. Despite a tradition of strength, local production of new knowledge is unlikely to have a positive impact on the lives of working-class people in the near future.

### Schools

Early in the 1980s two national programs distributed microcomputer hardware and software to schools (especially secondary schools) all over the United Kingdom to promote computer awareness in the general populace. Whatever misgivings people may have had about computers in labor sites, there was a clear national consensus regarding support for advanced technology in education, and the school computer was the core symbol of this consensus. Educators and government officials hoped that such programs would build on the popularity of home computers, which in the mid-1980s were more densely spread in Britain than in any other nation state.

Despite the presence of some dedicated personnel and innovative programming in city schools, educators at Sheffield University and Sheffield Polytechnic were discouraged with the results of these initiatives in the Sheffield region. They gave many reasons for their discouragement: for example, that one computer per classroom was just not enough, or that software use was undercut when support was eliminated too soon. The way in which computer studies instructors were often recruited—from among those existing staff with an interest in computing— meant that what was taught tended to be what the person already knew. All too often, these were technologically outdated programming skills rather than currently useful applications skills. Computer studies staff also tended to take a somewhat proprietary attitude toward the hardware, which made it more difficult to integrate computers as a tool into other areas of the curriculum.

The staff of the Sheffield Local Education Authority Computing Centre noted a related difference between the way computers were being used by primary teachers and the way they were being used by secondary teachers. Teachers of younger students tended to see computers as a tool to aid them in the development of classroom work. They taught their students to use computers as a way of gaining and organizing knowledge—building a data base for a science project, doing word processing to write more easily, or playing math games to improve computational skills. Primary teachers who had been on day courses to learn about computers were more likely to return to their building and share their knowledge with others. Likewise, the computer equipment was not locked in a separate room, but traveled from classroom to classroom. The cooperative structures in infant schools (grades K–2) and middle schools (grades 3–6) meant knowledge was shared among the teachers. The nonhierarchical view of education meant that computers were not regarded as a province of special knowledge, but as a means of doing an educational job more effectively. By the mid-1980s some comprehensive (secondary) teachers had begun coming to the computing center for help in developing specialized software to enhance the subjects they taught.

School-based computer initiatives clearly depended on the active collaboration of staff to be effective. Unfortunately for educational computerization, the national government chose schools, like mining, as an arena in which to implement its public sector industrial relations policies aggressively. Teachers' organizations resisted these initiatives through numerous strikes and job actions. By 1987 teachers' collective bargaining rights had been greatly reduced. Implementation of direct national control of school curriculum was begun in the 1990s. Some teachers who had taken individual initiatives to develop computer-based innovative programs have abandoned them out of frustration with the general school situation.

A number of initiatives in computer education were continued in adult education, but the initiatives were not well integrated. Staff articulated a desire to connect the teaching of computer skills with broader political and social education; a consensus on how to accomplish such integration had not emerged. At issue was the extent to which initiatives were to be primarily vocational, educational, or recreational in intent. A few exemplary training programs, like the Women's Technology Training Workshop, did develop an organic connection between training and broader social education. The general direction of computer-related training in adult education, however, was in the direction of more narrowly based skills.

In the 1990s adult education programs were cut back even more severely. Worker education was one of the important components of the vibrant working-class culture we experienced in the 1970s. The role of worker education, and especially its future, were unclear in the 1980s. The movement toward more narrow training and credentialing was general in adult education, not just in computer studies. All forms of adult, working-class education got fewer funds, and they have been swamped by the massive explosion of new Manpower Service Commission programs.[1]

In the mid-1980s, Sheffield began to reorganize adult education into a tertiary program. This was to combine into unified institutions three previously separate sectors: colleges of further education (similar to community colleges); sixth forms (university and polytechnic preparatory curricula traditionally carried out within comprehensive secondary schools); and adult education. Even this initiative was hampered by the national government's exemption from the reorganization of the wealthy southwest of the city, which contained most of the large sixth forms. It remains to be seen if the tertiary program will integrate computer and social education more effectively.

## Mass Media

New printing plants at Wapping in 1980s London were the site of the most spectacular public battle over new technology in Britain. Newspaper entrepreneur Rupert Murdoch, like the National Coal Board, used computer-based technology as an important weapon to break a traditional bastion of trade union power. After precipitating a confrontation, Murdoch locked out most of the printing staff of the *Times* and brought in a new workforce. The application of new information technology, by eliminating the need for traditional newspaper skills, made it possible to do this without disrupting production.

After the changes at Wapping, the national media tended to reflect a strongly computopian bias as well as aggressive support for the national government. The growing volume of mass advertising was particularly effective in promoting the anticollectivist message implicit in many national policies. A shift in the nature and role of the press was accompanied by broadened involvement of the national government in the mass media. The aggressive approach of the national state was especially evident in its attempt to suppress Peter Wright's *Spycatcher*,[2] but just as significant were its intervention into editorial decisions at public media like the BBC, which, for example, refused to run the program on the miners' strike that it had commissioned from Barry Hines.[3]

The nationalized character of many media, combined with the tendency of people to rent rather than buy telecommunications equipment, meant that Britain had an early advantage in moving toward a "wired society." This obvious next step in media computerization, the development of home computer networks for communication, shopping, and so on, was set back by the selloff of the national telecommunications system. Privatization of British Telecom, forcing it to pursue short-term profitability, precluded the infrastructural investment necessary to a universal information grid. Private competition also promoted incompatible hardware. This is yet another example of how potential early British social computerization assets, such as extensive distribution of home computers, were lost.

During the field study, a technology-related strike took place at the Sheffield *Star*. (The *Star* is one of the few large regional newspapers to support Labour consistently.) At issue was the refusal of journalists on the paper to operate new direct input computer technology unless the paper met various parity demands in wages and working conditions. Though technology was an important symbol in the dispute, it was not in itself the main point of contention. Rather, the strike replicated a pattern observable in other industrial relations contexts, where new technology provided a highly visible locus of battle, but long-standing structural confrontations were the real issue. The strike with the *Star's* journalists was resolved amicably through compromise, but the jobs of pressmen lost with the new technology were not recovered.

### Political Campaigns

Particularly on the national level, computers have had significant impact on the electoral strategy and style of political parties. The parliamentary campaign of 1987 was dominated by the reporting of the almost daily opinion polls made possible by computer technology. Direct mail fund raising and targeting of political messages were other incursions of computerization in the promulgation of what was often referred to as an "American-style" campaign. In contrast, the local Labour campaign in which we participated appeared untouched by computing.

On the policy level, however, the politics of the Sheffield Labour group were focused on computers in the early 1980s. At that time, new technology was presented as a necessary and central part of a new strategy for municipal socialism. In these politics, funds and programs to encourage the spread of new information-based technologies were to be a prime mechanism to extend the influence of the local state in the local economy as well as a means to repoliticize working-class people. To these ends, the Sheffield Council put considerable energy into the creation of a network of business and technology support organizations, from technology and product development through training and business advice to community computing programs. A vigorous promotion of information technology within the council itself was also envisioned. Unfortunately, the effectiveness of these initiatives was substantially undercut by adverse political, economic, and industrial relations circumstances.

### Neighborhood and Community Computing

A number of groups throughout the United Kingdom have explored ways in which computer technology could be used to promote grass roots community politics and to promote a proactive attitude toward computerization. One such group, Computers for People, has been active for a number of years in Sheffield. In addition to developing politically progressive computer games and carrying out computer "road shows" for labor and community groups, CfP helped generate such projects as the Polytechnic's Human-Centered Office Systems Group and others concerning progressive health efforts.

Despite these efforts, computers were not yet in general use among community groups at the time of our field study. Partly this was a problem of access to technology: Discussions between SPRITE and the organization providing support for Sheffield community groups about possibilities for expanding computer access for organizations were only just beginning when we left the field. Equally important were fundamental dilemmas regarding data—for instance, individuals' privacy rights versus the needs of community organizations for access to data in order to be more effective.

## Working-Class Culture

Substantial changes have taken place since 1976 in the patterns of Sheffield working-class culture and the way it is reproduced. By 1986 peoples' stopping at home to watch television, self-home-decorating, and part-time jobs were replacing leisure in workingmen's clubs and community centers, occasional evening classes, rambles in Derbyshire, and visits to traditional seaside resorts. The institutions of worker education had lost influence, although some innovative programs continued. Changes in employment were related to changes in gender role conceptions. In addition to changes in leisure patterns, gendering, and labor markets, patterns of semiotic reproduction had also altered. Sheffielder workers spoke of having to "struggle to find the culture we deserve," and some questioned whether existing working-class identities were sufficient to the new situations.

At least in part, the appearance of a search for a new model of class is a consequence of difficulties in the reproduction of the old model, which for many people was not compelling enough to win continuing active support. The old, "traditional" working-class culture did provide a self-identity for many working people, especially those living in Sheffield, the "workers' capital." As Mike the cutting tip factory trade unionist put it, "This is a bad period, but t'labour movement has had them before, and we will again. The important thing is to keep on with the struggle." Others who wished to identify with the working-class movement but had some difficulty, especially feminists and black activists, argued that new, broader conceptions of the working class and its movements were necessary to mobilize people. This discussion over basic questions of identity is clear evidence of change in the reproduction of working-class semiotics.

To what extent is there a causal connection between these changes in Sheffield working-class symboling and computerization? Clearly computerization cannot be seen in any simple sense as cause of these changes, which have much to do with national politics and the international political economy. Nor is computerization merely a contentless vessel, to be filled in whatever form people desire. There are real connections between computing and changes in the reproduction of working-class culture—in the coal mines, for instance. Yet even here the connection is complex; despite the loss of the miners' strike, disruption continues over introduction of the new technology.

There are connections between computerization and the changes in working-class symboling described above, yet the nature of the connections is not clear even in strictly semiotic terms. In Chapter 1, we presented many of the puzzling contradictory and diverse images of computers in the working class. The same person might

1. show a high degree of computer awareness and familiarity;
2. express the belief that computer technology is a profound source of social change, transforming fundamentally the world we have known and crushing the power of the working class;
3. say that computers and the new technology based on them represent the hope for reindustrialization and in general a better life in the future;
4. observe that computer technology has been integrated rather easily into her or his personal life; and
5. still maintain that "I'm daft when it comes to computers."

For many working-class people, computers were a locus of fear or derision. One satirist quipped, "I had a friend who wanted to do computers at school but he wasn't able to, 'cause he didn't have enough money for the lobotomy." Others, for whom computers do not fit easily within their social analyses, tended to downplay computers' effects. Sheffield data suggest that the most innovative and effective uses of computers occur in cooperative work, where hierarchies are diminished in favor of shared skills. Ironically, this runs counter to the macho and hierarchical image of the computer scientist or the individualist image of the computer hacker. Some young working-class people, like those in SPRITE, were attempting to create a new class identity centering on computers. Computers were often evoked as an attractive symbol of a progressive and less class-bound society. It was in political circles where these views predominated that progressive local authority computer policies were developed.

In a number of instances—for example, regarding changing gender roles—we saw both optimism and concern about the impact that new information technologies would have. As one of the women who had been in the leadership of the Women's Support Group in the miners' strike noted: "The new technology makes it more and more possible for women to be doing much of the work that a miner does. But we have not seen women flooding into mining." The question of why women do some jobs and not others has never been simply a question of ability, strength, or technological knowledge, but computerization has meant a change in the terrain on which the question is raised.

Such contradictory perceptions, and the performances based on them, suggest that the physical consequences of computerization—how the material characteristics of computers have necessitated change in the way work is done, and so on— are less important to the reproduction of employment social formations than the symbolic processes in which they are implicated. The experience of South Yorkshire suggests that computerization must be seen most fundamentally as a conceptual terrain on which is being fought a fundamental battle over how society is to be conceived. For someone in Sheffield, if the primary question of identity in 1976 was, "To which class do I belong?" by 1986 the question had become, "What classes are there?" Many people wondered, along with Andre Gorz (1982), if it were time to wave "Farewell to the Working Class," while they asked personally, "Can I cope with the computer, or will it make me redundant?"

## Summary

The third moment of computerization is computerization semiotics, the role of computers in the reproduction of the cultural categories in and through which humans perceive their lives. The connection between computerization and change in the reproduction of Sheffield working-class symboling is complex, but this complexity should not interfere with the recognition of its importance. A number of computerization patterns emerge from our survey of various loci of the reproduction of symbols. Education, research and development, mass media, politics, and community organization have been identified by very different groups as arenas in which new information technology would be of benefit. In all these areas, computerization has not as yet delivered what was promised. Often, this is because consistent computerization strategies have fallen prey to other, more powerful agendas, especially those of the Thatcher state.

Alternative self-identities, such as being "a computer person," have developed on working-class housing estates. These are based on activities such as playing and then programming elaborate games on home computers. One key to understanding computerization and semiotics in Sheffield is implied by Sherry Turkle's work (1980; 1984), which suggests that computers may be being used by contemporary peoples as what anthropologists call a master symbol, a kind of super metaphor that is the primary terrain on which are fought battles over collective identity and the shape of the future, or at least the ways it might be understood. Like other master symbols, computerization has come to stand for a very broad range of often contradictory developments.

Computerization must be seen in the context of the general reproduction of employment social formations, as a structure/process with its own "relative autonomy." Like other technological developments, the symbolic or ideological role of computers is as important as their material or physical role. Computerization is clearly an important terrain, one over which both those with power and those who wish to have it have tried to extend their control. How we think about computers is in this sense as important as what they do; computing is as much a result of how symbols are reproduced as it is machinery's impact on physical processes.

Recognition that computerization is implicated in the battle for hegemony in employment social formations carries with it certain implications for action. Involvement in programs to develop progressive forms of computerization is often useful in and of itself, in that such programs may result in more humane information systems. Involvement is important in another sense, however,—it can also impact the symbolic content or meaning of computerization. The symbolism of computing is implicated in, among other things, the way working-class people in Sheffield are trying to forge a new identity. Learning to use computers to pursue their own objectives may assist them in locating a viable future.

## Notes

1. The MSC is a branch of national government with a mandate to develop an "appropriate" labor force. To many in South Yorkshire, MSC programs had more to do with manipulating the rate of unemployment and instilling new models of labor discipline than with education.

2. In this book, Wright describes his experiences in the British secret service. In 1986, when the book was published in Australia, the Thatcher state made a clumsy and unsuccessful attempt to suppress it. During the trial, a British civil servant refused to acknowledge that he had lied but did admit that he had been "economical with the truth."

3. Hines is a former Barnsley miner who has published several successful novels and who previously had collaborated on a number of important television productions, including one on Yorkshire entitled "The Price of Coal."

# PART THREE

# Analyzing Computing Structurally

# 7

# Theorizing Computerization

Our ethnography of computing and social change in Sheffield documents the wide variety of forms that this relationship can take in social life and in peoples' consciousness. There, computerization was at least temporally associated with some rather profound changes in the nature of human social life. The ethnography also indicates that the way computerization is implemented influences its broader social consequences, even that the use of computers to create social relations independent of profit accumulation may eventually lead to a truly postindustrial civilization.

Still, ethnography cannot on its own answer the question with which we started: whether it makes sense to hold this technology responsible for the social changes we have documented. Answering such questions is an analytic task, which means abstracting the social change consequent to technology from the social change that has followed from other social forces.

Although to this point in our book we have focused on describing patterns of computerization in South Yorkshire, in the remainder we aim to explain where these ethnographic patterns come from by locating them in relation to phenomena that transcend any particular place. The essence of our analysis is that the connection between computing and social change is largely indirect, the direct connection being highly mediated by several other social structures and processes. The combined influence of these other social elements has more to do causally with the nature of the social changes taking place in Sheffield than do dynamics internal to computers as a technology.[1]

We present our analysis in two stages. The chapters of Part Three analyze the important structures within which working-class people—certainly in South Yorkshire, but, we believe, in many other areas as well—experience computerization. These structures—the national state, the international political economy, and the region as a labor market—are structural in the sense that working-class people in Sheffield confront them as built into the framework of social life; they operate, as it were, "behind the backs" of local groups and individuals in Sheffield.

In contrast, the chapters in Part Four take up influential processes, active human interventions that contribute meaningfully and directly to the creation of computer culture. These processes include local state policies to promote culture-centered computing, the reconfiguration of gender, and the creation of new cultural forms within the working-class, including labor freedom. These interventions, both conscious and unconscious, have important causal connections to the contours of computing and the social change associated with it, and therefore cultural analysis has a central place in the study of computerization.

Since analysis moves beyond questions of "what" to questions of "why," from *identification of* patterns to *accounting for* them, it necessarily involves the use of theories—related, articulated concepts that provide the general meanings out of which any particular argument is constructed. We present here in Chapter 7 the theoretical grounds for the descriptive notions that precede this chapter and the analytic notions used in the parts that follow. However, because in many contemporary accounts of ethnography, theorizing is a highly suspect moment since it implies claims that theoretical constructs have more general analytic validity than other discourses, we begin by explicating why we are committed to the theoretical moment of anthropological analysis.

## The Ethnographic Necessity of Ethnology

Cultural and social anthropologists, those anthropologists who study current cultures, share a commitment to ethnography, to grounding what they write or produce visually in actual human experience. Recent advocates of a "reflexive moment" or literary turn in anthropology (e.g., Clifford and Marcus 1986; Marcus and Fisher 1986) have radically questioned whether it is possible to go beyond this ethnographic moment. Though there are major difficulties inherent in theoretical discourse, such a "going beyond" is necessary if one wishes to address questions of general social process or to establish the relevance of any particular case to more general issues. We also believe, precisely because of the kinds of problems with ethnography to which reflexivists draw attention, that "going beyond" is equally necessary to ethnography itself.

Many of ethnography's problems grow out of the fact that its primary instrument, the human anthropologist, is flawed. Full participation in human life depends on possession of a set of cultural constructs shared with others, something that we get through entry into a specific culture; we are *encultured* into human life. Humans, including anthropologists, are thus innately ethnocentric—they tend to perceive what goes on in other cultures through the categories they know best, those of their first culture, their "culture of orientation." This limits their ability to experience other cultures without bias.[2]

To become useful observers of other cultures, anthropologists must act affirmatively to overcome the ethnocentric influence of enculturation, to *critique* the constructs of their own culture. By studying other cultures, they develop a lively sense of what is obscured by their culture of orientation and can better understand what tendencies they have as a consequence of their own enculturation. This is what it means to develop a sense of *cultural relativism*. This study of the culturally other, however, must itself be theoretically informed; otherwise, the study of the other is merely a reflection of implicit assumptions resulting from one's previous enculturation.

In Chapter 2, we discussed some of the problems that any ethnographer faces, including site selection and generalizing from single locale to an entire culture. Ethnographic description can be prejudiced inadvertently in a number of ways: using inappropriate categories to identify the problem to be studied, employing ethnocentric concepts in the field when deciding in which activities to participate, or by describing what events mean in theoretical language loaded with implicit, unexamined presumptions. For example, in Parts One and Two, we tried to avoid common descriptive phraseology—that is, phrases such as "the social impacts of computerization"—that *presumes* a simple causal connection between computerization and social change.[3] In order to describe what they experience in fieldwork, anthropologists must develop and master descriptive terms that privilege one type of social formation over others as little as possible. That is, it is necessary to complement ethnography with ethnology, the term used in anthropology for general theories of types of social relationships, the theory characteristic of cross-cultural research.[4]

Good descriptive constructs manage to reflect both the way informants talk about their lives and the broad concerns of social theorists. Terminology that reflects accurately the practice of both "sides" is less likely to be inadvertently ethnocentric. "The natives" can, of course, be as ethnocentric as analysts, so we cannot merely adopt either's terminology without considering its appropriateness first. Nor does the mere use of a term by both theoreticians and "natives" mean that it may be used descriptively or analytically with impunity. Good ethnography is a question of using the right descriptive concepts, but one can know they are right only by grounding them properly, with meanings both clear and intended.

## Is "The New Information Society" an Ethnologically Valid Label?

Consider, for example, the problem of how to describe, even to name, the era in which we live. Some notion of the overall characteristics of their "times" (an "ethno-era" [Hakken 1989]) is typical of human groups. Computers are used frequently in labels for the contemporary era, as in "computer society" or "information age." In many contexts, "computerization" is treated as a linguistic equivalent of "a new information technology-based transformation of society," a society produced by "the computer revolution." Should we as ethnographers use these labels, too?

There are several reasons why one might use "computer society" or some similar term to label our era. Empiricism suggests that we should derive theoretical constructs directly from the empirical world. Further, there is an ethnographic tradition, strongly supported by the reflexivists, that favors the use of "ethno-terms"—the terms used in everyday language—as analytic labels. As indicated in Chapter 1, working-class people in Sheffield also use such terms. The use of technology-related terms to refer to a stage in cultural evolution has a long history in anthropology (e.g., the bronze age, stone age, etc.). As referred to previously, there are also analytic arguments for the importance of computing to the contemporary era that constitute a prima facie case for its use as a label.

However, there are stronger reasons to avoid using "computer society"–type labels for our times. One is theoretical—to label our research in these terms would mean the risk of assuming what we want to discover. Such practice would also have run counter to the computing studies literature discussed in the Introduction, the thrust of which is to doubt whether contemporary society is all that different from its predecessors. We need to find analytic language that communicates an understanding of the potential social impacts of computerization but that at the same time allows us to question the presumption of social causation.

Perhaps most important, the descriptive use of "computer society" labels mystifies just the issues we wish to consider most carefully. Consider, for example, the implications of using "informational" adjectives to identify what is new about the kinds of activity of concern to Sheffielders; for example, as in Lenk's (1982) discussion of the present as an "Information Society." To the ethnologist, to call ours an "Information Age" makes little analytic sense. "Information" is an aspect of all human social formations, not just computerized ones. Indeed, most life forms are information dependent: They have derived adaptive advantage by formulating effective responses to conditions outside themselves. They react to or "process" "data" from their environment, "processed data" being a typical definition of "information."

Differences between the way humans and other life forms process data are ethnologically much more significant than differences among human "information" eras. Human data is processed twice, and on both occasions it is transformed. First, although humans sometimes respond to external stimuli more or less directly, this is often not the case. Rather, external data is "culturized"—has a semiotic dimension imposed on it—as it is turned into information, or, perhaps more appropriately, as information is *created*. Moreover, we also ponder, processing information a second time by comparing it consciously to systems of symbols; indeed, we may relate the same information to different symbol systems numerous times. In this second moment of the human information process, we evaluate information, testing it for its "knowledge" value. Thus, every human culture is doubly inseparable from information. Since contemporary human cultures are no more "informated" than those of any previous era, to call ours an "Information Age" is ethnologically misleading.

The extent of human dependence upon information does, however, suggest that any fundamental change in the way data becomes information may have broad implications. Through affecting how we *use* information, *could* computers be substantially altering how we *create* it? A "new information age" as opposed to simply an "information age" label for the new social formation might be justified, but *only* if we can specify the particular ways in which new techniques of handling data transform the nature of information. Thus, such terms are useful in posing questions for ethnography, but they are descriptively misleading.

For example, it is possible that computing could make the processes by which data becomes culturized into information substantially more transparent, such as by eliminating mystifications in existing cultural processes. That such transparency is the result of computing has yet to be established. Consider the comments of the WTTW trainee in Chapter 1 who wished to teach computing but felt held back by her lack of understanding. She wished she could see the "bus" pick up information from one place on a disk and "carry" it to another. Her comments should not be dismissed as unfortunately misplaced concreteness; rather, they indicate the set of profound mystifications (myths) introduced into social discourse along with computing, what Langdon Winner calls "mythinformation" (1984).

Through examples like this, a strong case could be made that computing is a *less* transparent data processing process than pencil and paper or files and cabinets, the information processes it tends to replace. The technicist, scientistic discourse of computerization hides more than it reveals about how data gets "informated" and in the process further alienates humans from an understanding of their own existence. It may also be that computing mystifies substantially more profoundly than other information moments, or that it basically replicates or alternatively merely speeds up the same human responses to given data, but the ultimate result is essentially the same information. Until we can be sure which alternative is more accurate descriptively, we had best avoid the descriptive use of terms like "new information society." Similarly, as argued above, adoption of the term "Computer Age" as a descriptive label must await demonstration that a substantial change in our basic ways of being human—change intimately linked to computer technology—has actually taken place, not just the possibility that this is the case.

In short, one must take care that analytic judgments are well reasoned, not hidden in empiricist ethnography. To avoid the use of unexamined categories, one must be clear about the problems one sets for investigation, and for this, ethnology is necessary. Without ethnology, ethnography is blind.

## Analyzing Computers as a Technology

However, we wish to use our Sheffield data for more than description; we want to evaluate a general proposition, the computerization hypothesis. To do this, we must have a concrete idea of what exactly is implied by the new information age proposition, to have conceptualized as concretely as possible the actual mechanisms by which computers *could* be causing social change. The argument above suggests that the most likely way in which computing could cause social change is as a particularly effective information technology. By altering the general way in which humans extract information from data derived from the environment and process it to create more information and eventually knowledge, computers are new mediators of the human link with the environment—that is, a new form of technology.[5]

Defined this way, humans have produced and used new technologies throughout their history. Computers are not the first technology to mediate the human/information link; tools for food production and books are other examples. In addition to seeing how computers alter the information link, our analytic goal is to determine whether such alterations are significant. This means that we require a standard by which to compare computing-induced changes in social life with changes induced by other new technologies, a theory that allows us to compare the extent to which different technologies alter the human/environmental link. When trying to say how basic a change is, one is driven to place the particular relationship in question in historical/cultural evolutionary context.

Human history provides several examples of new technology-related social change. These examples can be used to develop an *ethnology of technology*—that is, a comparative, historical typology of the kinds of things human technologies are. In our view, it is useful to identify several distinctive types of technology linkable causally to social change.

### Productive Technology

The first important forms of human technology were the artifacts and tools, work patterns, and cultural categories that substantially increased humans' ability to provide themselves with material necessities such as food, health, clothing, shelter, and energy. Indeed, there is good archaeological reason to see such *productive technology* as essential to the emergence of our species (Liebowitz 1980). All life forms have systems for providing themselves with material necessities and for altering their physical relations with their environment by changing themselves. What distinguishes humans from our immediate ancestors is the frequency with which we do these things in constructed social relationships and for social groups, as well as the extent to which we use deliberately altered material objects (tools) to change the environment.

The selective advantage provided by these proclivities was encouraged by and led to rapidly increasing brain size and more sophisticated symboling, which in turn meant more complex activities. Productive technologies are therefore complex, interwoven sets of subsistence-related activities, social relations, material objects, and symbols. Productive technologies get used in "work," as we used that notion in Chapter 4.

### Abstract Technology

About 10,000 years ago, humans developed modes of production involving primary dependence on domesticated life forms. Horticulture and pastoralism not only meant new productive technologies; they also involved the development of *abstract technology,* an approach to activity involving broad, conscious analytic concepts. The degree of abstractness eventually attained is perhaps best illustrated by the ability of New World humans to execute the genetic transformations necessary to derive modern (Indian) corn or maize from wild species. Abstract technologies may have developed first in production, but they were rapidly generalized into other aspects of human existence, including the development and systematization of the cultural constructs through which information is created and evaluated. "Science" is in this sense a form of abstract technology.

It seems reasonable to assume that in developing abstract technologies humans raised to consciousness the principles underlying one kind of activity (e.g., work) and then applied them to others, using new sets of activities, social relations, material objects, and symbols. The conditions that led to such developments are explicable, if not discoverable. For example, the absence of available domesticable animal species was probably an important condition selecting for the abstract thought necessary for New World humans to "invent" corn. Over the species' history, we can see an increasing gulf between specific productive technologies and abstract technologies, practitioners of the latter coming to see their activity as distinct from the provision of material necessities.

### Repressive Technology

An important new implementation of the abstract approach in technology occurred approximately 5,000 years ago, leading to *repressive technology:* the deliberate use of instruments and techniques, both physical and social, to enhance the power of elite social groups through control of the behavior of others. Also involving analogues of productive technology, repressive technologies were probably essential to the imposition of states, systems of permanent exploitation of one human group by another. Repressive technology allowed human groups to create and then dominate the new agricultural social structures.

It seems likely that the possibility of such exploitation would have been conceived on numerous occasions by humans. The technology of plant and animal domestication may have provided a model for brutal human "domestication"; the rise of derivative states rapidly followed the spread of domestication. Some of the tools of domination—spears, bows and arrows—clearly preceded the rise of the state. Still, the most important technologies of repression—armies, administrative structures, compulsive religions, punishment systems—involve new, more collective forms of human force to extract a material surplus from one group and permanently transfer it to another.

### Machine Technology: A Possible Fourth Form

Although it has not been around long, anthropologically speaking, it seems reasonable to hypothesize a fourth technology type, self-actuated "system" or *ma-*

*chine technology.* What we now call "automation" was also developed via the abstraction route. Though several machines were developed earlier, the first widely implemented systems of automation were developed to replace skilled labor in the manufacture stage of the late nineteenth-century labor process.[6] This new technology is associated with the consolidation of employment as the dominant social relationship.

### NIT: A Fifth Form?

Like abstract, repressive, and machine technology, new information technology, or computers, began as a commentary on previous technology. The earliest use of electronic, digital computers was in ballistics, an important modern form of repressive technology. Today, however, NIT is widespread precisely because of its flexibility—it can be implemented wherever the notions "data" and "information" can be applied. Indeed, computer technology is integratable into existing forms of all four previous technology types—productive, abstract, repressive, and machine. The prima facie argument that computers cause social change often draws explicit attention to just such polyvalent characteristics (e.g., Barron and Curnow 1979).[7]

Within technicist modes of thought, it is easy to believe that such broadly used instruments lead to great change, but ease of conceptualization cannot be substituted for analysis. NIT could turn out to be just another form of the preexisting technologies, or a mere recombination of them. Although ordinary people may speak of the "recent" emergence of technology or about how technology is "taking over the world," the comparative ethnologist is wary of such facile generalization. The plausibility of such talk often depends upon blurring together the several different preexisting types of technology. For example, computing studies suggest that organizational structure (a kind of abstract technology) is often changed at the same time as computerization, but such change—distinct from and not necessitated by computerization—is often more responsible for job loss and deskilling than is the computer technology itself (Wilkinson 1983; Gill 1985).

### Technology and Ethnology

What grounding in general justifies separating out one form of technology from another—for example, repressive and machine technology from abstract technology—and treating them as distinct? Our admittedly truncated review of the evolution of technology suggests that the most important ground is the association of the new technology type with fundamentally new social relationships. The emergence of productive technology is associated with the emergence of humanity as a species, abstract technology with the development of a new mode of production, horticulture, repressive technology with the rise of the state, and machine technology with the near universalization of the wage nexus. To evaluate whether computing constitutes a fundamentally distinct type of technology, we must specify emerging social relationships that are substantively distinct from previous social relationships and as closely linked to new technology. Thus, in addition to needing a broad history of technology types, we need a general theory of the types of human social relationships.

Anthropologists say that the more generally applicable a descriptive term is—that is, the more peoples to whom it is applicable without ethnocentric presumption—the greater its *ethnological* validity. ("Ethnology" is also sometimes used to refer to the main method for finding such concepts, the comparative or cross-cultural study of peoples, as well as to the theorizing on which such concepts are based.) Ethnological moments are also necessary for the anthropologist who wishes to illuminate broad social propositions like the computerization hypothesis.

### A General Ethnology

As suggested above, the brief ethnology of technology types we have just outlined leads to an important observation: Really new forms of technology appear in close conjunction with profoundly new social identities and substantial changes in social life. If computer-based information technology is a fifth, distinctly new, type of technology, we should be able to identify substantial new forms of social life linked causally to it. Thus serious consideration of the computerization hypothesis requires some general theory of social life, an ethnology that allows us to identify the degree of difference between social forms as well as their historical relationship to processes like technological change.

Perhaps the most basic structure/process contrast in ethnology is that between various structural totalities—social formations—and the processes by which these social formations are transformed from one into another. This perspective implies a notion of cultural evolution—that there is a limited set of basic social arrangements and that these entities are developmentally connected. A particular type of social arrangement can be described in terms of those structures/processes that are characteristic of it and not of the other types. Similarly, any account of the transition from one social type to another must explain why one set of characteristic structures/processes is replaced by another.

From this perspective, the relationship of computerization and social change can be seen as a question of what the relationship is between a new process—computerization—and the social formation, either within one type or as an element in the transition to another. In order to conclude that new information technology is a new stage in the evolution of technology, one must be able to specify the new pattern of social relations to which it is causally connected. To make such a judgement, we need a standard of profound changes in social formation. We can distinguish between a change in the basic ways of being human—for example, from gathering and hunting to horticulture—and less basic changes—from one machine technology to another. Even change from the "hand" form of employment division of labor (manufacture) to machine technology is "merely" a change from one stage to another *within* the same social formation type and therefore is not as profound. Evaluation of the computerization hypothesis, therefore, requires a general ethnology, a theory of types and a theory of transformation—that is, the important stages in the general character of social activity as well as what leads one stage to be transformed into the next.

## Social Formation Reproduction

The general ethnology that informs *Computing Myths, Class Realities* is a social reproductionist one. "Social formation reproduction" refers to the general process by which totalizing human social entities or cultures—social formations—are created, recreated, destroyed, and transformed through time. In the kinds of societies in which people live today, social formation reproduction is a complex process (Hakken 1987b).[8] "Reproduction" is the term used by social theorists to refer to the general process by which human life systems are perpetuated through time. One presumption of the ethnographic approach is that the way humans collectively *perceive* their world—the character of their cultural constructs—is likely to influence profoundly what they do, and what they do affects the nature of their life system. As argued in Chapter 2, anthropologists study society ethnographically because of the highly probable importance of cognizant human action to the processes through which social formations are reproduced. Following from our "social reproductionist" approach to understanding computerization, we directed a great deal of attention while in the field to the possible roles of symboling in laying the basis for and in relation to collective human action, "politics" in the anthropological sense.[9]

The main advantage of a social formation reproduction model of social process is the emphasis it places on the contingency of particular social arrangements. Any social formation has no necessarily independent existence; its perpetuation depends on being reproduced or actively recreated from day-to-day and era-to-era. By the same token, any particular structure is dependent for its perpetuation on the reproductive dynamics of the social formation or formations in which it is embedded. This contingency means that social formation reproduction is a dynamic process, one characterized by frequent change.

Social reproductionist ethnology has roots in both neo-Marxist social theory and realist philosophy. On this reading, social formation reproduction is explicable at the most abstract level in terms of culture, on the one hand, and political economy, on the other. Culture and political economy are held to be related dialectically, in that they both constitute and are constituted by each other, the purpose of empirical research being to grasp this dialectic in particular situations.

One form of mechanistic Marxism, metaphysical materialism, contends that material, political economic factors, those which go on "behind the back" of people, not mediated to any significant extent by peoples' perceptions or their conscious action, have causal priority over more "cultural" structures and processes, at least, in Althusser's (1971) phrase, "in the last instance." Such views have much in common with simplistic technological determinism, against which we have argued that technology is embedded in culture, economic relations, and so forth. For the metaphysical materialist trained as an economist, it is difficult to avoid the mechanistic reductionism of political economism, the tendency to think of economic phenomena in overly structural terms, as contextually given. On this reading, symboling-based behavior is more contingent, something whose possibilities are more *determined by* political economic parameters than determining of them.[10]

What we experienced in Sheffield was a situation in which the theoretical problem of the relative importance of cultural practice and political economy was being worked out in a particular case, the social terrain of computerization. We participated in a "real" experiment in the relative power of conscious human action, on the one hand, and political economy, on the other, to determine the course of social formation reproduction. As described in Chapter 1, informants sometimes conceptualized the current situation in Sheffield as determined by powerful political economic context factors, such as the international division of labor, the decline of capitalism, computer technology, and so on. Among them, such factors were perceived to oppose the healthy perpetuation (in theoretical terms, the extended reproduction) of the Sheffield of working people, shrinking of the manufacturing base, increasing problems due to the absence of a regional base for the alternative service economy, increasing tendencies for people to think of themselves as individuals rather than collectively, and so forth.

For various reasons, we are critical of political economistic interpretations. For one thing, contemporary social formations are just too complex. In Britain, for example, the political practice of the Conservative Party is difficult to explain in terms of some universal economic structure. That is, whatever the abstract validity of monetarist economics, the decisions to shut not those but these particular mines or steel plants, or to privatize these specific activities now performed in the public sector, and so on, are more explicable in terms of ideology than "external" economic structures. For people in South Yorkshire, the miners' strike and the nature of policing manifest during it are the clearest examples of action determined by class more than economic and structural reasons. Displaced miners and steel workers in South Yorkshire experience unemployment as about class, as a consequence of adverse *political* events—as *dis*employment rather than as personal failure—and thus as much an internal, deliberate human action as an external, economic event.

## Combined Structural and Processual Models

Mechanistic conceptions of social formation reproduction are forms of theorizing that treat social structures and social processes as ontologically distinct. For sociologist Anthony Giddens, structures and processes are not different kinds of things so much as alternative moments of the same thing. Thus such entities as a sex role structure and the gendering process should really be discussed as if they were fundamentally the same, merely alternative phases of what he calls a "structuration" (1986).

The problem that Giddens has pointed out is an important one. Large social structures like "states" and "political economies" are used abstractly, often in language that implies that they are little affected by the daily actions of human beings. Conversely, descriptions of human action are often abstracted from structural contexts. However, we have decided not to follow Giddens's terminological suggestion. The structure/process contrast is still useful if one recognizes that it is a relative rather than an absolute distinction. It is true that structures like states are from one point of view only a residual effect of human action, their influence permitted through certain forms of human inaction. Yet structures cumulatively place real limits on what humans can normally accomplish. That is, nation states are more structure- than process-like, but the converse is often true for local politics. By describing computerization ethnographically before addressing analytic issues, we hope to avoid both overly structuralist and overly processualist readings of our analysis. Like Giddens, we wish to emphasize the ultimate connections between structures and daily practices. The computerization experiences described in Parts One and Two are not reducible to the dynamics of structures alone; people do have an impact on the nature of their own experience. To gauge how great this impact is, however, one must grasp the constraints on action imposed by the structure-like entities that constitute the broad context for the reproduction of computer-mediated social formations. We begin our account with structures, but it should be borne in mind that this is an expository strategy only.

## Class and Social Formation Reproduction

The need to view computerization in social reproductionist terms can be illustrated ethnographically. In South Yorkshire, working class peoples' behavior and speech reveal a strong sense of the kinds of human actions that improve or interfere with the quality of their lives and that of the region as a whole. In our theoretical language, they have a developed cultural construct of the process of social formation reproduction, the key symbolic component of which is "class." One senses the importance of "class" as a symbol, for example, in the frequently articulated sentiment that people are most likely to find their personal situation improved as the position of their class improves.

Different classes have different symbols and build alternative value associations on them, and there are substantial disagreements among Sheffielders of different classes as to the relationship of the dynamics of the reproduction of the region as a whole to the dynamics of class and therefore to the proper way to conceptualize and talk about class. "Class" is key to an appropriate understanding of social reproduction in South Yorkshire, in that it is class rather than any particular technology that ties together the way in which individuals experience the various structures and processes described in Parts Three and Four. Thus, as our title *Computing Myths, Class Realities* implies, "class" has validity as an analytic construct as well as being an important element of the way the "natives" conceptualize social reproduction.

In the remainder of this chapter we will clarify the way in which we use "class" analytically. Some of the characteristics of "class" relevant to an understanding of the computing/social change relationship, as well as how class and computing are both important parts of lived experience, are indicated in the following vignette.

The rally had been publicized on a widely circulated leaflet as another event in Sheffield peace week. When we entered the assembly hall in the local office of the Engineering Workers' Union, however, we saw few of the local peace activists, such as the people David had seen at the Campaign for Nuclear Disarmament meeting the night before. As we waited for the speakers, we read the posters on the wall, most of which were advertisements for the *Morning Star,* the daily newspaper of the Communist Party of Britain. The posters meant that those putting on this rally were "traditional" Communist Party members, *Morning Star* readers, not Eurocommunist readers of *Marxism Today.*

The meeting chairman spoke in a broad Yorkshire accent, a sign that he felt among friends: "I'm very pleased to see all you lads and lasses coming out after a hard day on t'shop floor. Of course I wish we had a larger crowd tonight, but the *Marxism Today* crowd and their middle-class supporters, the ones responsible for sabotaging the miners' strike, appear to have boycotted us tonight, along with the cause of peace."

A similar tone was struck by the first speaker, a national official of the miners' union: "We must separate ourselves from those armchair socialists who say the solution to working people's problems requires a change in political strategy. The class issue is the basic one, and the old approach, collective action through struggle, is still the most important thing for us to be doing. Of course, as a consequence of new technology and multinational corporations, capitalism is different, and there is a need for new tactics, but not fundamentally different goals. The main role of working people is to struggle to defend our heritage and eradicate Thatcher's values."

The meeting ended with a financial appeal by a prominent female party member. She had been sitting on the platform during the speeches but had kept an eye on her eight-year-old daughter. "Why do we still need the *Morning Star?* That poster on't wall puts it clear for me sen [self]. It asks, 'Is this the age of New Technology?' The answer is there, printed inside that VDU screen: 'Murdoch's New Technology Means the Sack.' "

"Rupert Murdoch knows about computers; he used them to build a "high tech" printing plant at Wapping in London, so he could fire all his workers who were not members of the scab Electricians' Union. To us, the new technology is just another way to confuse the workers and keep 'em down. Like it says on that other poster, 'Read the Truth About Wapping in the *Morning Star.*' Support the *Morning Star* because it gives us the truth."

The vignette illustrates the "class" concerns relevant to the ethnology of computerization of at least some "natives." For the woman addressing the rally, computerization is clearly an important problem. Her "take" on computerization, clearly not computopian, is that it is a "class" problem. The consequences of computerization are seen as determined less by a technical than by a social relationship, that between the working class and the ruling class. The combined actions of Rupert Murdoch and the class of which he is a part, not some abstract social factor labelable as "technology," are viewed as responsible for what happened at Wapping.

There is a close connection between people's sense of identity and their shared ideas about why daily life takes the shape it takes. The speakers have a theory of the role of new technology that connects it to their sense of identity. Technology itself is not a threat. Rather, the impetus for new technology and its negative consequences are viewed in terms of what they perceive to be a larger context, class. Class is not just an abstract force; it is evident in the motives of individual industrialists, readable from their actions. For them, the experience of technology is not separable from the experience of class; indeed, it is almost reducible to it.

As indicated in this vignette, the terms people use to discuss such issues as new technology, highly charged with symbolic value, contain analyses, answers to "why" as well as to "what." Though one cannot ignore them, if one wishes to express successfully what one has learned about an issue as contentious as computerization, one needs to be more precise in how one uses words than is generally the case in everyday speech. To explore what relevance class had beyond its considerable role in perception—its broader relevance to social formation reproduction—we need an ethnologically valid concept of class.

Our previous ethnographic experience had persuaded us that a concept of class was likely to have continuing relevance to the way working-class people in Sheffield apprehend their lives. As well as a term widely used in Sheffield, "class" is a preoccupation of social theory. Without a notion of class, it would be as difficult to talk social theory with a British sociologist as it would be to discuss computerization with a *Morning Star* reader. Still, one can accept the need to incorporate human action into one's model of social formation reproduction without assuming that it is predominantly class through which humans "proact." Indeed, there is a loudly made, if flawed, attempt to convince people that class is of decreasing relevance in contemporary society, as in the following comment from the *New York Times:* "Most analysts agree that … [a reshaping of Labour Party ideology] … is necessary because of the decline of organized labor and the shrinking size of the working class" (*New York Times,* March 25, 1988).

This "end of class" view holds that a working class with a distinctive culture and politics is of declining social relevance. Theoretically, this end of class view conflates an economic judgment (decline of organized labor) with an apparently demographic observation (shrinkage of the working class). The result is in effect a statement about social theory on the declining influence over social reproduction of a particular social formation element. The political and cultural creations of working-class people will eventually become irrelevant to emerging social situations. In a typical end of class view, a technology-led transformation in social reproduction, a change manifest most vividly in computerization, will push us inevitably toward a postlabor, postindustrial society—one in which "worker," specifically, and occupationally related social identities, in general, are no longer of great relevance.

Consider the following comment attributed to Margaret Thatcher: "This business of working class is on the way out. After all, aren't I working class? I work jolly hard, I can tell you" (Margaret Thatcher, 1969, quoted in *News on Sunday*).

"End of class" views suggests that those at the lower levels of industrial social formations, even if they are there as a consequence of not owning or controlling means for the production of profit, have little to gain from organizing collectively or pursuing broad forms of collective identity or class culture. Because of rapid technological change, a shared practice based on identity as members of a working class is no longer viable. Instead, more individualistic pursuit of personal goals is presented as more likely, in the long run, to produce personal satisfaction. Though such arguments have been a common part of the political process in industrial social formations, they have been justified more insistently in recent times.

"End of class" arguments are refutable. Marxists tend to do so simply by pointing out how views that denigrate collective struggle are patently in the interest of socially dominant groups. Mavis's experience in the Data Shop constitutes a convincing ethnographic argument for the continuing relevance of class in the era of the computer.

Perhaps of greater difficulty to the analyst who wishes to continue to use class analysis, however, is another problem hinted at in the vignette: The nature of the class/computerization link is controversial *within* the working class. For example, whereas for *Morning Star* readers the computer is of interest primarily as a tool of domination, for others computers are symbolized very differently. The issue of *Marxism Today* current at the time of this rally, for example, carried on its back cover an advertisement for a computerized information service/data base, claimed to be "a necessity for every informed Marxist." Indeed, one's stand on computerization became an important issue in the struggle for leadership.

Computerization is a highly *politicized* issue. In one sense, the politicization of one's issue is an advantage to the field-worker; it means, for example, that informants are likely to talk about and act in relation to one's issue on their own, and thus ethnographic data are likely to be abundant. As the dilemmas explored in Chapter 3 suggested, however, politicization can also be a difficulty. Informants were wary until they judged our position was compatible with theirs. In any case, they made presumptions about our interest that on occasion hampered our work.

It was only by being able to communicate that our research problem was important in terms of some of the values we shared with informants, while at the same time indicating that our views were not necessarily the same as theirs, that we developed an ethnographic relationship with space for real dialogue. Development of an ethnology of computerization involves more than finding language that does not offend. To be adequately ethnological about computerization, we have to find a way to talk about computerization and describe its consequences holistically, to include the technological, political, and social dimensions of computerization in a single analytic frame. This must be done in a manner that not only avoids prejudging the basic social processes involved in it but also allows dialogic access to informants.

### A Cultural Construction of Class

The preexisting dialogue regarding the class implications of computing gave us the ethnographic entrée we needed in Sheffield. We also feel that, analytically, computerization in Sheffield cannot be understood separately from class. In our view, class, far from being opposed to culture, must be seen as a cultural process as well as a social structure. It is only through seeing class in sociocultural terms that the changes in the lives of working people, and the relationship of those changes to computerization, make sense. When informants assert that computerization is a class issue, they mean that class is a major social mediation between technology and daily activities. The consequences of any particular implemented technology, like computing, depend on the particular, class-structured ways that technology is connected to the general process of social formation reproduction. In short, computerization is a question of class culture.

One way to conceive of this class culture is to see it as constituting what Bourdieu calls a "class habitus." For him, an individual's set of characteristic habits or behaviors is his or her habitus, "a durably installed generative principle of regulated improvisations" that generates "practices which tend to reproduce the regularities immanent in the objective conditions of the production of their generative principle"; in other words, habitus is tied to material conditions (1978:82). In regions like Sheffield, the class character of habitus is particularly evident. Arguing for the class character of habitus in general, Bourdieu comments on social relations:

> [B]eing the internalization of ... objective structures ... 'interpersonal' relations are never, except in appearance, individual-to-individual relations and ... the truth of the interaction is never entirely contained in the interaction. ... [I]t is their present and past positions in the social structure that biological individuals carry with them ... in the form of dispositions which are so many marks of social position. (1978:81, 82)

There are clear advantages to this conception of culture. Ortner (1984) and others have argued that it directs analysis to practice rather than structure, whether that of a political economy, a set of immanent linguistic antinomies, or a framework invented by the analyst/observer. However, Bourdieu's approach is ultimately inadequate because it is a mechanistic model of social formations, whose reproduction is merely simple replication of both habitus and structure.[11]

Our Sheffield research was cast in a broader mold, with an emphasis on extended or expanded, not simple, social formation reproduction (Hakken 1987b). The reproduction of culture is held normally to involve change; in the process of reproducing themselves (or being reproduced), social formations are the locus of shifting relations, hegemonies, and adaptations among the various moments, from the semiotic to the productive. The implicit goal of any collective action is to influence the pattern of this reproduction, a matter particularly important, and difficult, for subordinate social groups.

## Theories of Class

Class has been an important although controversial element of social study at least since the nineteenth century. Its relevance as a purely *descriptive* category—as a way to chart the stratification present in the reproduction of complex social formations—is generally accepted by social analysts, as in data on the increasing stratification of income and household resources in the 1980s on both sides of the Atlantic. If it is to be used as an *ethnological* category, however, "class" must point to an underlying social dynamic important to *accounting for* the broad outlines of social reproduction in the social formations under consideration. In Marxist theory, for example, because class is important in understanding history, it carries important implications for how groups should orient their actions in the future. Such analytic uses of class are the ones questioned most sharply in recent times, as in the "end of class" views described above.

We take the position that class remains an important determinant of people's experience, particularly with regard to computing. To make our case, we must separate our view from a perspective on class alluded to in the vignette and implicit in "traditional" working-class politics. As described in Chapters 2 and 6, appeals to traditional working-class values are decreasingly successful at mobilizing action. This does not in itself invalidate the relevance of class, however. From the reproductionist perspective, any notion of a "traditional" class is suspect, because the cultural content of a social group normally changes, "tradition" regularly being invented and reinvented. One can argue for the general relevance of a "working class" as a social actor in various periods in the history of employment social formations without committing oneself to any particular constellation of working-class characteristics as essential. Indeed, to do so would be to privilege a particular class moment over all others.

Analytically, our task is to specify the relationship of computing to the "really existing" working class of today, not to a "traditional" working class fixed at some point in the past. Still, to justify the use of "class" as a term of general analytic utility relevant to computerization and to changes in the lives of working people today, we need to specify more exactly what we mean by "working-class people," to identify which classes exist and, if there is a working class, to determine who is in it.

These issues have exercised social scientists for a long time, but they are very much a part of the way people in Sheffield argue about events as well. It is very common for political commentators to identify a comparatively rigid class system as a distinctive feature of Britain among industrial societies, and it is equally common for economists from both the left and the right to implicate class in the problems of the British economy. Yet a consensus on the relevance of class to social process does not mean there is consensus on how class is to be understood. In addition to ambiguity about who is in any particular class, there is disagreement about how classes relate to each other.

What things are characteristic of the working class, not merely a temporary manifestation based fundamentally on some other social structure? In a particularly revealing discussion of class, English feminist Anne Phillips (1987) identifies three ways the term is used. She speaks first of a "common sense" usage, as manifest most frequently in the descriptive use of "middle class," "working class," and other elaborations of these basic categories. She correctly stresses the extent to which these notions are used to draw attention to the way we perceive our own and other peoples' lives, common sense usages of class having an important semiotic dimension.

Second, she refers to the notions of class involved in government statistics, notions that, as in the United States, rely primarily on occupational groups such as "unskilled manual" and "professional." These are also descriptive models of class, but they operate on a more abstract plane and are less a part of everyday language than the first usages. The third type of class usage to which she draws attention is the theoretical type, of which the Marxist theory of class is an example. Such theories of class contain notions about the underlying dynamic that generates class relations, the Marxian theory being based on relations of production as a primary generator of other social relations. Thus laborers and capitalists are the two important classes in an industrial society. Although Phillips points out that the different levels on which these views of class function complicate the discussion, her main emphasis is on how important elements of the class phenomenon are grasped by both the Marxist political economic and the more semiotic "common sense" approaches. The ethnological problem is to combine the positive features of both into an adequate class construct.

### The Philosophical Presumptions of Our Class Analysis

The materialist, realist philosophical approach of Roy Bhaskar (1979) allows us to develop just such an integrated class construct. Bhaskar argues that an important job for philosophy is to help the social scientist be clear about the presumptions that inform problem selection. Realism, an approach in philosophy with a long history, has recently come to renewed prominence, especially in Britain. New forms of realism developed initially in response to philosophical critiques of the adequacy and clarity of the theoretical constructs that underlie scientific, especially social scientific, research. They have also been pushed further by those interested in providing an alternative approach to issues raised by postmodernism (e.g., Bhaskar 1989).

For Marxists, realism provides a way to avoid both the economic reductionism of many previous Marxisms and the idealism of many poststructrualisms, for example, Foucaultism. From materialism, realists accept the existence of underlying structures that influence human events. From cognitivists, realists accept the argument that the way people conceive of their situations, the cultural phenomena that structure their perceptions, have material consequences. Marxist realism is perhaps best understood as an outgrowth of attempts to apply the rigor of analytic philosophy, without its idealist presumptions, to Marx's dictum about how "men [*sic*] make their own history, but not just as they please."

The main value of a realist approach to the social scientist is as an epistemological guide; that is, as a tool to help us be sure we are clear about why we have chosen to do what we find ourselves doing. Realism critiques empiricism; it is critical of the assumption that unexamined common sense categories, those used in social life, are necessarily the best for purposes of analysis. This is why realists reject definitions of class that equate class with occupational groups. For the same reason, realists are unwilling to pretend that the problems they select and the ways they pose them are not themselves directly influenced by social processes; rather problem selection and statement are to be guided by explicit theory, not implicit prejudice.

In the realist perspective that we use, class is understood to operate on three levels. First, there are the "empirical" manifestations of class, such as occupation, whose class aspects are observable and frequently remarked upon by "the natives." Losing your manual job when a computerized machine tool comes into the plant, while white collar workers retain their jobs, is such an empirical class event.

Second, there is class in the "actual" sense, particular structures and processes that underlie and constrain the perceptions and actions of particular groups. According to Roger Burrows, the domain of the 'actual': "refers to those elements of the 'social' which are not observed (either because they cannot be, or because there is no human agent available to do the observing) but which nonetheless constitute events which have an impact upon the 'social'" (1987:7, 8). Arguing that the reason you lost your job was because your union wasn't strong enough to force your employer to negotiate an effective technology agreement is to make an argument in terms of "actual" class.

Third, there are "real" classes, social entities that "constitute the necessary basis for the actual and the empirical, and [are] constituted by a given set of relatively enduring historical and spatially *intransitive* social structures which have real *causal powers."* Such causal powers, however, are "conceptualized as tendencies which only generate events when activated by essentially contingent events" (Burrows 1987:8). Were one to argue, for example, that management refuses to negotiate over new technology because of immanent tendencies that encourage dominant social groups to avoid practices that threaten the conditions of its domination, one would be drawing attention to "real" class.

From the above it should be evident that the value of any realist theory of class depends strongly on the validity of the way this third level is handled. In our case, these conceptions are built out of a broad reading of historical, anthropological events, like the characterization of technology developed above. There, we spoke of the need to distinguish repressive from productive technology, and we connected the emergence of the former to the application of abstractions from the latter to human social process itself, in the form of the extraction of a material surplus from one human group and its appropriation by another. In Part Four, we make a similar argument with regard to gendering. These are among the theoretical justifications for considering emergence of permanent social stratification, or "class," as the most significant event in human history. At the level of the real, a class can be conceived as a transcendent (Bhaskar 1989) social structure with real causal powers activated by contingent events.

Such a general understanding of the importance of class to social process in complex society must be translated methodologically into a set of procedures to identify the actual manifestations of class in relation to the particular social process in which we are interested.

When we turn to the question of computerization, we arrive at the "actual" level of reality. "Computerization" is an actual structure with substantial consequences, a structure in which empirical manifestations are a consequence of numerous technical, industrial relations, political, and semiotic contingencies, themselves all influenced by underlying "real" class. In order to account for what we experienced in Sheffield, we find it useful to conceptualize at least provisionally a set of "actual" classes—a working class, a middle class, and a ruling class—that manifest "real" class more directly. As actualities, each of these classes is contingent on the character of a number of factors in historical and current social formation reproduction, including work, human biological reproduction, the international political economy, the state and its various dynamics, and multiple symbolic or semiotic processes.

### British Use of Class

As Phillips suggests, a high proportion of those in British society use the language of class to describe events. Coherent at the "empirical" level, Britons talk as if their society has a more or less stable class structure. There is a dominant or ruling class with roots in the monarchy, aristocracy, and nobility that over the years has incorporated into itself the top elements of rising strata, such as commercial, financial, and industrial elites. There is a large working class, composed primarily of factory and office workers. Between these two is a middle class of professional employees.

The basic characteristic attributed to this class structure until recently was its stability, a consequence of each class having recognized its social role and having contributed appropriately to the reproduction of the general social formation. In this view, often articulated by former Conservative Prime Minister Harold MacMillan, the working classes provided their labor and produced the commodities that resulted in profit and therefore the wealth to run both the private and public economies. The dominant or ruling classes made the basic decisions that guided the mixed economy, while also participating in and funding a wide range of voluntary activities to promote a decent existence for all. The middle classes had their own interests but also made tactical alliances, sometimes with workers and other times with rulers. An ideology of civility was an important element in this general structure of reciprocity, a structure that was held to provide opportunities for each group to pursue its interest while recognizing the contribution of the others.

Although perhaps a useful point from which to initiate discussion, when such empirical class is treated as "actual" class, it obscures as much as it reveals. To understand what is actually happening with computerization in Sheffield, a more dynamic, complex model of class is necessary.

In terms of the working class, it is clear from the *Morning Star* vignette that at least some people in Sheffield have a different notion about what it means to be in the working class and how the interest of this group is to be pursued. As a consequence of the history described in Chapter 2, this is a notion of a traditional working class, the industrial working class, whose members have jobs in large extractive and manufacturing industries. In line with the processes described by Marx and Engels in the *Communist Manifesto,* this class is held to be growing bigger and more militant. Through economic militancy at the point of production, this traditional working class will eventually come to control the reproduction of the industrial social formation. Occasionally, this traditional working class can make alliances with other social groups, even fallen-away middle-class or ruling-class elements, as long as these take on a worldview appropriate to the traditional working class.

In the Sheffield of 1987, another conception of the working class was emerging. As yet phrased primarily in negative terms, the alternative conception drew attention to the failure of traditional notions of the working class to give adequate attention to the needs of women, minorities, youth, the unemployed, and so on, and argued for a more open conception, one without a unitary focus on industrial militancy.

In terms of numbers, there were essentially two ways in which the working class was changing, or the traditional working class eroding and a new working class emerging. First, an increasing proportion of working people, or at least those traditionally conceived of as the "natural constituency" of the industrial working class, were no longer "working" in the sense of orienting their lives and self-identities around a paid job; indeed, many (e.g., housewives) never did so orient themselves. For example, a greater proportion of United Kingdom men between the ages of fifty-five and sixty-five were unwaged than were waged. And a series of questions was raised regarding whether the interests of these people were adequately served and servable by the methods of traditional working-class militancy. A second actual problem for the traditional conception of the working-class culture was the increasing proportion of workers with educational or technical credentials. The vignette suggests some of the hostility of the working-class traditionalist to those often referred to as the middle class. Yet an increasing proportion of those in employment have some ability to use their individual employment situations to pursue what in the past were effectively pursuable only collectively. In this respect, they are "middle class." British trade union membership is growing in only a few areas, and these are primarily technical and managerial, whereas membership has fallen most, both absolutely and proportionally, among those in unskilled or semiskilled work.

The following contradiction has arisen: To the extent that traditional working-class culture depends on industrial militancy, its reproduction is dependent on the willingness of an increasing proportion of those people labeled "middle class" to act militantly. Yet it is these people who are in the best position among employees to pursue an individual, rather than a collective, interest. Though in the "traditionalist" view, the working class should be hesitant about accepting such people until they renounce their individual advantages, it is just these advantages that are the basis of any increasing trade union power.

In short, the actual working class we encountered in Sheffield was growing more complex. In terms of perceptions, it is useful to speak of "traditional" and (as yet largely unarticulated) "alternative" views of the working class. In terms of groups, the working class is differentiated, with neither the nonwaged nor the more securely employed fitting neatly into the traditional categorization. It is this complex, differentiated conception of class that we must use if we are to understand the consequences of computerization in Sheffield.

## Actual Conceptions of Other Classes

An empiricist approach is no more appropriate when discussing the dominant social group in Sheffield. Although not the direct focus of our research, some model of the ruling class is necessary for posing the question of computerization properly, because of, rather than in spite of, one informant's contention that the local ruling class had "disappeared." This contention does have some validity on an empirical level; most of the large, locally owned industries had disappeared by 1986. Though the Hallam constituency in West Sheffield remained one of the most well-to-do areas in the nation, the growing economic divide between the South of

England and the North, especially areas like Sheffield, made Thatcherism less popular even among some of the affluent in the region.

There have been numerous attempts to explicate the political phenomenon of Thatcherism in class terms. The influence of the ruling class was mediated politically through Thatcherism, a mediation made possible by the willingness of large numbers of nonruling, middle-class people to vote for it. Like Reaganism, Thatcherism was in many ways a program of most benefit to transnational capital, through its emphasis on capital mobility, deregulation, and so on. Such policies have had profound consequences for at least some elements of the "old" ruling class in Britain; investment in British manufacturing has been stagnant since 1979, for example. Thatcherism included a radical attack on the organizations of the working class, especially unions; Margaret Thatcher herself described as her long-term goal the elimination of socialism from Britain, meaning the elimination of structures and policies conducive to large-scale collective action. At one point, she argued that "society" itself was a meaningless abstraction. Her successor, John Major, is equally committed to creation of a "classless" society. Despite its openness to transnational capital, the heart of Thatcherism was really an appeal against the old notions of reciprocity and civility and in favor of the individualism most characteristic of the petite bourgeoisie, or old "middle class"; its hero was the "Sloan Ranger" or yuppie, making a killing on the stock exchange "without conscience," as the Conservative Party chairman is reputed to have said.

Empirical uses of "middle class" vary even more than those of working class and ruling class. Sometimes the phrase is a reference to economic status, such as income. Sometimes it is a reference to life-styles (what one eats or wears, where one lives or shops, how long one has been in an area). Sometimes it is a reference to the background of one's parents or grandparents; sometimes it is a label of self-identity. We think of the actual middle class as composed of people dependent on selling their labor for an income, but this income is relatively secure, at least perceived to derive more from personal attributes than from collective action.

To think of themselves as sharing an interest with "working class" people is obviously not the only option open to "middle class" people in Sheffield. Another is to see their interest as linked directly to that of the ruling class. Wealth can be held to be generated through profit; therefore, any increase in the size of the total profit generated in the political economy is likely to mean an increase in the part of that surplus that the middle-class individual is able to capture for her/himself. One imagines something like this consciousness as characteristic of brokers in the city of London whose wages have grown since the 1986 "Big Bang" of share market computerization and internationalization. This argument is one basis of the Conservative Party's appeal to the middle class.

Such an appeal is often not persuasive to the middle-class person in Sheffield. Most jobs in the region with middle-class security attached to them derive ultimately either from manufacturing industry or from public spending on public services, maintenance of which depends on collective action. These sectors of the economy have been hit particularly hard by Thatcherism. There is a third alternative for the middle-class person: to perceive her or his interest as separate and distinct from that of either the working class, on the one hand, or the ruling class, on the other. It is to this view that the Social Democratic/Liberal Alliance attempts to appeal.

### Class in General

In brief, the surface or empirical manifestations of class among people in Sheffield are in part a consequence of underlying "actual" classes. These underlying classes are complex, having both conceptual and behavioral aspects; they are changing, as a consequence of the dynamics of the reproduction of the broader social formation, and they are subject to substantial contextual mediation. Thus the nature of the "actual" working class is a function of the increasing proportion of working people who are either unwaged altogether or "unwaged" in a salaried form. Similarly, the impact of the "actual" ruling class is affected by Thatcherism as a political phenomenon. The influence of computer technology is also mediated by these complex class phenomena, the particular manifestations of which are a consequence of multiple actual structures and processes. The underlying entity within which all of these connections and mediations can be best explicated, however, is the real entity of class.

Our orientation toward class as the most important general mediation of the computing/social change connection in South Yorkshire derives from our general model of social formation reproduction. This ethnology identifies "real" social inequality as the distinctive feature of complex social formations. Though mediated in actual social formations by a variety of other factors, real social inequality does not disappear. As argued by Harris (1968), it is the ultimate problem with which any theory of complex social formations must deal.

This theorizing results in a defensible set of notions that allow us to illuminate the computing patterns described in the first half of our book. In the following chapters, we use these ethnological constructs to analyze how specific structures and processes, themselves generated in class, affect most strongly the relationship of computerization and social change.

### Notes

1. Any discussion of causes in social science confronts several knotty philosophical issues. Parts One and Two presented the ethnographic evidence for the co-occurrence and likely connection between computerization and substantial change in the lives of Sheffield working-class people. The mere fact that these processes occur together does not in and of itself mean that computerization *is responsible for* the social changes; establishing social causation is logically much more difficult than demonstrating co-occurrence. Andrew Sayer's *Method in Social Science: A Realist Approach* (1984) makes an effective case that despite

the difficulties, causative argument is a necessary element of social analysis. Jon Elster's *Explaining Technical Change* (1983) is an interesting exploration of the philosophical dimensions of causal argument in terms of our topic.

2. Ethnocentrism is also a problem when studying one's own culture. One is even more likely to "take for granted"—that is, assume to be cross-culturally valid—what is merely cultural presumption, because everyone one interacts with does the same thing.

3. Such presumption is an important flaw in the technicist academic literature critiqued in the Introduction.

4. To some extent, theory grows out of ethnographic experience, as the empiricists recommend. Our initial, groping efforts to comprehend field experience are also strongly affected by our preconceptions—firmly ensconced in grant applications, among other places—that themselves emerge from our personal experiences, our conversations with others, and our reading of theory. In short, the relationship between the ethnology of computing articulated here and the experience of computerization is a dialectical one: The theory grows out of fieldwork, description, and analysis, which in turn are affected by theory.

5. Bernard and Pelto (1986: Chapter 13) use "technology" to refer to material artifacts alone, an overly restrictive usage. In an article on educational technology published some time ago, we defined technology somewhat more broadly, as any combination of techniques and equipment to accomplish a given end (Andrews and Hakken 1976). Most definitions of "technology" refer to basic patterns in the instrumentalities, both physical and social, that humans use in relating to their physical environment. After our experience in Sheffield, we feel that such general definitions, because they merge together processes that need to be kept apart analytically, are too broad and of less analytic value than the more specific notion presented here.

6. Although many people in employment-based social formations believe that machines were the cause of the new industrial society, a new *social* arrangement—the detailed division of labor of the employment relationship—was generally present earlier. It thus makes sense to see the general spread of machine technology as more a consequence than a cause of a new social relationship. (Braverman 1974; Clawson 1980)

7. Defined technically, computers are merely electronic devices for storing and manipulating large amounts of data, whether linguistic or numeric, in order to extract and organize information. With the development of less expensive and more powerful computers in the 1970s, a nearly universal information technology, unlike previous technologies, could be implemented almost simultaneously in a wide range of economic and social contexts. Thus, there is at least a prima facie case for special concern about the relationship of computing to the character of our times.

8. Indeed, probably since the rise of state-level social formations about 5,000 years ago, social formation reproduction has operated on an immense, if not world, scale. There is often, however, at least some autonomy in social reproductive dynamics at the community, regional, and national levels as well. Therefore, it is justifiable, in order to actually do empirical research, to treat particular reproducing social groups for a time as if they existed in relative isolation from more general levels of social reproduction, as long as this isolation is eventually removed.

9. We believe that culturally based, collective actions can have profound influence on the general process of social formation reproduction. By coordinating their actions, humans can *transform* their life system. Though more successful at transformation than any other species, humans exert varying degrees of influence and can lose control of the consequences

of their actions. How people try to control and transform their life system is politics in the anthropological sense. Our Sheffield research was in part an attempt to explore the extent to which a particular set of conscious human actions in one local social formation had an impact on the social correlates of a particular example of computerization.

10. At least in part out of exasperation, the tendency of the Marxist anthropologist is to argue the opposite—that culture is more determining and that political economy is contingent. This itself is of course very close to the position of the classical idealist philosophies and of many religions. We see social formation reproductionism as distinct from both.

11. Perhaps Bourdieu's mechanical model is a consequence of his preoccupation with education as a social process. Like Margaret Mead, he tends to treat education as an essentially unidirectional process, involving the enculturation of naive youth with the cultural constructs of experienced elders. Such enculturationist approaches fail to see education as a significant point for potential social transformation (Hakken 1978).

# 8

# The National State
# and Computerization

The ethnography of Part Two indicates that computing in Sheffield was associated with rather profound changes in social life but that the patterns of computing were quite diverse, suggesting substantial interdeterminancy. Clearly one of the most important (and unanticipated) divergences was that between computing in private and state institutions.

## Patterns of Computerization

In predominantly private sector work activities, such as food provision, the making of mining machinery, and new housing construction, computerization tended to be ancillary, introduced primarily into or restricted to separable tasks such as accounting. Computers were fit into existing patterns, perhaps moderately accelerating trends already present, such as centralization or labor reduction, but not altering general characteristics. Manufacturing manifested similar patterns: a gradual approach, piecemeal purchase of equipment, the evolution of systems to accomplish discrete tasks, and low levels of investment.

More extensive computerization, associated with greater degrees of social transformation, was manifest in national state activities. In mining, computerization transformed the nature of production and had profound effects on local communities and the contours of British industry and social life in general. Although less visible, computerization was becoming important in national health care and social service delivery initiatives. It was also in public sector primary productive activities that worker resistance to new technology was most manifest. Computing had the most dramatic effects in some local state actions—the housing strike, on the one hand, and, on the other, projecting a radically different NIT policy with regard, for instance, to health. However, in others—education, research and development, politics—extensive computerization was not associated with great social change, computerization strategies being less persistently pursued in the face of apparently more powerful political agendas.

The patterns of computerization in services were also more divergent, like those in state-mediated activity and unlike those in subsistence-related work or manufacturing. Though some computing—for example, in cooperatives—enhanced skills, some computing deskilled. In other cases—for example, building societies—the process had moderate impacts with regard to skill and employment levels. Even in cases of apparently more adverse impact on skills, computerization highlighted certain social features of the labor process, such as the "human interaction" skills of employees, which may have protected existing jobs as they were transformed.

Thus how jobs changed with computerization depended on (1) the extent to which their content was connected to basic production and (2) the character of the organization within which they existed. When a job was part of an organization involved in a material, subsistence commodity or service, the impacts of computerization were muted. Similarly, in organizations tied closely to a "productive" imperative—that is, the creation of physical things that have to work as they are supposed to—"piecemeal" approaches were most frequent. Also, when a job was computerized in an organization like a cooperative—whose goals involve the creation of new social relationships—the results deviated substantially from the deskilling and disemployment often associated with new technology. Conversely, national state sector subsistence producers and private sector organizations whose commodities were not material or subsistence tended to introduce the most radical forms of computerization and were associated with the most drastic social change.

The importance of state mediation suggests a relationship between computing, politics, and class: that the social power of relevant groups and individuals is an important determinant of the course of computerization. Human priorities may have as much to do with computerization as machines, as important as the "computerizability" of an activity from a purely technical point of view. Among the most powerful priority-forming institutions is the national state.

## The British State's Computing Policy in the 1980s

Early in the period of new information technology, there was much about which British computopians could be optimistic. As a result of the pioneering work of such computer specialists as Alan Turing, Britain was an early entrant into the computer world. Inexpensive personal computers were quickly and widely available; even as late as 1986, it was presumed in the press that there were more personal computers per person in Britain than anywhere else in the world. Such British firms as ICL were major actors in information technology. The future looked bright as well; an integrated public sector telephone, telegraph, and mail service, for example, was envisioned as providing the basis for a "wired society" (Barron and Curnow 1979), universal access to new information technology effectively creating and opening up a range of new computing possibilities.

Arguing that substantial state support for development would be necessary to keep British manufacturing competitive with world computing developments, the

Labour government of the 1970s established a public sector firm, Inmos, to underwrite research and development on forefront technology items such as the transputer, "a network on a chip."

Conservative politicians embraced computers as an important symbol of the "modern" postclass era into which they wished to project society. After coming to national power in 1979, they developed several policies regarding computers, including the showcasing of computing in such state sector institutions as mining and social services. They also financed such programs as "computers in the schools," which placed a BBC brand microcomputer in every classroom, and a follow-up school software distribution program. By 1987 the Tories' election manifesto proclaimed that "British schools are world leaders in the use of computers in the classroom."

Other policies tended to undermine these procomputing activities, however. Commitments to privatization of public sector enterprises and the shrinking of the public sector in general led to a breakup of Inmos and a substantial reduction of public support for computer research and development, especially in the universities. The collection of statistics on the size of the domestic computer market, information essential to the maintenance and orderly development of a domestic computer industry, was eliminated. The telephone and telegraph systems were privatized and "competition" was encouraged, leading to the loss of the technological compatibility necessary for a "wired society."

Some contradictory images of computing were built into the policies themselves, but poor results were more a consequence of factors less directly related to computing per se. The contradictions of the Thatcherite project are particularly evident in its policies toward the production and sale of computers themselves. By 1985 British computer technology had lost its market competitiveness; IBM-PC compatibility was becoming standard in the business world. Though such developments may not have been avoidable forever, the shrinkage of state means to cope with economic change was certainly a contributing factor to their acceleration. Because international market contours were ideologically held to be determined by forces largely beyond national influence, the Alvey Commission, a public body convened to examine the state of computerization, concluded in 1983 that there was no point in attempting to maintain a comprehensive, broad-range domestic computer industry. Alvey redirected efforts into a few specific areas in which the British might still be competitive, but by 1986, there was pessimism about whether even narrow goals could be achieved. The computer technology that most excited computer users in 1986 were the low cost, IBM-configured Amstrad products of Alan Sugar, most of which were designed elsewhere and manufactured in the Far East.

### Computing and General State Policy

Thus, certain procomputer policies were undermined by ideologies with substantial effect on the course of computing. Most important were the contradictory consequences that flowed from the ambitious social change goals of the Thatcher state, the policy with perhaps the greatest impact on computerization being privatization. Privatization has had three major consequences for computerization. First, the Tories clearly believed that investment in computerization was a way to make state enterprises more attractive on the private market. However, as in mining and social service, the Tories stimulated investment in forms of computerization that centralize control and information. This resulted in less flexible, less efficient information systems for those organizations remaining in the state sector.

Second, privatization tended to absorb much of available British capital, thereby limiting money available to the private sector for investment in such things as computing. Third, privatization decreased the number of modalities available to the state for carrying out procomputing policies (e.g., Inmos) and increased the difficulties of further computerization (e.g., incompatibility of telecommunication networks).

Other examples of the negative consequences of state action for computerization include the way in which new information technology in the coal industry undermined the long-run energy independence of Britain by effectively reducing usable coal reserves. Equally important has been a general centralization of authority in the national state, despite the desire to reduce the size of the state. As it becomes more powerful, even if formally smaller, the state influences an expanding component of the wealth-creating capacity of the economy. In particular, the state becomes increasingly the source of funds for innovation and expansion into new areas, through organizations like the Manpower Services Commission and Department of Environment Urban Enterprise Zones. This leads to a condition that one informant described as "pseudo-entrepreneurship, where everyone appears to be acting as if they were in a marketplace, but it's government money they're all after anyway."

In a capitalist economy, the spread of any new technology is dependent upon available investment resources. A technology like computers requires both massive capital and instruments to promote compatibility; these in turn imply instrumentalities to promote a long-term time perspective. Privatization has brought the opposite tendencies to the fore.

## The Mass Media, the State, and NIT

The mass media are another aspect of information technology in which national state policy has played a critical role. In public perception, the private national press was the battleground on which the major battle over new information technology, at Wapping, was fought. The electronic media are more in the public domain, the state having direct control over the BBC and control through regulation of other electronic media in the private sector. These regulatory mechanisms were changed to promote private sector interests. Ironically, as a purchaser of "adverts on the telly" to promote its privatization campaigns, the state became the single most important source of revenue for private electronic media during the 1980s.

During the field period, there were no systematic attempts to privatize the public mass media. It is understandable that states will give particular attention to the messages communicated over the mass media, and public ownership of such media potentially gives the state additional means to pursue public persuasion. It appeared to us Americans that there was a concerted campaign through the entire field period to use national state influence over the media to shape public opinion in a manner favorable to the state. This campaign included slashing political attacks on the BBC by a Tory party leader, "skinhead" Norman Tebbitt, political vetting of BBC employees, and several direct acts of government censorship. Though the *Spycatcher* affair reached an international community, an equally notable intervention was the suppression of Duncan Campbell's film on Zircon, a (badly kept) secret satellite intelligence program. David saw the film at the Sheffield Trades Council, but formally the government prohibited its showing, even trying to block the right of members of Parliament to see it. Censorship was consistently directed against the broad range of perspectives that Margaret Thatcher identified as "socialist." Particularly disturbing from a political point of view was her refusal to pursue evidence that agents of MI-5, the state foreign intelligence agency, were involved in a plot against Labour Prime Minister Harold Wilson.

## Civil Rights and Computerization

Similarly, although many public activities, such as housing and mass transit, were short of funds, the instruments of state repression, especially the police, were massively expanded during the 1980s. The details of the battle for Orgreave described in the vignette below illustrate the extent to which the conception of "proper behavior" on the part of the state has been greatly stretched, if not transformed. Although the miners' strike was certainly a singular event, Orgreave was only one example of the confrontational use of the technologies of repression by the "government of the day," with which the police confronted those whom Thatcher referred to as the "enemies within."

It was the first opportunity that David had to spend time with Bill, a full-time trade union official, since we had arrived back in Sheffield. Bill and David had spent the day in Bill's office while he made final preparations for a peace rally. "This rally is the kind of thing that the trade union movement does more and more often now. There is less of the normal membership support to do, there being fewer and fewer members."

While they were driving back to Sheffield, they passed a coal mine on the motorway and the conversation turned to the miners' strike. "Everyone tells me that Orgreave was the decisive event in the miners' strike," David said. "What do you think?"

"I'd say that's true," Bill responded. "Orgreave is one of the main coking plants for the steel industry, and it's actually in the city limits of Sheffield. The confrontation at Orgreave was early in the strike. Once it was clear that the police wouldn't let the pickets into Nottinghamshire, the only way to win the strike was to disrupt industries dependent on coal, like electric generation and steel. That's what the miners had achieved at Saltley Gate [Birmingham] in 1972, when they stopped the coal lorries.

"The action at Orgreave went on for weeks. I was there, you know, with Arthur [Scargill, president of the National Union of Mineworkers] on the day he was arrested. When it was all over, I was crushed. I knew the strike was lost. I went home and I had a breakdown, couldn't get out of my bed for weeks. Since then, I've felt like I was in a fog."

To the extent that the confrontation with the miners was a battle for state power, the Tories must be deemed successful. The contrast between the results of Saltley Gate and Orgreave was cited repeatedly by working-class people in South Yorkshire as an illustration of the difference between the 1970s and 1980s. At Saltley Gate, a mass picket of miners was able physically to block coal deliveries; the Conservative Heath government was unwilling to run the risk to its national legitimacy that the mass use of force to move the pickets would necessarily have entailed. At Orgreave, the government of Margaret Thatcher demonstrated its willingness to use force openly, almost brazenly; the miners were unable to find a sufficient counterforce, and their strike was lost.

The failure of the miners to stop deliveries by coal lorries (trucks) at Orgreave was the beginning of the end, although the strike went on for several months. Orgreave was dramatic not only in its results. The following section of a pamphlet published by Sheffield Policewatch, a group organized to monitor the policing of the miners' strike, vividly illustrates the central role of state violence in pursuit of the Thatcherite program:

### Police Attacks on Pickets with Horses and Riot Equipment

29 May, Orgreave: Arrived at 7:30 A.M. About 1,000 pickets and several hundred police awaiting arrival of coke lorries. Police include dog handlers and mounted police. Approximately 8:00 A.M.: six mounted police charge down the road on which we are standing, scattering miners and nearly pushing us down a bank. Just before 9:00 A.M., when the lorries started arriving, red smoke bombs went off and police started a series of charges with horses and riot shields which drove the pickets back from the plant entrance. Stragglers were picked off and arrested. At 9:00 A.M. we saw one picket standing in a field about 100 yards away suddenly snatched by two policemen (closely followed by two more) who ran up behind him. He wasn't doing anything to provoke arrest. He was pulled to the ground and dragged away. We saw another picket disappear under a pile of policemen. By 9:20 A.M. we had been pushed back 500 yards by waves of police, mounted and with riot shields; we then saw an incident where mounted policemen galloped up the road on which a picket was lying down

after being knocked over, so that he narrowly escaped trampling. About twelve police horses then galloped into the field where some miners (and at one point ourselves) had retreated for safety and tried to round the pickets up. 9:30 A.M., the situation calmed down; we saw one miner being led away, covered in blood.

1 June: 9:45 A.M. Most pickets standing on the road. They push forward as the lorries come out of the plant. Some missiles are thrown from the back; pickets appeal to mates to stop. Police surge forward; several people are crushed and fall to the ground. ... Police pursue pickets, kicking/punching from both sides. 9:50 A.M. twelve mounted police ride into the crowd. This in my view was unnecessary and dangerous. J. saw four pickets being dragged off by the police. P. saw four or five policeman kicking/hitting a picket on the ground. One policeman had his truncheon out. When a camera crew came up, another policeman told him to put it away. The picket was arrested.

18 June: The police lines opened up and a charge of the first batch of what turned out to be forty-two horses came galloping up the hill. ... Panic spread and everybody was running, including ourselves. No sooner had the horses moved up than the riot police, with all the other police lines behind them, moved along the road and the fields in one sweeping line and literally mowed down anything which stood in their way.

Some aspects of the strike implicate computing directly. During the coal strikes of the 1970s, flying pickets from coal districts strongly supportive of militant action had been used to bring out pits in other regions. Early in the 1984 strike, police prevented the use of flying pickets. This was done, on the one hand, by physically surrounding and effectively cutting off coalfield regions from interaction with each other and the rest of society. On the other hand, roadblocks at motorway interchanges and on major trunk roads were used to interdict miners' cars and those of their supporters and turn them back from nonstrike areas. Remote access to the national computer data base of motorcar registrations enabled the police to identify these vehicles. Indeed, the miners' strike marked the coming of age of a wide variety of new computer-based electronic repressive equipment and technologies, many of which had been previously tested in Northern Ireland (BSSRS Technology of Political Control Group 1985).

## Centralization

National state strike policies centralized control over the police, reinforcing a general bent toward centralizing. For example, forms of computing introduced into the welfare system reinforce a centralizing, often dominating, apparatus, contradicting both the explicit desire to shrink the influence of the state and counter to the technological potential of microcomputing. The tendency to centralize is particularly evident in the government's Data Protection Act (DPA) of 1985. Justified as a vehicle to protect the individual against the electronic abuse of data bases, the act required state registration by anyone, including anthropological researchers, using computers to store data about individuals. The DPA's high registration fees, combined with exemptions for nonelectronic storage of data, inhibited the use of new information technology by small users like tenant's associations. However, the DPA provided no protection against data abuse by the state, as in the case of the miners' strike.

## Computing and State Policy Goals

In sector after sector, computing was centralized. This, in turn, was at least partly the reason for both the contraction of personal computing noted in Part Two and the contraction of the British computing industry. These results came about in spite of real government attempts to promote popular computing. To comprehend why these contradictory developments were allowed to come to pass, one needs an analysis of the broader goals of state policy under the Tories. The radical nature of Conservative national policy, aimed at changing the fundamental basis of popular government from franchise to property, and the radical methods used, including a higher level of state violence, emerge in press reports on Conservative Party policies.

First, the policies had a clear proximate target: "socialism," effectively equated with the actions of local governments run by Labour Party majorities. "The Prime Minister lashed out at 'tinpot Socialist republics' in local government, with their intimidation, harassment and anti-police activity" (*The Star*, Sheffield, December 31, 1986).

Stuart Hall of the Centre for Contemporary Cultural Studies argues that the fundamental Conservative project was much more ambitious—to change culture, everyday British social life as it had functioned at least since the end of World War II; to reverse "ordinary common sense." To understand this project, Hall claims, one had to begin with the basic shared values of the British populace:

> The "common sense" of the English people had been constructed around the notion that the last war had erected a barrier between the bad old days of the 30s and now: the welfare state had come to stay; we'd never go back to using the criterion of the market as a measure of people's needs, the needs of society. There would always have to be some additional, incremental, institutional force—the state, representing the general interest of society—to bring to bear against, to modify, the market. ... I'm talking about the taken-for-granted, popular base of welfare social democracy. (Hall 1987:17)

It was precisely these cultural presumptions that Margaret Thatcher set out to eliminate: "Thatcherism was a project to engage, to contest, that project, and, wherever possible, to dismantle it, and to put something new in place. It entered the political field in a historic contest, not just for power, but for popular authority, for hegemony" (Hall 1987:17).

Second, as well as a target, the policies have a clear conception of a base of social power, popular capitalism, alternative to the welfare state: "Our goal is a capital-owning democracy of people and families who exercise power over their own lives in the most direct way" (1986 Conservative Party Election Manifesto). "Stressing that 'power to the people' would be a theme of her campaign, Mrs Thatcher said: 'We intend to spread ownership of houses, shares and pensions even more widely than we have already done'" (*Financial Times*, May 20, 1987). "Mrs. Thatcher moved quickly to ... her crusade for 'popular capitalism' through wider share ownership as the centerpiece of her keynote [election] speech" (*Guardian*, May 21, 1987).

Hall labels Thatcherism as "regressive modernization," a refashioning of British culture by abolishing the type of society that Labourism built and that Margaret Thatcher labeled socialism. Yet the state was not only crucial to the reproduction of Labourism; in developing a program to eliminate socialism, Thatcherism found itself trying to use the state to abolish itself. Moreover, though Mrs. Thatcher stated a desire to shrink the size of the state, increased unemployment and the kinds of confrontations with social groups whose power she wished to curtail led to larger social welfare and bureaucracies of repressive technology. This was only one of the several contradictions manifest in the ideologies and policies through which the Tory government's transformations of society were articulated and implemented. Another important contradiction was inherent in their conception of democracy. In a society based on share ownership, one's influence is limited to the number of shares one owns. Unequal ownership of shares means results are frequently undemocratic.

These contradictions suggest that the difference between the Heath and Thatcher governments was more than merely one of tactics. There was clearly a change between the 1970s and the 1980s in the nature of state action. Given the profoundly placid character of British social life that we had experienced in the 1970s, it is appropriate to speak of a change in the cultural conception of the proper role of the state and its relationship to the individual.

The contradictory outcomes of computerization initiatives suggest strongly that new forms of state action were responsible for at least some of the social change in South Yorkshire. Contradictory outcomes are compatible with analyses that place causal priority on politics rather than technology, yet they don't in themselves provide a sufficient account for the particular policies pursued. Consideration of this issue requires an understanding of the nature of states in general as well as the particular history of the British national state, one particularly susceptible to the use of such radical methods.

## Theories of the State

At the core of the state as a social form is a claim that only the state has the legitimate right to resort to violence, the ultimate sanction. When to use this state monopoly was clearly at issue during the miners' strike.

Anthropologists generally divide human social formations into two great types, the small "simple" societies without states and the larger "complex" societies with them. Complex social formations generally cover a large territory and integrate several settlements and peoples into one social formation. Present in complex social formations but not in simple ones are substantial social stratification, extensive social role specialization, and the development of large, special institutions of control and repression. Anthropologists differ over the prime impetus for the development of the state. Some (e.g., Pfeiffer 1982) place primary emphasis on the functional requirements of technology, such as the need to coordinate complex institutions such as irrigation systems. Others (e.g., Carniero 1970) stress the importance to the state of institutionalized social domination. This includes structures that create a social surplus via extraction from a dominated group and promote reproduction of classes.

Like theories of the origin of states, theories of current states vary in the degree to which they assign primacy to coordinating or exploitative functions.[1] Christine Gailey identifies two processes, state formation and ethnogenesis, as the fundamental moments in the reproduction of complex social formations. "State formation" is more or less identical with exploitation:

> State formation involves the political subordination of a majority of the population, redirecting part of the production of most people toward the maintenance of at least one nonproduction class. As a process, state formation is not the history of rational management for the sake of social progress and prosperity, but a tense and contingent way of reproducing class relations. (1987:35; see also Milliband 1973)

"Ethnogenesis," the formation of authentic human groups and identities, takes place in contrast to and conflicts with state formation.

In general, anthropologists tend to take a dualistic view of the state, one similar to that described by Nicos Poulantzas (1978) as the characteristic Marxist view. In the dualistic view, the state has a positive role, its function in the reproduction of the basic system for obtaining necessities, but it also has a negative role in reproducing social inequity.[2] Contemporary state theories have also developed a relatively broad conception of what should be considered part of the state.[3]

Recent theory in political sociology suggests a third view of state action, a view that contrasts with both the class exploitative and the functional views. This "state-for-itself" view builds on the broader notion of the state as well as the Weberian critique of bureaucracy. In this third view, the state is held to have a certain autonomy from both functional necessity and dominating class; the state is oriented most to serving its own ends. This, we believe, is the model that best accounts for the impact of state policy on South Yorkshire computerization. Such an interpretation is compatible with contradictory state policy results. Indeed, state action may be quite contradictory, a consequence of the complexity of modern society, the contradictory pressures of class reproduction, and the trajectory set by a state's own particular history.

### The British National State-for-Itself

As a component of a social system, the characteristics of a state are a consequence of its past relationships with the other aspects of the broader social formation of which it is a part—that is, its history. The current British state takes its form from several events, including the signing of the Magna Charta and "the Glorious Revolution" of the seventeenth century, the restoration of a monarchy along with Parliament. Although the nature of the state has certainly changed since these events, the British state still retains much of its medieval character. Individual rights are not guaranteed by a written constitution and are subject to the dynamic of current politics. Free speech, for example, is a situational right that can and has (recently as well as in the past) been withdrawn from certain categories of people simply by act of Parliament.

To Americans used to a national state with a clearly federal basis and "checks and balances," the British national state appears to be a particularly powerful institution. First, the prime minister and the leaders of the various cabinet departments are all members of Parliament, so there is a close connection between legislative and executive branches. Further, there is no longer a national middle tier of government, comparable to U.S. state government. (In South Yorkshire there used to be, but it was abolished by the Thatcher government.) Not only is it possible for legislation to be introduced and passed in a very short time, but centralization of the administrative structure and compactness of the national territory mean swifter implementation of policy. The expansion of the public sector, especially since the war—to include coal and steel as well as housing, water, and electricity—has given the state powerful fiscal instruments. Finally, the "first past the post" system in parliamentary elections tends to exaggerate the influence of the largest party grouping. Despite the theatrical quality of parliamentary debate, Her Majesty's loyal opposition is more a gadfly than a force requiring compromise. A particularly striking aspect of the British national state is the Official Secrets' Act, which makes it illegal for any government official to reveal publicly any information about very broad aspects of government action, including, for example, the menu at military canteens. Moreover, the British state has a built-in elite bias; the effective composition of the largely hereditary House of Lords is easily manipulated by Conservative government. Though the ability of the House of Lords to influence legislative and executive actions is limited, it is the court of final appeal in the judicial system.

In short, the British state is an unusually powerful instrument for influencing social process. This potential to use the state as a powerful instrument for policy was one element that made the British scene seductive to us as 1960s-era activists anxious for radical, popular change. Indeed, many British social change ideologies, like Labourism, give central emphasis to the national state as an initiator and the most powerful guarantor of social transformation. Any use of such a powerful state to bring about democratic social change, however, may have equivocal results, because it risks reinforcing the power of the state as against the individual.

## The Contradictions of State Policy

A powerful state instrument makes possible the pursuit of a radical program in the face of contradictory results. To specify how the contradictory character of state action works out in practice relevant to computerization, we return to the issue of privatization.

Inmos was not the only entity that was privatized. The following newspaper account, published after the Conservative victory in the 1987 national election, conveys the scope of privatization:

> We have already privatised a fifth of the state sector of industry we inherited. In the next parliament we will privatise most of what remains.
>
> This is the pledge given by the Chancellor of the Exchequer Nigel Lawson at the Tory Party Conference last October [1986], and now they are returned to office, the Government looks set to press ahead. ...
>
> Since the privatisation programme began the Government has raised more than 12 billion pounds by selling off state-owned industries, including BP, Amersham International, British Aerospace, National Freight, Cable and Wireless, British Telecom, British Gas, Rolls-Royce, Associated British Ports and sundry other smaller concerns. ... The money raised ... has helped to fund tax cuts. (*The Times*, June 6, 1987)

In order to grasp the consequences of privatization on computerization, one must first understand the social intent of the program. The *Observer's* industrial editor puts it this way: "[T]he central privatisation drive has been powered by the Conservatives' desire to enroll as many new private shareholders as possible, each a potential Tory-voting capitalist, and each in danger of losing out to a Labour tax campaign against unearned income" (December 7, 1986). Thus privatization must be understood as a consequence of a Tory strategy to create and bind to themselves an electoral majority composed of those who perceive a material interest in continuing Tory control of the state. In addition to tax cuts, fueled literally by profits from the sale of North Sea oil, the prime means of extending the potential voting coalition of stock market share owners was through the sale of state-owned facilities for the production of goods and services, all of which were at least potentially salable commodities. To do this, public sector activities were divided up into marketable corporations, the most desirable, of course, having gone first.

This is clearly a "state-for-itself" act, that of a state aiming to insure its own reproduction. The act also cut to the heart of "traditional" working-class culture. "The family silver," as Sheffield workers said, "was flogged at jumble [rummage] sale prices." The purpose, as perceived in South Yorkshire, was to induce big private capital to support the government by giving them "free" profits and small capital to buy into state policy. As argued in Chapter 2, the mediation of work by the public sector is an important part of the working-class culture, which was the distinctive feature of the Sheffield region. Privatization, whether of such enterprises as the British Steel Corporation, of services as home helps, traditionally provided by local authorities, or of such organizations as the health service, provided by an independent national bureaucracy, was perceived in Sheffield as a direct threat to "the culture which the working class deserves." Further, privatization was seen as a primary cause of the rundown of the local economy, a rundown thus politically motivated rather than a consequence of some technical economic necessity. Privatization had major impacts on working-class peoples' perception of unemployment and other changes in the labor market.

Although a success at the polls nationally, it is less clear that the share-owning democracy strategy has accomplished the democratic transformation of which the Thatcherites spoke. Nor have its results been that positive economically. *Guardian* columnist Hamish McRae argues that the economy was distorted by the inflated profits going to the big capital interests that bought up controlling ownership of the enterprises. He also suggests that the mass of new investors were being badly socialized into imprudent market behavior:

> How can you persuade people to spread risk when by building up an unbalanced portfolio of the companies which happen to have been in the U.K. public sector you make more money? How can you persuade people to use shares to save for their retirement, when they make large profits by selling at the first possible opportunity?
>
> People are being led in the wrong direction, a direction which a large segment of professional opinion in the world of finance feels will damage the creation of a broadly-based, long-term investment community. Investment is not gambling. The Rolls-Royce share scramble will, alas, help persuade people that it is. (May 21, 1987)

At least in Sheffield, purchase of shares in such entities as the Trustee Savings Bank (TSB) was generally treated as "a good wager, one where you can't lose," a bizarre extension, as it were, of the action found by "punters" or bettors at the ubiquitous private-sector betting parlors. As a state-chartered enterprise developing out of the cooperative movement, no one knew that the TSB could be sold, because no one knew that it was property. Nor was there any idea of its value. The government bet a price at which the imagined shares would sell; those that bought were able to turn around the next day and sell for twice what they paid. Many Sheffield workers had chosen the TSB because of its connection to the working-class movement, and those with savings accounts at the TSB were given priority access to shares. As one analyst in the *Times* put it, "It's not an investment, it's a gift." The leader (editorial) in the *News on Sunday* was equally blunt: "The workers are as keen as anyone to have a flutter on a hot tip. At that level, putting your money into British Airports shares this week is little different from backing a 'dead cert' in the 3.30 at Doncaster [horse track]" (July 12, 1987).

Here we have another example of the contradictory impacts of the British state: In the short run, the accumulation of capital is served, in that public revenue flows have been given over to the private sector twice—first as capital, then as tax cuts—and in the transformation of bank capital into finance capital by enticing new small investors into the marketplace. In the long run, investment is diverted from production of necessary commodities into financial activities. In this way, a strategy to keep the state in power has a contradictory and negative effect on the capitalist political economy in general. The strategy affects computing in particular by decreasing available investment capital.

## Summary

Computers have a prominent place in Conservative images of contemporary society, but they also have a prominent role in the national state's technology of repression. It is little wonder, therefore, that the computer has become a potent symbol of domination to those who, through lack of wealth, have little influence in the Thatcherite national state. Despite its expressed desire to shrink the state, the state under Thatcher expanded its influence over the reproduction of the social formation. The course of computerization has been bent to these dynamics. The results have been contradictory, leading to slower rates of computerization in general, the dissipation of a favorable computerization position, and the implementation of less productive forms of computer technology.

Taken together, the forms of computerization that have followed from these national state influences have had at best an ambiguous, possibly even negative, impact on British capital, let alone the reproduction of the British social formation. Despite the apparent commitment of Margaret Thatcher to big capital, such developments seem to us to be more compatible with "state-for-itself" theories than class domination theories of the state. Whatever one's ultimate analysis of the state, however, the action of the national state has had a major impact on the course of computerization in Sheffield, an impact better understood in political than in technological terms.

## Notes

1. Because of their insistence that premodern social formations be taken seriously and their emotional identity with the Third World people they study, few anthropologists manifest statism—the presumption that the state is *in itself* a good thing. Still, Gailey is as extreme in her opprobrium toward the state as are Dahl and others in the Americanist tradition of political science in their celebratory "pluralistic" characterization of the state in contemporary "democratic" social formations.

2. Poulantzas also points out that often this dualism is tilted into a prostate essentialism, in which the state is presumed to have a good "core" surrounded by "the rest," which is bad. In the Marxism characteristic of the Third International, for example, the core is composed of functionally necessary state actions to coordinate production; it is surrounded by a periphery of accreted additional activities, these latter tending to be more implicated in exploitation (see also Draper 1977). Most often, the peripheralness of the "bad" elements is merely assumed, not demonstrated; statism is in this way brought in from the back door.

Poulantzas's critique of "core/periphery" metaphors for the contemporary state leads to an important insight of contemporary state theory, that of the relative autonomy of the state.

3. Ralph Milliband (1973), for example, includes as elements of the state system the government of the day, the administrative apparatus or "bureaucracy," the military, paramilitary, and police, the judiciary and criminal justice system, the local state, and such representative assemblies as Parliament. He also argues that the broader political system, which includes parties and pressure groups, must also be viewed as part of the state. He includes as well a "legitimation system," labeled by Louis Althusser "ideological state apparatuses" (1971).

# 9

## Sheffield Computerization and the World Political Economy

Regions such as South Yorkshire are employment-based social formations; that is, societies in which institutions of wage and salary labor are primary mediators of most social processes, including those which provide necessities. These institutions constitute the most visible terrain of social process in such social formations because of their importance to the patterns of social reproduction. In employment societies, the bulk of social surplus is created through the production and sale of commodities for profit. "Political economy" refers to the institutions for profit accumulation and to the system under which such institutions function.[1]

Substantial change took place in the accumulation process between the mid-1970s and the mid-1980s. The fundamental result of these changes has been to undercut the importance of national boundaries. Such changes had a major impact on the course of computerization in South Yorkshire. That these changes, and the differences they make in conjunction with technological and political factors, are of ethnographic importance emerges in the vignette that follows.[2]

"Emelyn," the managing director of the mining tip manufacturer discussed in Chapter 4, was describing the firm's current market position: "We make a wide range of specialty producer goods for manufacturing industry. We try to produce a line of tools which is available to the customer at the best price at the time they need it, which is usually now. That makes us basically a service business. At any given time, we have to have 95 percent of our catalogue offerings available in stock. When we get an order, we often have to alter the basic tool to fit the customer's needs, but to stay in the market, we can only charge a small additional fee for this service.

"Our customers are not as good or sharp as they ought to be. We need to educate the people who consume these products. The price of a product is related to its quality, but many consumers are ready to buy throw-away products because the cost is less."

Using a soccer metaphor—"This works is really a Second Division side in the League Table of machine tool firms"—Emelyn described the firm as a lower-level participant in its market, "even though it's the largest in the U.K. in its speciality." He then discussed the implications of this market situation for the firm's strategy: "To survive, we should pick a winner in the product range, concentrate on it, and do it better, but in the short run, we're going to have to attempt to aim for both service and diversity of products. The problem with this business, and with U.K. engineering firms in general, is that they relied too long on a fragile U.K. market. Instead, there's a need to go out and find new markets, especially in the U.S. and in Europe. I don't believe tariffs or import duties are any help, because it's a buyer's market—has been for twenty years. We are under constant pressure to make the product cheaper so that we can get a return in a competitive market."

In response to a question about finding markets in the nonWestern world, Emelyn argued that the Third World is more a source of competition than a place for future markets. "When Third World countries buy technology or begin new businesses, they do so with newer technologies than the ones we possess.

"Because of our market, we need a totally flexible workforce, one where the workers can do one job in the morning and another one in the afternoon. Technology can reduce cost, but it does not necessarily make you more flexible. Before you invest fifty thousand pounds in a new machine, you should have a market. In the past the company purchased new machinery without an assessment of what it could really produce; consequently, the machinery has stood idle. If and when we buy more computerized machines, it'll have to be for a clearer business purpose, like our new order and stock control system.

"We are now attempting to rationalize our operation, to have the right equipment and the cooperation of our workforce: the right workers, in the right place at the right time. I've been with the company for eighteen months and I'm proud of my relationship with labour. One of the reasons I'm glad to be here, despite our difficult position, is because this is a place where people are not afraid to work.

"Now the parent company is a paternalistic enterprise where most of their operations were not unionized or they were unionized in a weak way. As you probably know, our convenor is a member of the Communist Party. That isn't a problem for me; it means we have a strong union, and I think a strong union is an advantage, but I'm relatively in a minority in management with that opinion. I just believe that you can't get things done without organized workers."

Mike, the convenor, listened to Emelyn silently but later expressed agreement with the market strategy, the foolishness of some previous investment in technology, and the need for flexibility. He separated his noncommittal attitude toward computers from "those things I truly regret, such as the loss of trade union power. This means that it is more difficult to pursue the broader political objectives of rising living standards, peace, and internationalism through the working-class movement. Too much of the time I'm only able to protect the pay of a few remaining workers, or make the process of redundancy [lay-offs] more humane for those whose jobs could not be saved."

To Mike's way of thinking, this situation had little to do with computers or even management strategy. Mostly, it followed from the change in working-class politics that made Thatcherism possible. We knew Mike and his family from our previous fieldwork; he is a friend as well as anthropological informant. Because he is a competent and forceful person, he might have risen to great heights had he chosen a different career or political party. Mike had no regrets about his life choices, however—he was a respected member of an important, citywide organization, a political leader in his council housing estate and at his labor site, and an active participant in the attempt to rejuvenate the Sheffield economy. He continued to express confidence in the future of the Labour movement—"This is a bad period, but t'Labour Movement has had them before, and we will again. The important thing is to keep on with the struggle."

These comments illustrate several ways in which the world political economy is and is not perceived to be important to what happens in Sheffield. Emelyn sees the centrality at several key points—commodity markets, product lines, and profit maximizing strategy. The transnational character of the marketplace has consequences for the organization of the labor process, compelling a flexible workforce and "modern" management practice, instead of "bloody minded" or narrow trade unionism and paternalism. Emelyn poses questions of technology in general, and new information technology in particular, inside this political economic framework rather than separate from it, a position at which he has arrived after some negative experience with technology.

Mike is less willing to articulate his concerns directly in terms of a changed world political economy. Partly this is because an international perspective has been a taken-for-granted aspect of his worldview for a long time anyway; a global perspective is not a change. He directs his attention to national state processes. Still, he accepts many of the implications drawn by Emelyn, including a recognition of the need for labor process change; he only wishes for a stronger position from which to negotiate. Both share a conception of an important trade union role in the current era.

In the following vignette, a South Yorkshire worker places more emphasis on the importance of world political economy to workplace and trade union dynamics, connecting national state and world political economy:

On a blustery February evening, David drove to a District Trades Council meeting outside Sheffield. The unemployment that had hit the area was personified in the person chairing the meeting. An energetic man in his forties, Reg was no longer able to find a job in the mining industry; he now worked organizing centers for the unemployed. Reg moved the meeting very quickly into a report on the recent British Telecom strike by introducing "Brother Ron," an engineer and a man known to many in the audience as a long-time union and political activist.

Relaxed and at home with the audience, Ron's talk was punctuated by the kind of energy, humor, and analysis generally a part of working-class discourse in South Yorkshire. "When I was first invited to address this meeting, we thought our action might last as long as the Miners' Strike [one year]. Fortunately, it didn't. I think that, on the whole, we came out of it better than we might have. I want to talk about the lessons of the strike for the working class, especially about the impact of new technology, but you need to understand the background first.

"You all know about the privatisation of the post office-telephone system in '84, and the splitting off of the telephone into British Telecom. When the Tory government set it up, they brought in a new management which was supposed to be very aggressive, so it's no accident that Telecom was chosen for the first major dispute in a privatised public service. Also, the new technology in telecommunications allows the system to run more on its own; this diminishes our members' skills and shifts the balance away from us. Although the telecommunications industry has expanded 100 percent over the last ten years, the size of the workforce has declined; this is true in high technology industries in general. Finally, a right wing leadership was elected in the National Communications Union last year, sweeping out the left. So, all in all, it looked like a good opportunity for the Tories to push their assault on the working class even further."

He paused during a murmur of assent from several delegates in the audience. "In March '86, the union submitted its yearly wage claim. In September, management responded by demanding greater flexibility from labour, which would have destroyed many remaining demarcations between jobs. They demanded this even though they already make 160 pounds in profit per employee per week—that's a 50 percent increase in two years, out of which they financed 80 to 100 percent increases in the directors' salaries. Even though there have been 25,000 jobs lost since 1981, they wanted 24,000 more now and a commitment to 70,000 fewer jobs by 1992. That was managements' response to our claim.

"It was outrageous, but the new union leadership didn't even respond; instead, they sent the proposal out to ballot, like the Tories want. The membership rejected it three to one, but the leadership mumbled something about it only having been a 'pretend' vote; when they sent it out again for a 'real' ballot, it was rejected four to one. Still the leadership did nothing.

"In the January, some workers began industrial action on overtime, and management responded by instituting all kinds of provoking actions, like insisting that pay telephone kiosks be fixed on the weekends. Fancy British Telecom making public telephones a priority!" A ripple of sympathetic laughter crossed the room. "When the men refused to do this because of the overtime ban, management locked them out. The right wing union executive voted twenty-two to one against taking any support action, even though 38,000 members were already out on strike in protest; by the end of the week, 100,000 were out; it were glorious. Finally, the Union Executive backed them.

"There were very few scabs during the whole action, although the union president tried everything to undermine the strike, like saying 'We're going back, it's settled,' when it wasn't. Despite this, we got a settlement in only a couple of weeks. The workforce was well mobilized; the workers won the public argument during the strike, such as by making sure the emergency '999' phone service was manned.

"We in the trade union movement have to look at the way industry is going. We see a decline in the workforce, but the new technology is producing tremendous wealth. As a society, we need to find a way to switch this wealth from industry alone to funding the services we want and need. We can't do this anymore only through jobs, or through just fighting for higher wages for those in employment. The international trade deficit of the British economy means that the ball game has changed completely in the last ten years, for increases in wages no longer lead to an increase in the number of jobs.

"The Telecom strike is a lesson in this new industrial world. For some, the pay increase of about 6 percent a year was decimation, considering the profits, but we have retained central pay bargaining and fought off the worst of their flexibility demands. Unfortunately, we lost ground in the Telecom equipment factories, where they now have separate, and lower, pay rates. As has been so often the case, the traditional greed of the working class got in the way; it was this greed which led people to accept the splitting of the Post Office from Telecommunications and the loss of a telegram service in the first place, rather than preserving services. All our people's services are under threat. As it is, British Telecom gives cheap rates to business, so the wealth created is going to profit instead of people."

The chairman asked if there were any questions, and one craftsman, disemployed two years before, asked about support from other unions. Ron responded: "The right wing president refused to try to coordinate our action with the organizations of clerical and management grades in Telecom, but we did try to build alliances with them on the rank and file level. We didn't get hostile, so we can work with them in the future, something especially necessary with the breakdown of demarcations between different jobs in the industry. Whatever was going on in Wapping, the Electricians' Union refused to cross our picket lines, and the General, Municipal, and Boilermakers' were supportive."

The Chairman congratulated the telephone engineers on the way they had conducted their strike and asked the speaker to sum up. Ron ran his hand across his balding forehead thoughtfully: "The way I see it is this, that in the face of belligerent management—which we will get more and more—put there by an ideologically motivated government, we need to fight hard to win, but we can win. Information technology is the biggest possible growth area in our economy, so it is the biggest source of expanding wealth. We need to fight to take this back into public ownership, to insure that wealth goes to people's services. To do this, we need to build stronger alliances with other workers, to fight for renationalisation. We were lucky this time, but the only way we will be successful in the long run is to understand what is happening with the new technology and introduce political demands into our movement again." He sat down to strong applause from the forty-odd delegates.

For this trade unionist, the world political economy plays a key role in his analysis of national politics. In the past, Labourism stressed as one of its basic strategies high wages for private sector workers. Such high wages would tend to draw up the wages of other workers, and progressive taxes on wages and salaries could be used to finance public services. Now, the existence of a deficit in international trade means this strategy no longer tends to produce a general improvement for the working class. Fewer private-sector workers have the strength to win higher wages, and those that do have much less impact on the wages of other workers because of the increased ease of capital flow across national boundaries.

Further, Ron sees new information technology implicated in these changes. First, the technology undermines the forms of worker control of production characteristic of the previous technology. Further, the technology changes the political economy by itself becoming the center at which profit tends to accumulate. Ron concludes from this that even greater emphasis must be given to an older element of the Labourist program, nationalization. Indeed, nationalization is to be given a new role, the direct financing of public service through expropriation at the point of profit realization, as opposed to higher wages leading to greater income tax revenue.

These perspectives underline the fundamental point of this chapter, that changes in the world political economy strongly influenced the course of computerization in Sheffield. Yet each of those whose views we have presented approach world political economic and technological change somewhat differently, just as the effects of change may be diverse, even contradictory. In some ways, technology changed the accumulation process, but in more important ways change in the accumulation process has determined the technology implemented.

We begin with a discussion of some of the ways in which technology has directly affected accumulation. We next examine some contemporary academic theories of world political economic change and then analyze the Sheffield situation in terms of them. We conclude by specifying the interactions of political economic, technological, and social changes. We must separate out the consequences of changes in political economy if we are to specify the extent to which technology is a direct cause of social change.

## NIT as a Cause of Political Economic Change

There are many ways in which NIT appears to be causing change in the world political economy. As suggested by Ron, technology does change power relations within the labor process, and such changes do affect how profits are accumulated as well as the place where profit is realized. High-technology companies, most of which have a strong connection to computing in their manufacturing or in their products, were among the profit-making centers of the 1980s, whereas other sectors lost profitability. Ron also sketched out some of the implications of this change for working-class culture, both in labor strategy and in declining wages.

Additional instability in the world political economy can be traced to rapid cross-border movement of capital, movement made possible by the instantaneous communication capabilities of new information technology. London has become the center of international currency speculation as a consequence of its previous role as a source of Eurodollars being combined with the new technology. Sheffield University sociologist Angkie Hoogevelt argues that with the 1986 "Big Bang" in the city of London, the various forms of money are no longer separate, with London handling over 60 percent of a three-trillion-dollar international currency market. As a consequence, Britain became the second largest net capital exporter in the world; Hoogevelt argued in 1987 that capital exports combined with international debts and assets were greater than the entire British gross national product. A *Financial Times* article estimated that 1987 purchases of overseas stocks brought "towards two billion pounds the amount of institutional liquidity being exported to the U.S. rather than recycled in London." (Another important diverter of capital from investment, of course, is the policy of privatization.)

Finally, some economists have argued that investment in advanced information technology tends ultimately to decrease the total amount of wealth that is realizable within a political economy. This is because such technology tends to save labor, and these economists see labor as the ultimate source of wealth. The tendency to invest in machinery that radically reduces the amount of human labor power used in industrial production of commodities tends to decrease both the wages available for consumption and the surplus value available to be converted into profit. In previous eras, the introduction of new technology gave a firm, industry, or nation an advantage over its competitors and therefore raised profits, at least temporarily. The rapid spread of computer-based technology throughout the world, however, tends to reduce the time over which these relative advantages hold.

Such considerations are less relevant in the eyes of economists who see capital as a more important source of profit than labor. Thus, one's sense of the direct implications of new information technology on political economy clearly rests on one's political economic perspective—for example, labor versus capital theory of value. In order to develop some perspective on these issues, we turn to a discussion of more general trends in contemporary political economy.

## The Disorganizing Contemporary World Political Economy

Contemporary political economists generally share the presumption that the dynamics of their subject must be conceived globally, as part of a "world system," rather than nationally.[3] They differ on how long this has been the case as well as on what the implications of this condition are. One of the most provocative analyses of the world accumulation process today is that of the German sociologist Claus Offe, who places stress on the increasing degree of *dis*organization manifest in the global political economy (1985).

The developing monopolies and concomitant national state interventions of the first half of the twentieth century appeared to such political economists as Rudolf Hilferding (1910) as indicative of an era of increasing control and institutionalization in political economy. In retrospect, the post–World War II period in general, and the 1970s British "social contract" between labor, capital, and the state in particular, appear to have been similar relatively "organized" periods. Offe argues that more recently such stability has been eroded.[4]

Marx suggested that accumulation in capitalist societies has two dominant moments, that of *production* of commodities and that of their *circulation,* through which profit is realized through sale and reinvested as capital. At a 1987 conference in Sheffield sponsored by the Conference of Socialist Economists, Kees van der Pijl argued that the relative influence on reproduction of these two moments changes over time. Times when the production moment, a real process involving material objects, is dominant are generally conducive to planning and organization. In contrast, during times when the circulation moment is dominant, individuals and firms emphasize competition with each other, and accumulation "action" is moved to maneuver and speculation. Such times are more conducive to anarchic political economy and thus to relative disorganization.

Throughout their history, capitalist political economies have alternated between relatively organized and disorganized periods. To argue that the current period is one of disorganization, then, is to argue that circulation is currently more dominant than is production. For van der Pijl, the relative political organization of détente and trilateralism of the late 1970s has been replaced by the disorganization of a "post-Fordist" world subjected to what he calls "the neoliberal project."[5]

"Disorganizing" is certainly an apt way to characterize the economies of the former Soviet states; it is one of the important conditions necessitating *perestroika.* In what follows, we attempt to explain why we feel Offe's characterization is accurate as a description of political economies based on private accumulation as well.

## Disorganization and Public Policy

The relative disorganization of the current capitalist political economy is manifest in a number of ways. *First, the world political economy is less amenable to public policy.* This is true with regard to the actions of all current governments, on local, regional, and even national levels. Even superpowers can at best use policy to adjust to rather than to control basic political economic forces. Supranational bodies such as the World Bank and the General Agreement on Tariffs and Trade (GATT) also find the world economy more difficult to influence.

In other periods of industrial capitalism, dominant nations or institutions have provided a coherence to the system, controlling tendencies toward instability and providing mechanisms for long-term planning. This does not appear to be the case in the current period. At first glance, the increasing prominence of transnational corporations in employment-based societies like Britain seems to imply greater organization than disorganization. Such organizations in reality undermine the control or even influence of particular nation states or even of corporate groups. Far from being conducive to planning and organization, they often amplify the economic distress of local regions through competition on a world scale.

There are several possible (and partial) exceptions to the disorganization tendency, such as government and corporate cooperation as in Japan. It is also conceivable that disorganization will decline in the future in sectors of the world political economy dominated by single, extremely powerful transnational corporations. In the long run, development of new trading blocks like the Euromarket of 1992 and the United States/Canada/Mexico free trade agreement may bring new forms of stability, but for the moment these appear to be more disruptive of world economic order; witness the United States and European trade skirmish in early 1989.

In a disorganized situation, the consequences of any major development, such as a technological change like computerization, are less controllable by normal public policy (e.g., regulation, support for research and development, training and education, regional policy) than might otherwise be the case. Indeed, disruptive technological effects may be magnified by general disorganization.

### Disorganization and the New Transnational Division of Labor

*Second, the international division of labor is being transformed.* "The last three decades have witnessed the growing integration of the world system of production on the basis of a new relationship between less developed and highly industrialized countries" (Nash and Fernandez-Kelly 1983:vii). As suggested by Emelyn, this new division of labor accompanies a shift in the Third World away from dependence purely on resource exploration and toward manufacturing, especially in export processing zones, a geographic dispersion of productive stages, plant closings in the "core" nations of the developed world, and an increasing fluidity of international capital. As a consequence, economic conditions both locally and internationally are difficult to predict.

### Disorganization and Instability

*Third, there are tendencies toward instability built into the contemporary world political economy.* In addition to the tendencies toward instability articulated by traditional Marxism (e.g., a tendency of the rate of profit to fall), an additional instability appears to be characteristic of the present period. As writers such as Mike

Cooley of the Greater London Enterprise Board have argued, the current political economy is not very good at insuring that work necessary for the reproduction of the broader social formation is performed, even when that work is profitable. Indeed, there are various forces that tend to concentrate investment in nonproductive activities, like conversion of flats (apartments) from rental properties into owner-occupied properties, rather than investment in manufacturing or wealth-producing services. Underinvestment in what has come to be known as social infrastructure (e.g., bridges, education, public utilities) results in more major disasters (Three Mile Island) and other crises (e.g., solid waste disposal) that require substantial social investment and/or diverted investment from economic growth.

## Disorganization and Uneven Development

Although the tendencies listed above are general trends, how they work out in particular instances is dependent on a number of factors. Consequently, *fourth, the development of the world political economy is increasingly uneven.* Some regions of the world, such as the Route 128 corridor of Massachusetts, "Silicon Valley" in California, the M4 corridor of England, the "Third" Italy (Zeitlin 1987), and the Grenoble region of France (Dunford 1987), recently experienced periods of expanding accumulation resulting in widespread regional, but not general, economic benefit. Developments in other regions, such as Scotland's "Silicon Glen" and South Wales, are more equivocal, and the Route 128 bubble appears to have burst. Conversely, one sees in certain regions, like South Yorkshire, economic contractions that outlast the "normal" business cycle.

## Disorganization and Corrosion

*Fifth, this changing, uneven, unstable world political economy tends to be corrosive of existing social relationships and the cultural patterns related to them.* Again, according to Nash and Fernandez-Kelly:

> Decaying industrial cities of the United States and Europe have in the last decade become characterized by breakdown of municipal services, marginalization of large segments of the workforce, and the atrophy of the democratic operation of trade unions and community interest groups (1983:vii). The wages and benefits won over decades of labor struggle are undermined in the old regions while militarization, which often accompanies industrialization abroad, prevents the mobilization of collective action to win gains on the frontier. (x)

These changes are directly related to changes in "the sectoral composition of labor" (xiv), as for example, the increasing proportion of the workforce that is female and employed in less secure, part-time jobs.

It is not always the regions of highest unionization and greatest social benefit that suffer the most. Both Boston and Bologna were recently centers of growth even though they are traditionally strong areas of unionization and working-class

organization. What is important to stress is the volatility of economic expansion
and contraction and therefore the impermanence of the cultural patterns built at
previous centers of accumulation.

### Disorganization and Continuity

There are thus several good reasons for seeing the current period of world political economy as different from its predecessor. How fundamental are these
changes?

We have argued at length against labels—for example, computer age—that
overly stress the technological discontinuities between the contemporary era and
the previous one. Similarly, this disorganizing world political economy is still primarily *industrial* in character. The wage nexus remains central to it. Its dynamic
remains based on commodities, the production of physical goods or activities
(services) predominantly for sale rather than for self, family, or community
consumption—that is, consumption within the producing unit. Further, commodity production continues to be dominated by large organizations, such as factories and corporations. (It is the combination of commodity with large organization rather than the specific notion of "factory" locations for the production of
physical goods that is the most useful meaning of "industrial."[6])

Though there clearly are shifts in kinds of employment, these shifts are not necessarily profound from a theoretical viewpoint. The shift from "manufacturing"
to "service" employment, of which so much is made by Daniel Bell and other
scholars, is just as accurately described as a shift from factory production of goods
to factory production of services. The political economic shifts do not justify the
label "postindustrial" as a characterization of these societies.

Moreover, the world political economy remains dominated by a *capitalistic* accumulation dynamic. That is, the surplus that is generated through economic activity is appropriated by privately owned organizations, largely corporations, and
this profit is generally held to be reinvested in production for purposes of accumulating more profit, thereby becoming capital. In general, this surplus still comes
from the surplus value created when the cost of purchasing human labor power is
less than the value created by that labor power (Marx 1967). There are
noncapitalistic aspects of the world political economy, such as the remaining
state-owned corporations and worker cooperatives of both East and West and
family and community-based subsistence and barter production. However, these
kinds of economic activities do not set the basic dynamics of the world political
economy. Moreover, as in Britain, there is currently a tendency for national states
to disengage from production of goods and provision of services and to return
them to the political economic sector. Although the increasing control of capital
over investment contributes to disorganization through its tendency to promote
underinvestment in infrastructure, capitalist control of investment is not a new
thing.

Thus, the context within which South Yorkshire reproduces itself remains industrial and capitalist.What has changed is that the world political economy (1) is less amenable to public policy, (2) manifests a new international division of labor, (3) is unstable, (4) develops more unevenly, and (5) is corrosive of existing social and cultural relationships. In a sentence, the world political economy is increasingly disorganized.

### Disorganization and the Decline in Investment

The disorganizing tendencies of the world political economy place clear limits on accumulation in the British economy. One consequence of the current stage is the flight of capital from both the manufacturing activities like those which were characteristic of Labourist South Yorkshire and the newer private sector service activities. Hoogevelt estimated that for the national economy, 1986 investment in manufacturing was still 20 percent below the 1979 level.

The decline in domestic production investment is not due to the absence of capital but its diversion, which has reinforced the profound regionalization of the British political economy. This regionalization was clearly geographic in the 1980s: wages, investment, and house prices were substantially higher in the South, and unemployment and plant closings were higher in the North. Only 6 percent of the two million manufacturing jobs lost between 1979 and 1985 came from the South (Routledge 1987). Moreover, as a feature in the Sheffield *Star* points out, the "great divide" in British society is social as much as it is regional. Those able to plug into the speculative "casino economy," even in South Yorkshire, are doing well, but those unable to make the connection are losing out.[7]

### Political Economic Disorganization in South Yorkshire

John Field (1985) offers several indications of how political economic disorganization hit the Sheffield region:

> Between 1978 and 1981 alone, the County of South Yorkshire lost around 49,000 jobs out of a total of 552,400. ... The years since have seen a further dramatic collapse of manufacturing, particularly in steel and heavy engineering [metalworking]; and since 1984 the National Coal Board has embarked on a major programme of closures in the mining industry. (p. 4)

A Sheffield Employment Department pamphlet indicates that in addition to manufacturing losses between 1979 and 1982, over 4,500 jobs were lost in the service sector (DEED 1983). A "Regional Development Programme" report on South Yorkshire from the national Department of Trade and Industry describes the situation in the following terms:

> A direct consequence of an economy based on old traditional heavy industry is the obsolescent and degraded physical environment and infrastructure which is found

in many parts of the area. Colliery spoil heaps and waste lagoons are an unfortunate part of the coalfield landscape, whilst the closure of large steel works has produced extensive areas of dereliction in the urban centres. These examples of specific problems are on top of a more general problem of obsolescent urban environment. (1986:1)

Ken Curran, a full-time official for the National Union of Public Employees, comments, "Unless there is a dramatic change in the Economic fortunes of the Rotherham area [of South Yorkshire] we shall bear witness to the greatest decline in the standard of living ever seen in a modern nation"(1986:2).

## An End to Regional Disorganization?

During the field period, there were signs that this economic upheaval had bottomed out. In an article entitled "City is Dragged into the Age of Technology," (1987) the Sheffield *Star* chronicled the apparent stabilization of several reorganized steel and metalworking facilities, such as Sheffield Forgemasters and the privatized United Engineering Steels, albeit at vastly decreased levels of labor and through government support. Unemployment dropped fitfully, and jobs began to expand again in the service sector. A centerfold in *Chartered Surveyor Weekly* (1986) speaks of a "Retail boom in steel city ... [T]he retail sector is now seeing something of a property boom, and in the past year some 500 million pounds worth of retail schemes have been submitted to the Council." A internal memorandum for the Employment Department argued "many of the cities [*sic*] manufacturing firms remain and are still key U.K. multinational producers which are surviving and even prospering in international markets, but they are no longer major employers" (DEED 1986:1). This document suggests that "private sector service employment in the city is set to expand further ... It is a complex picture to grasp, but the point is that the city is not everywhere in terminal decline" (p. 2).

It must be stressed, however, that these changes in local political economy do not mean a return to the status quo ante. "Retail workers are among the lowest paid in the national workforce," with almost 75 percent earning less than the official poverty wage (DEED 1987). Many of the new jobs, such as those related to the real estate boom, are part of the speculative economy. Such economic change increases the difficulty of pursuing progressive social policies on the local level: It is difficult to push antiapartheid policies when "the bulk of South African ferrochrome and nickel imported into Britain is used in the Sheffield and South Yorkshire steel industry—including British Steel Corporation Stainless, United Engineering Steels, and Forgemasters" (Sheffield Anti-Apartheid Movement n.d.).

On the local level, then, disorganization in the world political economy results in numerous specific difficulties and, in general, complicates the problem of social reproduction on the regional level: "A highly segmented labour market thus produces much more than one clearly defined 'employment problem' and once this is understood it is easy to grasp why the Employment Department has such a broad and at times contradictory programme" (DEED 1986:3) John Darwin concludes that the region must find new ways to integrate itself into the world economy. Just as for the modern firm, the key for the region is a flexible political economy. Moreover, given the nature of state policy, any local initiative will likely have to be carried out in partnership with the private sector (DEED 1987:27, 46).

## Technology, Political Economy, and Social Change

There is a tendency in popular discourse to treat new information technology as a singular factor causing social change. In this chapter, we have looked at NIT in relation to political economic structure. There are some senses in which NIT has played a key role in political economic change, as in the boost that it gave to the emergence of London as a center of world financial speculation. Indeed, NIT has played a direct part in disorganization, as with the "Big Bang" of 1986, when London financial institutions became instantaneously connected to their counterparts in other capitalist nations. This technology, combined with substantial deregulation, led to some temporary but still major lurches in international financial traffic. More important in the long run is the way in which this event increased the ease of capital flow out of the British economy.

The main thrust of our argument, however, is that the political economy has followed its own "relatively independent" dynamic. This dynamic is disorganized, and we have tried to show how a disorganizing political economy mediates NIT. The kinds of world economic factors discussed above are examples of just such mediators (see Rosenberg 1982): It is within the context of a world political economy with these characteristics that individual firms make decisions about whether to invest in information technology and in which form. The individual firm may choose information technology to improve its position vis-à-vis its competitors, but as numerous firms take similar decisions the consequence is to exacerbate already pronounced tendencies toward instability in the political economy as a whole.

The current world political economy, because of increased uncertainty, encourages the development of flexibility in organizations. In a context of the destruction of instrumentalities for public influence, increasing flexibility at the level of the individual firm means increasing levels of disorganization at the level of the social formation. Through increasing access to information, computer technology could just as easily provide means for increased overall control of the system, but the national government has destroyed many of the structures that might have been able to use such information.

Such national policies have also placed limits on the ability of local people to influence the reproduction of their social formation. In addition to privatization and its failure to develop an effective policy to maintain British standing in new information technology, the Thatcher administration also failed to develop positive policies for transnational bodies like UNESCO and the EEC. These factors similarly decreased the ability of British society on the national level to influence the reproduction of the world political economy.

Taken together, the cumulative effect of change in both politics and technology was to reinforce tendencies toward disorganization. Thus there is a link between technology and social change, but a link mediated heavily by state and political economic structures.

## Notes

1. The use of "political economy" can be traced to the arguments of the eighteenth-century Scottish moral philosophers. Adam Smith and Adam Ferguson conceptualized a "civil society" or emergent set of social relationships with dynamics somewhat independent from the moral action of individual humans and best freed from the encumbrance of their states. The basic relationships in the sphere of civil society were political economic ones. Adam Smith argued that when civil society was freed from the constraint of states or other social institutions, the result was the maximum social benefit. In contrast, Marx argued that conflict between the private appropriation of wealth and the provision of public necessities would get worse.

Though largely abandoned in the nineteenth century, the term "political economy" has returned to some popularity in contemporary social science. On the right, the phrase is used to refer to approaches that harken back to the laissez-faire economics articulated by the founders of political economy. On the left, "radical political economics" refers to critiques of mainstream economics that stress how broader social relations, such as those between classes, as well as the state must be integrated into models of civil society. In *Economic Development: Value, Wealth, and Job Creation,* (1987b), John Darwin from the Sheffield DEED places strong emphasis on how wealth is created in various sectors of the economy, including the state sectors, not just the profit-oriented sectors. Much radical political economy draws inspiration from substantive economic anthropology, which emphasizes the social context of economics.

Although clearly part of this radical tradition, we nonetheless opt for a more restrictive definition of political economy, one that uses the term to refer to the institutions of accumulation alone rather than to the broader institutions of production. The expository value of the distinction is illustrated in the differentiation between the subject matter of Chapter 4, work, and our stress in Chapter 5 on profit-related or "political economic" institutions. The issue is related theoretically to the various positions among political economists on the Labor Theory of Value (LTV) articulated by Marx and others. Authors such as Darwin justify abandoning the LTV because of its limited applicability. In contrast, our position is that Marxist political economy, including the LTV, is of continuing value in understanding precisely profit-related dynamics like those to which we wish to draw attention in this chapter. The analytic error is to proceed, as Marx does on occasion, as if political economic dynamics constitute an adequate model of all the essential elements in the reproduction of the entire social formation (Hakken 1987b).

2. Political economies operate on a much broader scale than the region; consequently, ethnography is not necessarily the best research methodology for apprehending the dy-

namics of political economic change. Still, informants in Sheffield frequently resorted to political economic arguments in their attempts to account for both social and technological change, and many of the changes that struck us most strongly on our return to Sheffield in the 1980s appeared to be related to the kinds of broad processes that are traditionally considered by the political economist. Since one of the dangers of political economic analysis is the reification of structure consequent to an overly macro perspective, the method followed in this chapter has been to frame our analysis of the political economic dimension with arguments put forward by Sheffield informants.

3. The phrase "world system" has been popularized by sociologist Immanuel Wallerstein (1976) and his colleagues at SUNY Binghamton, who have argued that the emergence of a political economy operating on a world scale as early as the sixteenth century must be recognized. In his important work, *Europe and the People Without History* (1982), anthropologist Eric Wolf argues persuasively for recognizing the existence of an integrated economic system stretching across much of the globe even before this time.

4. Offe does not intend to develop an elaborate model comparable to Hilferding's, but rather to suggest the possibility that in the current era "the procedures, patterns of organization, and institutional mechanisms that supposedly mediate and maintain a dynamic balance between social power and political authority (i.e., seek to *organize* coherently the socio-political systems of contemporary welfare state capitalism) actually fail to perform this function." His aim is therefore to identify "the symptoms, consequences, and potential remedies of such failures of the process of mediation" (1985: 6; emphasis in original).

5. Many radical political economists, building on the work of Antonio Gramsci, characterize the present era as "post-Fordist." Gramsci (1971) developed the concept of "Fordism" to characterize a social formation based on production of physical commodities in large, integrated organizations. After World War II, Fordist societies in Europe and North America tended to reach an accommodation with organized labor, an accommodation that is now breaking down. In the sense used by Gramscians, Fordism refers to a social totality, not just a political economy. Though post-Fordist is a term more acceptable than "postindustrial" to describe the entire current social formation, "disorganizing" is preferable as a term to describe the current world political economic system, both because it is a narrower description of political economy, just one aspect of the social totality, and because it is more precisely indicative of the nature of the political economic dynamic.

6. When we say that the contemporary political economy is still industrial, we mean that it is characterized by large-scale commodity production. To characterize this world system as "industrial" does not mean that large-scale commodity production is the only form of economic activity. There is substantial activity within what is often called the domestic economy, in which, for example, housewives produce meals for families or unemployed working people improve their houses. Such activities, however, do not generally fit into an international pattern or system, nor are they the primary source of the surplus, capital, characteristic of this type of complex social formation. Here, surplus is generated in industrial (large-scale commodity production) activity, and it is the reproduction of the structures within which these activities take place that provides the basic dynamic of the current international political economy.

7. Regions with declining employment institutions and those that are less well situated with regard to the economy of share, real estate, and other forms of speculation have to search out other options for development and/or reindustrialization. Many have hoped to find the key in attracting investment from multinational firms (the basic strategy of the

Scottish, Welsh, and Northern Development Authorities in Britain), and others have tried to discover the key for "growing the next Silicon Valley" (Miller and Coté 1985). Case studies of such regions as "the Third Italy" (Zeitlin 1987; Blim 1988) or Grenoble in France (Dunford 1987) document the extent to which the notion of such a key is a myth (Saxian 1987; Darwin 1987b). In many sectors of the economy, the only way to get investment capital is via the national state—through involvement, for example, in enterprise zone schemes that circumvent local government.

# 10

## Computerization and the Region

The term "region" is used in many different ways.[1] For example, "region" is occasionally used at a macrolevel to refer to groups of nations. In this chapter we refer to a more limited, intranational pattern of regular social relationships. For our purposes, "region" means the arena of potential "day-to-day" social interaction, the set of normally available possible social interactions. The notions of "travel to work area" and "standard metropolitan statistical area" are spatial reflections of regional structures in the sense intended here.

It is one's *potential* rather than *actual* patterns of interaction that set a person's "region" off from her or his "community," the latter being the network of people with whom one regularly interacts. One's region includes all those social relations that one might have without being "away from home" or "on a trip" as these phrases are used in everyday language; one's region is thus highly dependent on available means of transportation. Regions are also different from broader social relationship patterns that transcend regional boundaries, such patterns as ethnic groups, classes, peoples, nations, or cultures with which individuals identify or in relation to which they are perceived as sharing identities. Thus regions contain multiple communities as well as components of such larger entities as ethnic groups or classes.

In employment- or labor-based social formations like Sheffield's, regions are an extremely important social terrain. It is within their own regions that people experience employment institutions most directly. Regions in a geographic sense correspond increasingly to the employment opportunities or *labor market* within commuting distance of the bulk of residents. Regional labor markets have identifiable dynamics, which can change. With regard to gender, for example, the regional labor market in South Yorkshire has changed drastically.

What happens at the regional level is also important to political activities. Interaction with others is essential to reproducing shared worldviews. It is also within regions that organizations have the kind of day-to-day interactions that make forms of broader cooperation possible. Here people establish the kinds of relationships that can transform their experiences through *collective action*—voting, creating new organizations, demonstrating, striking, consciously promoting particular patterns of consumption but discouraging others, and so forth. Thus it is within the framework of regions that individuals and groups reproduce the particular inclinations that give them a distinct identity.

Sheffielders perceive major changes in the institutions of employment within the region, both in the structure of jobs or labor market and in such workplace organizations as trade unions and employers' groups, public and private. The region is the structure through which changes in the national state and world political economy most directly impact the daily life of working-class people, having a strong impact on what is possible as computer use spreads. On both individual and collective levels, the characteristics of jobs constrain and channel action, so any change in these characteristics is likely to be closely related to technology-induced social change. Further, any plan to develop policy to influence the social correlates of technology must take into account changes in the labor market.

At the most general level, one can see regions as being important meeting points between semiotic and material processes. Regions are affected directly by changes in such structures as the national state and international political economy, but they are also strongly affected by the forms of human action described in Part Four. Like British geographer Doreen Massey and her colleagues, we conceive of regions as important structural elements in employment-based social formations, emergent forms whose reproductive dynamics are closely tied to the meeting of the political economy and the labor market, on the one hand, and collective human action, on the other.[2]

There are thus theoretical as well as methodological reasons for focusing on regional dynamics as an important constraining structure.[3] In this chapter we will identify changes in reproduction on a regional scale so that we can assess the region's relationship as a structure to computerization. After we have identified some of the dimensions of regional change, we give particular attention to worker skill and to gender, two aspects of the labor market, and to an important form of collective action, trade unionism. We summarize these changes in terms of what they imply both for computing and for the economic and social revitalization of the region.

## A Contemporary Statistical Picture

A useful initial picture of regional change emerges from *The State of the Nation: An Atlas of Britain in the Eighties* (1985). Because people still gather government statistics using the units of regions, Stephen Fothergill and Jill Vincent can place South Yorkshire in graphic perspective. If we examine computer-generated maps, we can compare South Yorkshire to other British regions.

- South Yorkshire has been heavily towned, yet it still has a high proportion of land plowed for crops.

- Into the late 1970s more that 50 percent of its workers were in manufacturing industries, with only 15,000 in banking, finance, and business services.
- It has had relatively high proportions of single pensioners (with several Local Authority old people's homes and many home helps), one-parent families, and low-skilled manual workers, but not a comparatively bad housing shortage; almost half of South Yorkshire's housing has been provided by the council.
- Only a relatively small proportion of its students stayed in school beyond the statutory leaving age.
- Into the 1980s more than 50 percent of South Yorkshire households were without an automobile and it had high subsidies for public transportion (this changed in 1986).
- It has had a low proportion of police officers.
- It has had poorly or badly polluted major waterways.

There have recently been several changes in the region.

- It has declined moderately in population between 1971 and 1981 due to out-migration; the immigration of blacks and Asians has also been moderate.
- South Yorkshire has changed from a low-unemployment region in the 1970s to a high-unemployment region by 1984.
- It has lost heavily in manufacturing employment, including more than 10,000 jobs lost from British steel works between 1974 and 1981 and over 47,000 jobs lost in the Yorkshire area in the coal industry between 1965 and 1982.

These changes appear to be closely related to the following regional characteristics:

- South Yorkshire has been the home of few of the nation's political, military, or business elite. (It is the location of the headquarters for only twenty-one of the country's one thousand largest corporations, and despite its large population, Sheffield supports only one daily newspaper, which is nationally owned.)
- Despite its problems, South Yorkshire has been receiving only moderate regional aid from the national state.
- It has continued to give most of its votes to Labour, including control of all local district councils, all of which have also been rate capped and punished by cuts in state grants because of "high spending."

## The Dynamics of Change in the Regional Labor Market

As these data suggest, the labor market in South Yorkshire has changed considerably in the last fifteen to twenty years. In 1985 Ian Linn, the research officer at

Northern College in Barnsley, studied the impact of political economic change and drew the following conclusions:

- The industrial structure of South Yorkshire is historically biased toward industries such as mining and steel, which have been in decline both because of national trends and because of low levels of investment.
- The services base of the South Yorkshire economy is smaller than the national average, although capable of expansion.
- The process of decline in the traditional employment industries of South Yorkshire is forecast to continue, whereas the smaller-than-average services area is forecast to expand in terms of jobs.
- However, the South Yorkshire workforce, which is disproportionately skewed toward skilled manual jobs, very low in professional, intermediate, and skilled nonmanual jobs, and less well qualified academically than the national average, is poorly equipped to take advantage of an expanding services economy. (1985:7)

### Regional Change and Computerization

Something of the way in which these regional conditions and changes relate to computing emerges in the following vignette involving Albert the programmer. Though obviously very proud of his own work, Albert's more general reflections on Sheffield labor sites tell a more troubled tale of recent structural changes in the region. For example, he is scathing about the current attitudes toward unions of:

"The female secretarial staff, who have their eye exclusively on the two pounds-fifty weekly deduction for dues. The young male engineers are no better. They accept miserable pay, as little as 8,000 pounds a year, even though they are graduates, designing control systems for multi-million pound rolling mills and the like. They justify not paying attention because in a few years, they will be gone to better jobs; two have gone to the States just this week. This is partly why I have to spend so much time stitching together systems—their parts were designed by people who are long gone."

David asked Albert if what had changed over the last ten years was the people or the attitudes. "The people have definitely changed. What you're getting now is the people who had never been in unions, because companies have weeded out the pro-union people. Like Davy Highstreet, the previous convener of shop stewards at my works."

Davy had been convener when we first came to Sheffield in the 1970s, when the factory, still locally controlled, had been pictured in the newspapers with a red flag hoisted above it to celebrate a deal closed with the Soviet Union. The factory's shop stewards' movement played a prominent role in regional trade union and industrial events, and its workforce was connected tightly to the work site, through its own sports center and organizations on the adjoining council housing estate.

"Davy was the first victim of the firm's 'night of long knives' in 1983. On the Wednesday, the firm announced that it was going to save 20 percent on the wages bill by laying off 20 percent of the workforce. The blue collar union leadership made a mistake by proposing a motion to strike with the first redundancy, but it went down by a margin of four to five. The next day, I made a motion to the white collar members that they agree to take a 20 percent cut in pay to save the jobs, but this was defeated by a similar proportion.

"On the Monday, Davy was called in and told to be off the premises in ten minutes; all but five of the union stewards were made redundant in a similar manner. Over one hundred staff jobs were also lost. Mostly, they got rid of activists or those close to retirement, who got substantial government grants to encourage voluntary redundancy. A second lot of redundancies occurred two years later, when anybody who enquired was automatically put on the list. One skilled engineer with a responsible position as a project director is now wasting away; he never got another job.

"Now the unions have had to rebuild their organizations almost completely, so they have been very tentative about any action. The plant recently announced purchase of a computer-aided engineering system which will remake much of the engineering work. The union members are refusing to work with the system, and the management is complaining bitterly, but I expect the opposition to fold soon; it's coming up to time for the annual wage rise.

"It's wrong for the company to introduce change in this manner, without discussion with the unions. The engineers involved wanted to keep the technology issue to themselves, but I urged them to bring in all the workers for support, to explain the importance of the issue, and so on. That's the way they handle it at Smiths, where they still have an active [Communist Party] Branch. There, when management expressed to the union their intention to introduce an automated system which would lead to two hundred redundancies, the Branch asked me to do an educational. I got them all to subscribe to automated equipment trade publications. At first they were scared, especially after the firm got them to tour an integrated manufacturing facility like the one being proposed. The convenor told the membership that, if it's what they wanted, he could get jobs with the highest wages in the world, but there would only be four workers left! Just this week, they announced agreement on a system which will mean only sixty redundancies; that's quite a success.

"You see, the big change is not really in the attitudes of workers, nor does it have that much to do with information technology. Rather, it's the 'Rambo' attitude of management, supported by Thatcherism. Employers are arrogant. They can't even be bothered to come to the North to take advantage of lower wages; they are fat and comfortable in the South, where they don't have to work hard."

Albert's concluding geographic comments illustrate how the issue of social change is conceptualized in regional terms. Like his Communist Party comrade Mike, Albert tends to account for the changes in regional status in terms of national state policy. Whatever the source, he outlines a situation in which workers clearly have less collective power at the point of production. Although some, like the engineers, maintain a certain degree of individual power, this individual power has little impact on the nature of computing systems, except in the negative sense of complicating Albert's work. Even the relative successes of collective worker action, such as Smith's, manifest much lower levels of influence than in the past.

Albert's perspective, combined with Linn's conclusions quoted above, suggest something about why labor market changes have been so disruptive to individuals in South Yorkshire. Because such groups as trade unions depend on workplace organization, such great changes in the structure of jobs have obvious implications for their influence as well.

## Region, Skill, and Computerization

What is the relationship between labor market changes and computerization? We have chosen to approach this aspect of computerization from the perspective of skill, which is relevant in several ways to recent changes in the labor market.[4] In employment-based, industrial social formations, the job is often the cornerstone of individual identity and group culture. A typically important component of any specific job or occupation is the set of skills required for and recognized as part of it. If we can specify how computerization is associated with change of skill at the regional level, we can infer much about what has happened to jobs, working people's access to them, and to their culture.

Skill has a number of aspects: how it is acquired, how it is perceived, and how necessary it actually is to the physical acts of commodity creation. "Skill" has a clearly substantive or "real" element—the degree of physical or mental dexterity shown in or required for completing a purposeful activity. Skill also has a formal or "symbolic" dimension. In employment-based social formations, jobs generally come to be associated with one or another skill label—for example, "skilled," "unskilled," or "semiskilled." The formal label does not necessarily correspond tightly to the substantive skill actually used or needed in the job, yet the formal label often does have important implications for the self-identity created, quality of life experienced, and degree of prestige and recognition enjoyed by those who perform it. In a phrase, both substantive and formal skill are important to class culture.

Much recent sociology of work (e.g., Zimbalist 1979) has drawn attention to the dialectical relationship between the two sides of skill. Partly this has meant paying attention to the substantive side of skill as opposed to the formal "job title" models of industrial sociology. Focus has shifted to production itself, especially the degree of actual worker control over the labor process. Skill, like the general character of any labor process, is determined politically as well as technologically. Degree of skill is affected by the course of the day-to-day fights between labor and management about how work is to proceed, as well as by political battles over the local state. Like work-oriented social historians David Montgomery (1979) and Herbert Gutman (1977), work sociologists see the degree of control over labor processes and jobs as having crucial influence on the outcome of more general working-class economic and political struggles.

New approaches to the sociology of work direct attention to the importance of social ideology and prejudices, as opposed to substantive skill, in determining formal skill labels. In a particularly famous example, Louise Kapp Howe (1977) drew attention to the heavily gendered fact that, according to the then current edition of the U.S. government's *Dictionary of Occupational Titles*, the job of child care worker was "objectively" labeled as involving less skill than that of shoveling offal in a chicken factory.

### A Holistic Conception of Skill

The most impressive accomplishment of the new sociology of work is the creation of a unified, nonreductionist framework within which to deal with skill. Ken Kusterer's (1978) *Know-How on the Job: The Important Working Knowledge of "Unskilled" Workers* is an ethnography of the extensive and impressive mental and social skills involved in jobs generally labeled as "unskilled," particularly "pink-collar" jobs such as bank telling and machine minding in a paper cup factory. The theoretical center of Kusterer's book is his contextualization of skill in relation to labor site culture and "work community." Workers typically develop a shared "cognitive map" of the actual work process itself, and they develop a "communal network" of relationships with other workers. This takes place in necessary response to the alienation inherent in capitalist production.

The ultimate result is that workers practice their skills in labor processes that they themselves have actually helped to create. The practice of these skills, which draws on knowledge embedded in the map and on knowledge about fellow workers, is necessary for production to take place. Creation and reproduction of "know-how," necessary responses to alienation, become equally essential to production itself. In sum, skill is a very broad, cultural phenomenon, including more than the degree of dexterity needed in physical and mental movements. Skill is relevant to the formal label attached to the job, the self-identity, quality of life, and prestige of the individual who occupies it. Moreover, skill is linked to the character of individual and group alienation and how they are coped with, as well as to the "cognitive maps" or working knowledge, the work site communal networks, and the nonwork community associated with particular jobs.

### Effects of Computerization on Job Skills

If we organize the job-related computerization data presented in Part Two in terms of the theory of skill outlined above, the following patterns emerge:

1. The degree of physical dexterity needed in Sheffield jobs has not changed drastically—some manual skills have been replaced, although fewer than those replaced by mass automation, and some new manual skills, especially keyboarding, have been introduced.
2. The degree of mental dexterity required has changed a great deal.
3. Although the substantive skill needed to do jobs has not fallen as managements intended, the formal skill labels attached to jobs have changed and in many cases have fallen, accompanied by the institutionalization of several less-skilled new job titles.
4. Because of changes in the labor process, how workers experience and cope with alienation, in addition to what they consider relevant worker knowledge and labor site networks, have also changed drastically.
5. The sense of identity, quality of life, and feeling of prestige by those who have been able to keep the same jobs have also changed, sometimes in a positive direction, but these have changed drastically and largely negatively for those who have had to change jobs or who have lost them altogether.
6. The nonwork community has changed drastically, with the decline of housing estate, trade union, and working-class bases of social interaction; the emergence of "labor freedom" as a more or less permanent social identity, especially for the young; and with expanded part-time employment, especially for females.

### Computerization and the Causes of Skill Change

Should these changes in skill be attributed to computer technology itself? The correlations between computerization and skill changes in Sheffield are numerous and significant, but, as with the general pattern of computerization described at the beginning of Part Three, they do not form a simple pattern of impacts.

Obviously, the specific physical activities that must necessarily be carried out by workers were often changed when new equipment was introduced. Some skills important both to production and to class culture were being lost in Sheffield, such as those of the "skilled" machine setter. Yet more often than not, those jobs that remained were described by their occupants and were observable as involving roughly comparable degrees of dexterity. Partly this is because many previous skills remained relevant. Indeed, lecturers at the Sheffield Polytechnic argued that the shortage of cash in regional businesses rather than the lack of applicable skills was the reason for the relatively unambitious computerization actually implemented. Thus a weak regional economy also muffled the "change of skill" consequences of computerization. In short, computers have apparently not driven down substantially the average level of substantive skill in the region.

Computers are strongly connected to *formal* skill changes, however. Consider again the experience of Mavis in the Data Shop, a business offering one of the new services made possible by the development of minicomputer technology. Her work experience was in many ways similar to that of the women Kusterer studied a decade earlier and an ocean away—high substantive skill, poor pay and recognition. Though there clearly was a workplace culture, there was little work community, certainly little evidence of traditional Labourism. Rather, there was gendering in many forms, but it was evident particularly in the full-time employees' fear of job loss and family dependency and in the form of male privilege.

In contrast, skill with computers allowed Albert to maintain an identity as a worker, to keep his place in the work community, and to continue his political work. Albert was the chairman of a joint Trades Council–Employment Department committee on new technology for several years, and his conception of work and the nature of the working class informed his approach to programming; he depended on other workers to see the wisdom of his approach and, where possible, to build on existing skill, not to eliminate it. This approach was very much that of the new technology programs of the District Council, which he helped to shape.

Yet although Albert continued to pursue what he described as "the same objectives" on the new organizational terrain associated with computerized work, he felt his efforts were "a shambles." Much of this had to do with changes in the working-class culture, especially of organizations, into the building of which he had put much of his life energy. Ten years before, Albert had been the moving force behind the district CP's extensive educational activities. He wasn't involved much anymore, "what with all the factions and chaos." Though calling himself "a staunch supporter of the current leadership," Albert considered *Marxism Today* right wing and the *Morning Star* crew as "practicing working class blackmail, to the point where the paper was starved of funds by right wing printers. They forced the press to close, so that the paper is now printed by Trotskyists!" He found no group in the party with which to identify, and although he generally expressed support for newer political issues such as feminism, he felt many feminists were right wing too, "because they drive important issues to the periphery."

The organizations to which Albert had devoted his life, the regional trade unions and the Communist Party, were by 1986 severely limited in what they could accomplish. Many, like Albert and Mike, continued to "soldier on in the interest of the working class" and expressed a commitment to the traditional forms of collective action, yet their energies waned because they were pessimistic about whether traditional actions would prove effective in the face of rapid change.

In sum, although computerization had not had a major direct effect on individual substantive job skills, it had affected the formal side of skill and therefore the cultural categories through which individuals were perceived and the social relationships they created and reproduced. This indirect effect of computerization on skill was an important element in lessening the effectiveness of "traditional" working-class strategies for collective action, which in turn affected the characteristics of the regional labor market and the reproduction of the region as a whole.

## Gendering and Labor Market Change

The contrast between Mavis and Albert also suggests that an area of much significant change in regional employment institutions concerns gender. A series of leaflets by the Research and Resources Unit of the Sheffield Employment Department on the job conditions of women in Sheffield makes a number of points:

- Going out to work is now the norm in women's lives and not the exception (60 percent of Sheffield's women of working age are in paid work; the proportion working or looking for work rose from 30 percent in 1921 to 64 percent in 1981).
- Seventy-eight percent of women's jobs are in services.
- Over 74 percent of new service jobs are filled by women, but beginning in the late 1970s the growth in the service sector stagnated.
- Women work disproportionately in the lowest grades, with the poorest pay.
- Women's work is increasingly part-time—over two-fifths of all women workers work part-time—and the number of part-time jobs continues to increase overall, but the number of full-time women's jobs has decreased; indeed, the number of part-time jobs for women in manufacturing has actually fallen.

Fothergill and Vincent add that South Yorkshire still has a comparatively smaller proportion of its women in the workforce, and that earnings for both blue-collar and white-collar women are lower than average, although men's earnings are higher than average.

There appear to be intimate and yet contradictory interactions among these changes in the labor market, gender, and computers. An Employment Department pamphlet put it this way:

> New Technology is having a double edged effect: In some areas, e.g., shops, offices, banks, especially in the public sector, in health service, education, and local government, new techniques and natural wastage are replacing the jobs held by many part-time women workers, and lowering the wages of those who remain. In other areas, the use of part-timers is being expanded, e.g., in the micro-electronics industry, [and] contract cleaning. (DEED 1983:2)

### Accounting for the Gender Changes in the Labor Market

These changes in the local labor market are similar to those that are more generally characteristic of Britain as a whole and perhaps of other employment-based social formations. Their diversity suggests that any simple explanation in terms of technology alone is not warranted.

In an analysis of recent changes in women's labor market experience, Cambridge economist Jane Humphries, herself a South Yorkshire native, identified three popular institutional economic explanations (1987).[5] The "buffer" hypothesis suggests that various social arrangements create a "reserve army of potential labor" that is largely female and that functions to cushion the economic shocks due to technological change. In this view, women should be rapidly hired as economies expand and rapidly fired as they contract. Humphries argues that the buffer view is given little support by the recent experience of British women, whose employment has gone up or fallen slower than men's during the recent economic decline.

Especially when one takes into account the considerable constraints placed on trade unions during this period, such a pattern is more indicative of the second "substitution" view: Women are used as a substitute for male labor when male work organizations, such as unions, get too powerful. Indeed, the expansion of women's laboring has taken place in spite of national policies that make it more difficult for women to take jobs, such as a decrease in support for paid maternity leave, child care, and the dependent elderly.

A third or "segmentation" interpretation sees men and women as occupying essentially different niches of the labor market, with jobs so different that they follow different dynamics. For Humphries, the increase in part-time work can only be accounted for as segmentation. Segmentation, however, can be combined with substitution, as when full-time male jobs are broken down into part-time female jobs. Humphries concludes that combining segmentation and substitution offers the most satisfactory explanation for women's labor market experience in contemporary Britain.

Humphries's approach accounts for changes in gender in terms of changes in social arrangements rather than in terms of new technology. Patterns of worker knowledge, social relations, and work community are affected by major changes in the capacity for organized collective action, and these in turn have had a profound impact on the reproduction of the labor market. Computerization appears to be one of several media through which these changes are manifest. The comments of Mavis about men, and Albert's about women, indicate that the changes we have been describing are experienced in an active sense by both groups, that one cannot account for the way in which the region and its labor market have been reproduced without at the same time accounting for the reproduction of gender. Male trade union organizers, such as Jim Bucher of the National Union of Public Employees, find it difficult to organize women because "they have no collective culture and their relationship to work is looser; therefore, it's harder for unions to deliver for them." Women such as Cynthia Cockburn argue, however, that much of the problem lies in the failure of trade unions to address women's concerns, especially the relationship of jobs to work at home. Union officers don't have the experiential base to understand these issues—"89 percent of full time officials for the National Association of Local Government Officers have a full time spouse at home."

## The Limits of a Regional Structure Perspective

Although change in the process of gendering is manifest at the regional level, it is no more reducible to some process internal to regional structure than it is to technology. This means that there are important limits to a perspective that treats regions in strictly structural terms. To account for gender change, we must take into account human action, both in terms of perceptions and relationships. The following vignette depicts some Sheffielders who have found a more inclusive, holistic way to think about regions.

"Program officers" is the term used to describe people charged with implementing programs like those of the Sheffield Department of Employment and Economic Development. A group of DEED program officers were discussing the difficulties people have in coping with changes in the local economy. Tom had been trained in the structural approach of the economist, but he began by saying, "For us, strategy problems which at first appear economic often turn out to be more political. We want to develop a positive response to change, and we want to do it democratically, with the participation of all of the people in Sheffield. The problem is how to do it. For example: because we're in a run-up to a general election, the Labour Party needs an energizing left slogan. One proposal was 'social ownership,' but nobody knows what that means—besides, it sounds too much like the 'nationalisation' that nobody talks about any more. 'Democratic, locally-led economic development' is more prosaic, but it's safer. It covers things like Employment Departments and Local Enterprise Boards, different from the Urban Development Zones and other programmes of the [National State's] Department of Trade and Industry, because these latter take power from the localities.

"But whatever you call your strategy, you have to change the mind-set of many civil servants to allow for a real coordinated development strategy, one based on popular planning. Unfortunately, the politics of the situation means that the Labour Party nationally projects an exaggerated view of what is going on in places like Sheffield with regard to 'democratic development.'"

"You see, 'democratic, local economic planning' has been stumbled into," said Stuart, whose responsibility was working with the local polytechnic. "It's the only Labour Party economic slogan which looks very different from the other parties' rhetoric. Consequently, it has become a central element of the election Manifesto, but it hasn't been examined much, and people are getting worried about it. The only public debate about it is really a tangent, with M.P.s like Roy Hattersley really pressing for centralisation of development efforts. M.P.s like John Prescott use the language of democracy, but he's really talking of 'large region' development, similar to the Welsh and Scottish Development Agencies, which have very little local input. A strategy like Prescott proposes might include all of Yorkshire and Humberside, not just South Yorkshire, and this would allow little room for democratic participation.

"Both Hattersley's and Prescott's ideas are more compatible with indicative planning by bureaucrats, like what the French do. What we want—democratic planning with popular participation—is very different. There is no open debate about the differences among these approaches, about what is actually meant by regional planning itself."

Stuart went on to discuss differences in strategy among the program officers themselves: "Some here in the Employment Department accept the fact that their work involves an adoption of New Technology, albeit a skeptical one. They concentrate their energy on socializing the costs involved in adapting to it. Others, however, argue for a traditional defensive or 'trade union' posture: Any decision on technological change is the responsibility of capitalists, whereas the union's job is to fight change and only accept it when it improves pay, etc., of members. They won't participate in promoting change."

He added that the hesitation to participate has two roots: "One is in the history of militant manufacturing unionism, where the defensive strategy seemed to work. But the other, manifest in the public sector and mining unions, is more ideological. It's that involvement is a violation of the appropriate role of unions.

"This position parallels the 'traditional' position of hostility to promoting worker's control and worker cooperatives. The union within the Sheffield Council itself is officially hostile to any worker involvement in the introduction of new technology. Several Employment Department people got in hot water because they participated in a one month trial use of a new computer system."

"A good thing, too," interjected Tom, "because those 'Wampies' turned out to be crap, but we would have been lumbered with them if they not been tried."

"Issues are handled through traditional bureaucratic lobbying, instead of by a process involving as much popular participation as possible," added Clive, a technology specialist. "M.P.s argue over which plants to close, but no basic principles emerge. One can see the absurdity of the current situation in the cases of the steel and auto industries, where national lobbying and EEC planning have collided with local 'planning.' The trade union movement has favored national lobbying, because leaders think they are stronger there than with the local planners."

Stuart had read our grant proposal. "It's good that you bring up the cultural dimension of computerization in your research, but I think you romanticize the Sheffield working-class movement a bit. It's historically strong but defensive, not proactive. The attempts of the Employment Department to generate discussion of new technology have not had a big response. Some people in the trade union movement have even treated these attempts as a joke, though not in the health service and other state bureaucracies, where there is this mystique about VDU [video display units] hazards."

Mary, the team leader, sees a similar dynamic behind the difficulty of getting discussions going in the local trade union movement over conversion, not just from defense, to almost any new products. "Resistance to change is almost cultural, so economic change must encompass cultural change. Questions of planning are relevant problems of working class culture, but we can't address them directly enough, because we are frustrated by the absence of a debate over the mechanisms of participatory planning, over which groups in the working class are to have an influence and how to make sure they get it. And this means deciding who's in the working class."

Clive responded, "In order to develop regionally, we've got to have region-wide cooperation. But important aspects of traditional working class culture have to do more with locality than with region—living in one part of the city versus living in a class area established differently. I've lived in the city for twenty years and am still not considered a local. When I lived in a house on the edge of a Council estate, I'd watch children from the estate venture only tentatively across the boundary, like they were doing something very naughty.

"Sheffield is parochial. Unlike Newcastle, it doesn't even have an identity as a regional center—why Sheffield as opposed to Leeds or Nottingham? There's not a strong sense of regional unity. When the County Council died, we tried to set up a South Yorkshire and North Derbyshire regional economic development group, but this hasn't gotten anywhere. Once steel, coal—heavy industry in general—are gone, it becomes harder to argue that there should even be a large city here."

We asked about using "the new computer age" as a slogan to mobilize regional efforts. Mike was negative about short-run prospects for connecting computer enthusiasm to the existing working-class movement. "A positive perspective is necessary to any attempt to get involved in the design or early phases of new products. You've got to feel like you want to aim at helping a shift in the local economy, so you've got to believe that such local action can work, that your local organizations are powerful enough. But there's this deep pessimism within the trade union movement. Despite the failure of the defensive posture, bloody mindedness and work to rule still block positive approaches to new technology. The best hope may be in the development of new power groups, perhaps among a few white collar unions."

"You need new institutions to get progressive computer politics," Tom said. "In the early days of the Employment Department, the talk was of how the working class could control new technology, and how to build new technology-promoting networks was discussed at length. Such networks are in place in other locations and they've worked, but we couldn't get one going here. By now, the Sheffield working class seems to feel by-passed by new technology. New technology feels like a weapon aimed directly at them: through expropriation of the means of production from the working class, to remove the working class from history.

"Still, a fatalistic acceptance of this situation is not possible for the elected Labour City Councilors. They have to appear to be doing something, but all of the contradictions about how to relate to new technology are focused in their actions. They see a number of frightening signs, like an increase in the proportion of students from the Poly leaving the City. In essence, they operate out of a set of fears, about the death of a city, about loss of their political base, etc., so they set up units like the Employment Department and the New Technology Group. Politically, however, they continue to operate in a parochial, defensive manner, defensive about encroachments on their decision-making power and with no clear plan or regional policy. So we Programme Officers have to invent the region as we go along."

Although the region may necessarily be a primary unit in any plan to revive economic activity, as this vignette illustrates, the humans within it are not necessarily anxious to follow the regional "best interest." The program officers identify several issues that must be resolved if the working-class people are to assert control over South Yorkshire: new political styles, resolution of debates over class, and a more regional, less local, sense of identity. These mediating cultural factors are recognized as being much more significant than technology is to questions of class cultural reproduction.

There are clearly severe difficulties facing anyone who would try to develop a systematically regional approach to computerization and economic development. As the program officers' comments suggest, one can be a part of a region without being conscious of it, whereas a consciousness of shared identity is an essential component of ethnic group or class culture and a frequent component of community. Some degree of shared self-identity is necessary for political mobilization as normally understood—for example, as in the Marxist transition from a class "in itself" to a class "for itself." Sheffielders described themselves as "working class," but they tend to conceptualize this in terms of a particular area of the city— "Parson's Cross," "Greystones," "The Manor Estate." One was more likely to be "English" or "a Yorkshire lad" than to identify oneself by saying, "I'm from South Yorkshire."

One attempt to give some political identity to the region, through the creation of a South Yorkshire county council, was ended by the Tory national state when the metropolitan counties were eliminated in the mid-1980s. This is just one example of how conscious human action can have a real, albeit negative, effect on a region.

### Regions and Action

Still, most studies of economic regeneration identify a strong sense of regional identity as an important precondition. For the program officers, one aspect of the case for democratic as opposed to bureaucratic planning is that participation helps create a sense of regional identity and commitment. "South Yorkshire" is more than a convenient descriptive label; it is a creation of the institutions of employment, but these have been importantly shaped by human action, including the deliberate actions of working-class people. It was within this particular regional economy that the trade unions and working-class political organizations created Labourism and tried to create "the Socialist Republic of South Yorkshire" (Clarke 1987).

Today's South Yorkshire miner, if fortunate enough to retain to a job in the industry, might work at a job 30 miles from his home; the same is quite possible for the school teacher. They are still strongly tied together by the history described in Chapter 2, one which presents them with particular forms of employment. This history has also created within the region a "really existing" set of communities, organizations, and networks through which working-class people strive to participate actively in shaping the character of social life. There are good reasons to conclude, however, that these social relationships are less able to reproduce a high quality working-class life than they were previously. Changes in the dynamics of the region, especially in its employment institutions, have much to do with the inability of traditional, "trade union"-based strategies to affect positively the lives of working-class people. In Part Three we have shown how changes in the national state, the world political economy, and the region undermine the cultural basis of collective action based on Labourist principles. In Part Four, we examine the results of the various ways in which working-class people's conscious and unconscious, collective and individual actions also affected computerization and its relationship to social change.

## Notes

1. In anthropology "region" is a less developed ethnological concept than "people," "community," "ethnic group," or even "state" or "world system."

2. The conception of region that we use in this chapter owes a great deal to the recent reconceptualization of "region" in British academic geography. Doreen Massey's *Spatial Divisions of Labour: Social Structures and the Geography of Production* (1984) presents this new view of regions particularly well. Massey accepts the region as the proper object of geography, but she locates a central difficulty of previous geographies in the tendency to give the region an overly spatial referent. The subject matter of geography is more appropriately conceived of as people's social relationships within a physical area rather than as spatial relationships per se. As we assume in this chapter, spatial arrangements are more constituted by the social than constitutive of it. Similarly, though a given geography has an important economic component, this economic reality is culturally constructed as it is reproduced.

Massey takes as the most pressing task the understanding of what lies behind the recent massive changes in the regional geography of industry—for example, the movement of economic activity from the English north to the southeast and east midlands. Such analysis requires a shift in focus from simple patterns of employment in individual firms to the new forms of spatial organization, especially multiplant firms, and to a general attention to the new organization of production, both social and spatial. Massey also critiques political economistic Marxist models of regions because of their tendency to reduce people's actions—their struggles and their differences—to the accumulation process. Rather than seeking to normalize and eliminate difference, the main purpose of geography should be to develop models that explain difference.

Massey's most general claim is that behind the major shifts in the dominant spatial organization of labor within a country lie changes in the spatial organization of the capitalist international political economy, "the development and reorganisation of what we shall call spatial structures of production ... These shifts are a response to changes in class relations, economic and political, and national and international" (p. 7). Regional dynamics are also affected by the technical and organizational characteristics of industry—that is, all economic activity, all forms of paid employment—that often lead to new patterns of regional reproduction. Such relations are conflictual; thus the reproduction of a regional social formation reflects struggle. "Indeed, if we must think of regions spatially—any sub-national area is potentially a region—we have to recognize that the map of relevant regions in England is currently being rapidly redrawn" (p. 10).

The important task is therefore to study the reproduction of social relations, with geography used to study such reproduction in relation to a region. A number of factors—relative nearness or farness, environment, climate, distribution of labor power and skills, the constitution of social groups, and the class and cultural variations within national structures—are all relevant to regional reproduction and must be integrated to develop proper models, geographic or otherwise, of specific regional social formations.

3. The major shortcoming of existing empirical studies of computerization is their failure to bridge the gap between case studies of particular computerizations and aggregate studies based on national statistics. To be able to move more easily from the microlevel to the macrolevel of analysis, computing studies must develop regionally integrated studies.

4. Conceptualizing skill appropriately is probably the major "ethnological" preoccupation of recent work sociology. Robert Blauner's *Alienation and Freedom* (1964) argues that newly developed continuous-process technologies, which involve a change in type of substantive skill from more manual to more mental, increase skill level. Harry Braverman's *Labor and Monopoly Capital: The Degradation of Work in the Twentieth Century* (1974) argues instead that new technology continues the long-term tendency toward deskilling in capitalistic social formations because class is the primary determinant of which new technology is introduced into the labor process.

5. The major innovation in the academic study of labor market phenomena in the last twenty years has been the resurgence of institutional perspectives. Older perspectives, labeled by Berg "human capital theory" in economics and "status attainment theory" in sociology, were based on equilibrium assumptions, particularly the idea that unevenness in labor markets is only temporary, due to exogenous changes in technology that were the basic source of changes in regional labor markets. Individuals respond to "opportunity structures" by changing their personal investment in human capital or by altering their strategy for attaining social prestige, the main vehicle for both being formal education and training. Such individual changes ultimately lead to a new equilibrium. In the face of the continuing failure of the labor market to find equilibrium points, institutionalists have directed attention to a broad range of social patterns that appear to maintain differences among groups, whatever educational choices may be made by individuals.

# Making Computerization

# 11

# Culture-Centered Computing and Local Policy

Part Four concerns how the actions of particular human groups affect computerization. Here in Chapter 11, we examine one important action, the attempts of the Sheffield District Local Authority or "Council" to use social policy to promote particular forms of computing.[1] Careful studies of what happens in places that have well-developed computerization policies should illuminate the kinds of social groups—classes, occupational groups, regional groups—that may support computerization policy and highlight cultural dimensions of computing.

Our analysis of computing policy begins with its broader policy context, new municipal socialism or NMS. We present detailed descriptions of successful culture-centered computing projects followed by analyses of the broader failures of the new technology policy, relating to the structures analyzed in Part Three. Although the overall results of Sheffield computing policy may be limited, much can be learned from Sheffielders' efforts.

## NMS in South Yorkshire

In 1980 a new group came to prominence in the Sheffield District Labour Party. These activists argued that a "New Municipal Socialism" was necessary to reorient the working-class movement effectively. As described in Chapter 2, local politics in South Yorkshire overwhelmingly means Labour politics, but regional politics must be understood in relation to national politics.

After the victory of the Conservative Party in the national elections of 1979, the radical policies of Margaret Thatcher faced little effective opposition. An assertive rank and file in the Sheffield Labour Party developed a campaign to base opposition in local action. One participant claimed to have initially uttered "the Socialist Republic of South Yorkshire" as a money-raising catch phrase, but the campaign to center the Labour counteroffensive on such regions as South Yorkshire blossomed into a national movement.

Local elections in 1980 gave new municipal socialists control of the Sheffield District Council. By 1986 the ensuing politics were referred to as "the Blunkett

Revolution," after David Blunkett, a charismatic blind-from-birth technical college lecturer who was elected leader of the council's Labour Group. Drawing attention to the region's dependence on such "old" industries as coal and steel and its extensive public employment and services, Blunkett's supporters argued that Thatcherism and the major economic transformations of the period threatened social viability. Critical of the "welfare statism" of postwar Labour as well as of Thatcher, these activists sought to use the local state as a new way to intervene politically.[2]

### Labourism Critiqued

NMS politics claimed historical legitimacy through ties to the nineteenth-century locally based socialism that, for example, had legitimated the initial construction of council housing.[3] Yet by the 1940s Labourism, the dominant strategy of the Labour Party, gave little role to local politics. Instead, Labourism placed emphasis on:

1. controlled union militancy at the private sector workplace, to produce a general increase in wages and working conditions;
2. control of the national state through parliamentary victory for the national Labour Party;
3. the gradual expropriation of some of the ownership of industry from private individuals and its transfer to the state sector; and
4. provision of increasingly extensive public services at ever higher standards.

Because public enterprises and services were basically technical rather than political activities, highly qualified managers and professionals were to run them. Policy was to be determined nationally and only administered locally.

After the World War II, Labourism appeared to work in Sheffield, but by 1976–1977, some cracks had appeared. Analytic parallels were drawn between the bureaucratic forms of "really existing" socialism in Eastern Europe and the Sheffield Town Hall. The failure of the parliamentary Labour Party to oppose Thatcherism effectively was viewed as more proof of Labourism's inadequacy.

Labourism concentrated on diverting part of the surplus generated in the private sector to fund public services. NMS critiqued Labourism for taking the adequate operation of capitalism for granted rather than holding a "systemic crisis" view of the political economy. Increasing economic distress required direct intervention in the economy, "genuine alternative economic policies ... bridging the gap between the [public] provision of services and the [private] industrial manufacturing sector in local communities" (Blunkett n.d., ca. 1981:1). Bad national policy and failure to implement good national policies like industrial democracy had already led to local experimentation, as with the South Yorkshire County "socialist" low-fares transport policy. Several NMS elements were based on the *Social-*

*ist Republic* (Clarke 1987) experience of the new Labour-controlled county government in South Yorkshire in the 1970s.

It was necessary to repoliticize working-class voters because their low involvement in politics was the root of Labour's defeat by Thatcher. Labour had failed to use all of the possible instruments for socialist policy. An activist local state with new structures for popular participation was to become the means of "the genuine democratic control of total national resources" (Blunkett n.d., ca. 1981:1).

### Alternative Social Policies

Specific targets of those involved with NMS included the following:

1. the local private economy, in which strategic intervention would encourage production that met social as well as profit needs and would build on rather than replace worker skills;
2. the council's own contracting, purchasing, and other economic activities;
3. council services, to be decentralized and reorganized based on the notion of the council as both a popular democracy and a "model employer" promoting "workers' control"; and
4. the policy-making process, to be changed by addition of a set of structures aimed at increasing popular participation in policy development.

In rapid succession, the Sheffield Council opened several new units (including the Central Policy Unit and the Department of Employment); became much more publicly involved in local and national controversies (such as the attempt to prevent the shutdown of the local branches of nationalized industries, e.g., British Steel); and increased its internal committee structure, to the point at which being a councilor became for many a full-time occupation.

### Alternative Computing Policy

An officer high in the Sheffield Department of Employment and Economic Development argues about the Sheffield initiatives that "what was new was the emphasis being given to New Technology" (Darwin 1987b:3). NMS promoted new information technology while also influencing its social consequences. This approach was an innovation within the labor movement. The previous typical view was a scientific technical revolution computopian vision of, for example, "the white-hot heat of technological revolution." The minority "new left" tended to a more compputropian view, promoting resistance to new technology. NMS computing policy was also an advance on the British national Trade Union Congress and several national trade unions, which had tried to steer a middle course, willing in principle to accept NIT in exchange for guarantees over personing levels, union organization protection, and so on. The key element in their approach was the technology agreement, which failed strategically.

In Sheffield, the Blunketteers' more proactive approach saw new technology as an issue through which to demonstrate the possibilities of assertive working-class politics. A 1982 document from the Employment Department asserts that

> the challenge for the City Council and the people of Sheffield then, is how to gain control of the ways in which new technology is being introduced in order to protect jobs; how to identify those technologies, skills, and areas of research already present in the city which have growth potential for job-creation in the future; and how to attract and graft on those technologies and skills which could help to diversify opportunities and broaden the economic and employment base of the city. (Darwin 1982:2)

Eventually, programs relevant to computing came to include the following:

1. a model technology agreement with the council trade unions, including "no redundancy" (lay-off) and "prior approval" clauses to prevent implementation of computing systems without prior discussion;
2. a supplementary program that used local authority grant and loan funds to "develop within Sheffield the technology based industries which [would] preserve skills and jobs, and draw on Sheffield's resources of knowledge and expertise to develop new employment" (Darwin 1982:12);
3. a network of computing-oriented local services, including a product development center, a microsystem center, and a program to develop community computing;
4. the strategic promotion of new information technology within council departments, including conversion of the council's "Computer Panel" into an "Information Technology Panel" to oversee development and implementation of an internal council computing strategy; and
5. the promotion of general new technology skills and the awareness of potential social consequences through locally sponsored training, education, research, and conferences.

These policies were intended as a social response to computing, not merely a technological or economic one. Technological education, for example, was to be not only about preparing the Sheffield working class for new technology jobs; it also aimed to promote an effective political response to industrial transformation. A 1983 Fabian Society pamphlet by Blunkett and by Principal Strategy Officer Geoff Green in the Sheffield Central Policy Unit claimed some maturity for the council's policy: "Though 'new technology' often evokes feelings of uncontrollable change, we had paradoxically been able to plan our intervention much more systematically in this field than others" (p. 13).

### Alternative Computing Programs

By 1987 many of these policies had been implemented in programs. Our work site case studies revealed the existence of unique approaches to computerization in local organizations, captured in the following vignette:

Traffic Systems Cooperative is a business strongly supported by the local state in South Yorkshire. The co-op is located in a converted nineteenth-century "little mester's" workshop, a typical Sheffield industrial property. The one large room contains a jumble of traffic light equipment used to train workers from various local authorities to clarify appropriate spheres of responsibility. Training was referred to as an example of the co-op's orientation to cutting the cost of service rather than to making money.

Heather, the receptionist, quickly responded to David's question, about whether co-ops use computers differently from other businesses, by turning to the functions of the filing system, the primary computer application. Information concerning a piece of traffic equipment, including the relevant electronic settings and past faults, recent maintenance work, complaints, and so on, is entered into the system. This information is retrieved by an engineer before each visit to the piece, whether for routine maintenance or an emergency. Heather said the computer was also used for bookkeeping, auditing, working out bids, and word processing. When David asked why it wasn't used for designing, an engineer, Pete, responded:

"See, the Co-op is mostly a service business, not designing our own equipment but taking care of someone else's. Take a look at the form I'm filling out now. The piece of equipment in question is built by a multinational; it's no good, always faulting out, not enough room in the design for the minute time shifts, and so on; it's being taken off the market. This is the way we feel about microelectronics: as engineers, we aren't fascinated by them, but we use them as any other piece of equipment, with advantages and limitations. We like our computer filing system, because it means that engineers have much more time to spend on the road, or doing nothing. I'm in favor of anything which gives me mates more time to walk in the sun."

Another engineer, Steve, estimated that without the computer system the co-op would require a much-expanded administrative system. "Engineers would spend half their time filling out forms, digging in files, buried under paper. With the system, we can keep the bulk of our employees as engineers." When David asked if the system were used to monitor people, Steve said, "Bloody 'ell no! That would be using computers against people, the kind of thing which goes on in the States! The basic point of the co-op is to provide secure, decent jobs for people, plus to save taxpayers' money. Monitoring work, or using the computer to plan work flow to get the most out of workers, are both out. That's why we don't develop a work plan; it would lead to monitoring.

"Don't get me wrong. Computer applications which fit our view of what a co-op is about are taken on board readily, like our parts inventory data base. We have had this computer system for eighteen months and we're looking to expand, both to increase memory capacity and to switch to IBM compatible, because this is to be the standard in Sheffield City Council. We hope, in fact, to move to a direct fault report system, with a dedicated line from the District Council. We want to keep the pyramid of the company flat, with people as much as possible doing the same work. For example, everybody uses the word processing; if an estimate was asked for, Pete would work it up."

Gendering was clearly present in the co-op—for example, the pinup calendars of Samantha Fox on the wall, which Pete described as "sexist adverts." Heather was clearly responsible for office work, and so forth. Still, there was a relaxed atmosphere, a "first-name basis," a fluid sense of shared responsibility. With regard to the computer, several people had contributed to the design of the file system, both the early manual design and the final electronic system. All of the members David met seemed quite comfortable with applications work and talked about it enthusiastically; they shared the sense of frustration at the current system's slowness and looked forward to a 16-bit machine.

Steve and Pete traced the atmosphere and approach to computerization to the history of the co-op itself. It began "back in the early '80s, when most of them did," growing out of a strike at General Electric Company, Ltd. (GEC), where most of the original co-op members were working. Pete described GEC as charging outrageous prices for system maintenance—"700 pounds per annum for a simple system—we've cut it down to about 250. GEC could get away with it because of absence of competition; it was only them and one other Multinational, Plessey. Nobody thought that it could be done by outsiders, because it was 'very technical.' During the strike, we went to the chairman of the South Yorkshire County Traffic Committee and offered to provide emergency maintenance, to avoid traffic accidents, and so forth, as long as no money went to GEC. The service was accepted, and the Chairman asked us to come see him if we wanted to do the servicing on our own after the strike.

"We put together a proposal, coming in only slightly above Plessey. We got the contract anyway, and we went to the Co-op Bank for a float of 10,000, which we got. Unlike most of the new South Yorkshire Cooperatives, we have never had to go to the Councils for money, although they do purchase parts for us—off the counter prices for small numbers are astronomical. The equipment we service is all manufactured by large corporations, often the ones we compete with." David asked if this made them vulnerable, and they said that although by law corporations have to provide access to all new equipment and training in how to service it, they have tried to charge outrageous training prices, which the co-op has generally refused to pay. This caused some difficulty in the early days, but "we've proved our competence."

According to the engineers, in the twelve months before the case study business grew "fantastically; we've taken on Derbyshire, part of Humberside, and one-half of West Yorkshire as well as the South Yorkshire Councils." The co-op's primary difficulty was in the recruitment of necessary additional staff. They took on one Engineering Industry Training Board apprentice, but they really needed skilled electronic engineers. Most of the work involves being out in a van responding quickly to trouble; "we carry most of the necessary information in our head, aided by the computerized records." They've gotten inquiries from people with computer training, but they feel that one can't just train in computers.

Pete says, "You need substantive knowledge of electronic engineering as well. We use computers to save time and make people's work more enjoyable. Also, to contribute to the creation of dependable jobs—after all, creating decent jobs is what a co-op is all about."

Traffic Systems Co-op embodies many of the policy goals of NMS, including new technology. The use of computers is clearly influenced by the cooperative structure of the organization and the goal of "socially relevant production." The form of the co-op's success was indeed that of a genuine alternative to dependence on the new international political economy.

## Culture-Centered Computing

Traffic Systems Co-op was just one of several organizations that promoted progressive computing. By 1987 the network of technology-promoting training, advice, and promotion centers was in place and expanding. Council program officers had a much more concrete idea of what local economic intervention could accomplish and were more narrowly targeted. New information technology applications were spreading, albeit slowly, through council departments; an experienced senior program officer in the Treasurer's Department described Sheffield as a leading local authority in this area. Consultation through the technology agreement was institutionalized in council departments. The council had created the Information Technology (IT) Panel, which brought together council political and administrative leaders. Innovative approaches to training, such as the Women's Technology Training Workshop, received national recognition; these programs encouraged trainees to recognize the positive uses of IT and to fight against its negative potentials.

In what follows, we describe specific computing programs that *apply* a social understanding of computerization. What the programs and projects have in common is the high degree to which system conception, design, and/or implementation are based on broad cultural perspectives.

"Culture-centered computing" is a useful label under which to group some technical innovations in computing—various new techniques, computer artifacts, and information system designs informed by a broadly social conception of the information process—as well as a way of thinking more generally about information systems, as both "praxis" and "theory." As a term that attempts to generalize the kinds of praxis manifest in such projects, "culture-centered computing" is based in the tradition of American anthropology.[4] A computerization project is culture-centered if it increases awareness of how computing is a social and cultural activity, not just a technical one, and if such awareness is built into system design, implementation, and use.

### The Study Circle Projects

Study circles were implemented by the Human-Centered Office Systems Group at Sheffield Polytechnic. The group is composed of staff members and students from both the sociology and the computer studies departments. The long-term goal of the group is to develop an effective methodology for user involvement in office system development. They study both the "normal" process of information system development and the feasibility of alternatives.

The basic aim of the study circles is to prepare clerical workers to participate in the development of systems they will ultimately use, including decisions about design, hardware, and implementation. These projects graft techniques developed by such Scandinavians as Marja Vehvilaeinen (1986) with the tradition of workers' education in South Yorkshire (Hakken 1978). Workers are released from normal work activity to participate in monthly classes that cover basic characteristics of new information technology, critiques of the normal system development process, work process analysis, social issues in computerization, and women's personal experience. (Female clerical workers are seldom rewarded for initiative or for taking a long-range view, and previous negative experience with information technology is often ignored in system development. Consequently, the office study circles involve a substantial component of feminist consciousness raising.)

During the period of our field study, two study circle projects were initiated within local government. As a result of careful preparation, the projects had the support of the relevant trade unions and the Sheffield District Council, including the Department of Computer Services, which is committed to a structural methodology of system design. The project in the Libraries Department had taken off. After initial meetings, the clerical workers involved made a presentation to the top staff. As a result of this presentation, several of the study circle members were co-opted to (placed on) the Libraries Department's official team to develop new information systems. Some group members went on to lead additional study circles. Because new hardware had already been purchased in Personnel, discussion was limited to a set of guidelines for new system implementation.

### SPRITE

Sheffield People's Resource for Information TEchnology (SPRITE) grew out of Computers for People, a Sheffield group of computer professionals, educators, and community activists who shared an interest in progressive computing as well as a "compputropian" perspective. (CfP was itself an outgrowth of Sheffield Science for People, a 1970s group active in worker education [Hakken 1978].) Like the group in California that ultimately created the personal computer, CfP's initial aim was to "demystify" computerization. For example, its members raised a public alarm about the possible dangers of computerization; they developed popular computer games (such as "picket" during the miners' strike) to show alternative uses of computers; and they put on "computer road shows" at District Trades Council meetings and in community centers.

Especially at road shows, CfP members encountered in their working-class audiences an ambivalence about computing that paralleled their own feelings. CfP developed an action research project on "Developing Information Technology in the Community with Unwaged Groups" (Darwin et al. 1985). This research documented the strong Sheffield interest in collective rather than individual NIT applications projects. SPRITE was initially funded by the EEC's Social Fund.

SPRITE aimed to integrate community computing into existing centers and computer clubs. SPRITE was social rather than vocational in orientation and was designed to be strongly influenced by participating groups. After initial computer familiarization, SPRITE user groups were encouraged to develop applications for their own organizations. Each user group developed a unique direction (Cassell and Fitter 1987), several collaborated on the design of a data base system for the local Forum for People with Disabilities and others prepared a manual for an electronic bulletin board in local libraries.

By 1987 SPRITE had developed collaborative activity for people in diverse ethnic, gender, and employment statuses. Despite its nonvocational design, SPRITE led to further education and employment for several of its participants. For those unable to find paid labor due to the economy, it provided "leisure" skills that were both supporting and social, not individualizing like most computer games.

Still, SPRITE had difficulty addressing political issues proactively or creating a political constituency for itself and for progressive computing in general. Since initial funding for the project was external, SPRITE workers felt it necessary to ground the project more firmly in the council's institutional structure. It did this by joining the new "tertiary" sector of the Local Educational Authority, along with the Women's Technology Training Workshop and the Sheffield Information Technology Centre (ITEC), as "Tri-Tech." In 1988 some of the CfP activists who initiated SPRITE feared that these developments might compromise SPRITE's user governance and community orientation.

### The WTTW

The two-year curriculum of the Women's Technology Training Workshop included the study of a wide range of new technology-related skills in an all-woman context. It placed high priority on positive (affirmative) action, both by giving preference to older and minority women and by guaranteeing either a job with the

council or further education. Though the WTTW aimed to provide education in
social priorities as well as a model of best-practice training in skills, it depended
on local researchers to provide the social input. The overall understanding to be
attained was not clear to the participants we interviewed. Other aspects of WTTW
policy, in particular the intended relationship between individual vocational aspi-
rations and group and class needs of women, remained unarticulated.

## The CORU

The Community Operations Research Unit (CORU) was established by the
Operations Research (OR) Society of Britain, one of several groups that developed
out of the STR perspective.[5] The CORU aimed to provide technical support to
community organizations in the analysis of complex problems, to help such organizations clarify their goals and objectives, and to develop computer software using "soft" rather than scientistic approaches to problems, perhaps ones that identify "satisficing" rather than "maximizing" solutions (Rosenhead 1986). Its goal is
promote the application of OR to community problems and to establish a community OR tradition.

CORU was located at Northern College of Adult Education in Barnsley because
of the college's extensive links with community organizations. Like other culture-
centered computing programs, the unit was governed by a management committee that included nonspecialists. Implementation of CORU was slowed by changes
in personnel.

## The EPOSE

The European Poly-Office System Environment (EPOSE) was an experimental
research facility that was proposed for Sheffield's new science park. Using funds
from major private sector corporations like ICL and Nixdorf as well as the EEC's
ESPRIT (Experimental Research in Information Technology) Fund, the EPOSE
was to provide a prototype office information system to demonstrate how to relate
state-of-the-art computer hardware to the social and organizational cultures that
exist in the real world. The source of funding for both machine development and
research on sociocultural context, ESPRIT viewed the EPOSE as a way to apply results. The equal focus both on hardware and on culture was supported by the private sector organizations in the belief that the project would provide substantial financial advantages to businesses in the EEC member states.

The EPOSE was to include such computer professionals as Bjorn-Andersen on
its board. Forward movement was hampered by the British government's decision
not to release funding for research initiatives until it had gained more of its general fiscal goals within the EEC. In 1988 a decision was made not to fund the
EPOSE.

## Health Computerization:
## A Culture-Centered Computing "Best Case"

Several key informants identified health as a social sector in which prospects for progressive computing were particularly good. Access to health is necessary in any social formation, and health promotion is recognized even in the United States as too important to be left to an unregulated private sector. In Britain, the state is the major health care provider through the National Health Service. In Sheffield, a number of individuals with significant information skills are health activists. Something of their vision of a populace informed about health is revealed in the discussion by Sheffield health visitor Joan Harrison regarding new technology and nursing reform (1987). She responds positively to proposals in the national Cumberlege report for "neighborhood nursing teams" and parallel community "health care associations," but she doubts that the new forms will function well. Will the associations be democratic and independent, given that the only function described for them is "to generate resources of money and people" for the health care system? "Are health associations going to be supported in criticizing the organization and provision of health care? Where a health care professional is incompetent, will the health associations finish up with the power to fire them as a last resort? Are they going to be given access to health data which they can use politically?"

Harrison begins to sketch out what might happen if such associations were truly "informated" (Zuboff 1988) through well-developed use of new information technology. Data exist that illustrate inequities in health on a ward by ward basis:

> Let us suppose that the neighborhood nursing team (NNT) has [such] patient/client/community health information on a computer. Let us suppose a group of women who have had miscarriages want to start a group for all women who have had the same experience and ask the NNT to write all those concerned in the area and invite them to a group meeting in a local church hall to form a support network. Let us imagine they criticize the local NNT and General Practitioner [family doctor] and hospital services, they write to the M.P., the paper, they embarrass the National Department of Health and Social Services. Then a group of retired, older people come along, and want to use health information to expose the prescribing pattern of sleeping tablets in the area. ... I want local people to have this power, I wonder at what point they will be prevented from using it? Of course, community health councils should already have had such an effect—I wonder why, by and large, they haven't? This government has taught the public that health and illness are an individual responsibility, the medical profession retain their professional status (i.e., read power), and the ownership of information is power. The ownership of health data by neighbourhoods need not threaten confidentiality, but it threatens the status quo. A recent television programme showing that Asian people are more readily diagnosed as schizophrenic than white people is simply one example of the social context of health and disease. Is Ms. Cumberlege ready for the rapid exposure of issue after issue, or is

she perhaps hoping for the cosy coffee morning atmosphere of a health association
dominated by professionals, for which the non-professionals raise funds to buy basic
equipment like beepers and sphygmomanometers? (Harrison 1987:2, 3)

Harrison's computerization scenario identifies the potential role of computing
as a profound extender of democracy. She focuses on what is really at issue in the
democratic promotion of computerization, not so much a technical as a social
matter. Truly universal use of new information technology would increase awareness of social issues and would show that a humanist computer policy is indeed
feasible. Such a policy was embodied in the "popular computing" aspect of the
Sheffield Health Plan, a general program to promote health and provide better
health care in Sheffield.

## The Health System in Sheffield

The current organizational structure in health has problems. Relevant bureaucracies with direct involvement in the local health scene include the national state,
the government's Department of Health and Social Services, and the Trent Regional and Sheffield District Health Authorities, TRHA and SDHA, respectively.
Each layer of bureaucracy has its own responsibilities. The SDHA, in addition to
operating several large hospitals, includes the Department of Community Medicine. The latter employs staff in district nursing, health visiting, school nursing,
and family planning nursing; it also has a community medicine advisory committee. The SDHA has also recently created an information unit.

The Sheffield District Council has separate units with significant health functions, the Department of Environmental Health (coupled with Consumer Protection) as well as the Department of Family and Community Services. South Yorkshire municipal governments have launched several health-related campaigns.
There are also several strong trade unions, professional organizations, and activist
groups among health workers and consumers. For example, general practitioners
(GPs), the main providers of family medicine, are grouped into an autonomous
organization that bargains at the national level over the amount that they get for
each patient. Compensation is directly related to the number of patients registered
on each GP's index and to the services performed for them.

## Informational Critique of the Sheffield Health System

As developers of the IBM Sheffield Primary Care System, a computerized system for individual GPs, Mike Fitter and Bob Garber of Sheffield University have
carried out several studies of medical information technology in Britain. In a 1987
report, Fitter and Garber identify weaknesses in the health information system.
Because GPs are businessmen, their use of computers tends to follow small business needs. The pattern of uptake is extremely uneven and the information produced about health is extremely varied. The main problem in informating health

is not the creation of information but that much information already produced is incompatible. Because of idiosyncratic application by individual GPs, the new information technology actually increases incompatibility.

As a consequence of government reforms, a high priority has been placed on developing Management Information Systems in regional health authorities (RHAs) and district health authorities (DHAs), where a great deal of computer-mediated data exists. However, these data are primarily administrative in character and have little epidemiological value. Further, there is no overall information system that integrates service and administrative health data.

These computerization dynamics exacerbate preexisting problems of the health system in Sheffield. There is a long-standing lack of integration between the GPs and community health initiatives. Fitter and Garber argue that computers reinforce the influence of the acute care perspective of GPs in contrast to the preventative orientation of community health. The current information system actually makes it more difficult for health visitors or environmental health planners to access the GPs' indexes, the best information about nonhealth conditions experienced and services sought.

Computerization has increased the volume of information, but it is either the wrong kind or is incommensurate with other information. Health planners don't have the data they need and GPs can't communicate their data to others who could use it. This situation increases the likelihood that different policies will be pursued by separate bureaucracies and professions. Privatization of the NHS will increase the use of information as power rather than as a resource to be shared.

### Informating Health in Sheffield: Organizational Infrastructure

A strategy to informate the health sector in Sheffield was developed in 1986. The formal Joint Health Care Coordinating Committee was developed by the Sheffield District Council. Representatives of various health organizations met to develop plans, although members remained responsible primarily to the bureaucracies by which they were employed. Simultaneously, the Central Policy Unit of the District Council convened a Health Care Strategy Group (HCSG) to develop a new municipal socialism strategy for health care. This group included activists from the District Labour, practitioner, and patient groups. An early action was pressure to appoint a more responsive council representative to the District Health Authority. By 1987 representatives held prior discussions of DHA agenda items with the HCSG, and a subcommittee to develop a health information strategy was convened.

In line with the strategy of political decentralization, a great deal of effort went into creation of community-based health groups. A community health development project located near the city center began a local needs assessment. The citywide Sheffield People's Campaign for Health produced a pamphlet—

*Sheffield's Health—Could We Care Less?* (n.d., ca. 1984)—in response to the DHSS'
intention to "rationalize" local health facilities by eliminating several units. The
campaign encouraged development of constituency organizations, such as the Forum for People with Disabilities, and adult education classes on health gathered
information on public perceptions of health care needs.

### Informating Health: The Program

Parallel programmatic efforts reinforced this new organizational infrastructure. A "Healthy Cities 2000" initiative implemented this World Health Organization program. The council's Central Policy Unit led development of a food policy
for the city. Popular health planning culminated in a "Good Health for All" conference sponsored by the District Council, where two local analogues of the
underreported national "Black Report" were presented.

The SDHA prepared *Health Care and Disease—A Profile of Sheffield* (n.d., ca.
1986) to provide a baseline for planning health services in the future. It offered a
detailed picture of the variation in recorded deaths and diseases throughout the
city and also identified areas of the city that though they had higher rates of death,
actually had lower rates of health service. For the Environmental Health Department, Colin Thunhurst of Sheffield Polytechnic prepared a second document,
*Poverty and Health in the City of Sheffield* (1985). Thunhurst used regression analysis to demonstrate the causal relationships between inequality and illness, from
which working-class Sheffielders suffer inordinately.

### Informating Health: Health Information Technology

Sheffield has a substantial history of applied research, and city institutions regularly develop health-related information technologies of a standard "device" sort.
These include computer-based, voice-activated aids for people with disabilities.
Other initiatives take up NIT at a more strategic level—for example, the Environmental Health Department integrated GP indexes with a computer model of pol-
lution. The Sheffield DHA set targets for change to equalize services and hired a
full-time researcher to help health visitors reconceptualize their work and data
collection.

An example of how such initiatives can come together is the cervical cancer
screening program introduced in 1987, targeted to areas in the city with both high
rates of cervical cancer and low rates of preventive testing. Computer records were
first gathered from GPs. Women who live in high-risk neighborhoods were sent a
letter referring them to a new mobile screening unit, whose staff were trained in
procedures sensitive to the health beliefs and practices of Sheffield's minorities.
The basic strategy for the program was worked out in the HCSG, and difficulties
in implementing it were discussed by the Joint Coordinating Committee.

## Results of Informating Health

A number of contradictions arose during the implementation of the strategy. The South Sheffield Project found itself in conflict with the council and with local residents resistant to more "research workers" and the program was terminated. The centralized procedures used in the screening project seemed to imply less individual control. The programs of the HCSG were criticized as being weighted too much in the direction of standard medical practices by people in the alternative medicine movement. The program officer most closely identified with the information strategy left city service in 1988. His replacement decided to back off from the information strategy, arguing that the predecessor's strident political style had severely weakened the strategy's potential.

Still, the strategy accomplished two things. First was to put the problem of information at the center of the health discussion. In his conclusion, Thunhurst points out how the holes in his analysis "relate to the availability of suitable data sources. If the ... formulation of a comprehensive health promotion policy [is] to be successfully implemented, it is important that this is complemented by the parallel development of information sources and information processing resources to allow the monitoring of its effectiveness to take place" (1985:112). Similarly, the DHA working group concludes that data retrieval and analytical mechanisms are very important in responding to different needs (n.d., ca. 1987:111).

Second, the informating strategy incorporated a focus on equity into local discussions of health care. New technology was shown to make an effective action program on equity issues possible. The strategy gave working-class people a device for identifying and pursuing collective interests. Although its use may foster resistance, new information technology is a means through which working-class politics can continue to impact social agendas.

## Computing and Politics

The vignette that follows shows another way that computing policy aided political mobilization, but it also identifies some of the contradictions and difficulties of popular computing.

At a Computers for People meeting to discuss the implications of the government's new Data Protection Act, a dialogue developed between the speaker, an "expert" from the council's Computer Services Department, and two representatives of a tenants' association. The tenants were interested in the impact the act would have on their group's ambitious information activities. They described a data base system that they had developed on their housing estate with the aid of a SPRITE group. The tenants explained how, with access to all the data in the Housing Department's computers, their association could use computers so as to be much more effective in representing tenant interests, for example, by keeping tabs on empty flats and repairs, informing tenants of their benefit entitlements, and building their organization. They argued that such activities could become important politically as mechanisms of meaningful popular planning, which they pointed out was a major political goal of the district government. However, as the council's expert made clear in the discussion, such activities might violate sections of the Data Protection Act that were justified as protecting individual rights, sections that it was now also the council's obligation to enforce.

Here two public agencies found themselves advocating on opposite sides. The ensuing discussion brought out numerous other situations of future conflict as public groups implement new information technology. Popular or progressive computing is impeded by a hostile national state that imposes legislation like the Data Protection Act.

## The Failures of Computing Policy: 1987

Despite the creation of some progressive institutions, no one in Sheffield was generally enthusiastic about what had been accomplished. Unlike 1983, a 1986 Central Policy Unit pamphlet made no reference to new technology policy. When we talked with council officers about NIT policy, they often said it didn't exist. One argued that the initiatives described above cannot "be described as a coherent computerisation policy. In the early days we did consider attempting to develop such a thing, but it was quite clear that ... we lacked the resources to achieve this."[6]

The program of municipal capital for socially oriented NIT in the private sector had had little effect and had been abandoned, as had other attempts to develop a more interventionist role. Employment Department data on the local economy was meager, because research was focused primarily on meeting short-term needs, such as producing pamphlets against the closing of nationalized steel works rather than a data base for planning. The technology-support network had not had a noticeable effect on the local economy, and the innovative training programs reached only a tiny proportion of the workforce and other parts of the training system, such as the Industrial Training Boards. Conferences such as "New Technology: Whose Progress?" were abandoned due to lack of union interest, as were Trade Union Congress (TUC) courses and a Trades Council discussion group on new technology.

By 1987 council initiatives were restricted more or less to what could be accomplished internally, within the council departments, but even here progressive computing proceeded slowly. The technology agreement was the focus of a bitter strike in 1983. Although there is reason to see NIT policy as more the terrain for a general confrontation than the cause of battle, the strike exposed some embarrassing NIT practices, such as the bad working conditions of Treasury Department data entry clerks. After the strike fizzled, the new "Responding to Change" agreement was implemented unilaterally. Though the systems implemented have brought improved service in some areas, in others they have made preexisting bad practices more difficult to change. NIT development was more or less uncoordinated between council departments, implemented separately by individual chief officers. NIT was "application" not "information" driven—that is, people thought in terms of implementing discrete procedures, such as word processing or electronic filing.

Some council officers expressed belief in the council's NIT policy; this is the position taken in the only written NIT strategy document we located in the field. Brief (four pages) and very general, the document deals more with conceptual problems than with procedures; it was not generally considered an effective guide for action. Indeed, the document itself comments wryly, "It is interesting to note that in a value for money study undertaken by District Audit, the [Sheffield] Authority was marked 'poor' for its [NIT] strategy whilst Computer Services was marked 'excellent' for the way [the strategy] was implemented!" (Ardron 1986:1). Trying to be positive, a program officer argued that "each new implementation feeds into the strategy and helps us develop it," but this position implicitly accepts the view that the strategy was not as yet well defined. Another knowledgeable officer described the council's existing strategy as "cobbled together and irrational."

The political and administrative vehicle within the council that was to oversee progressive NIT policy was the Information Technology Panel. Originally called the Computer Panel, the name was changed in the mid-1980s to communicate the council's intention to take a more strategic view of technological change. Consideration of the cultural dimensions of computing, in the words of the director of Computer Services, "floats in and out" of the IT panel, but most talk focused on hardware. The panel was described as "a talking shop because it has no spending authority" and as ineffective at feeding political issues back to the Labour Group's general policy debate.

In a 1987 interview, the new leader of the Labour Group justified NIT policy strictly in terms of improved service to citizens, not improved quality of work life or influence over private sector practices. He felt that the council had failed to create an atmosphere in which discussion about the social consequences of computerization was ongoing. He doubted the ability of the IT panel to take up such issues effectively, doubts echoed by the panel chairperson and senior program officers in council Computer Services. Although Sheffield took NIT and ran with it because it was a good idea, these failures contributed to increased skepticism about what can be achieved.

Indeed, a 1987 council officer presented the connection between new information technology and improved quality of work life as axiomatic; by implication, no policy to control social impacts was really necessary. However, the presentation was criticized by a council agency director for ignoring the negative NIT experience that many council workers had already had. By 1990 the IT panel had folded.

In sum, a high initial political profile was given to computing, but initiative was lost, leading to frustration. Council computerization initiatives had only limited success, either externally or internally, in either economic or social terms. It is still probably the case that Sheffield computing practice is in social terms as good if not better than that of other large British local authorities, but the success of a policy should be measured at least in part in relation to its articulated goals.

## Technicist Fallacies in Computing Policy

In its attempt to develop NIT policy, Sheffield got caught in tactics, such as the following, that have failed in many other organizations.

1.  Computopian "NIT promotion": Precipitous computerization, without adequate analysis of informational needs and organization structure, ossifies bad informational procedures and makes them even harder to change in the long run, ultimately requiring whole systems to be abandoned. We quite frequently heard "rubbish in, rubbish out," the Sheffield variant of an internationally known computer phrase.
2.  Dependence on administrative staff for program initiative: Administrative strategies for computerization tend to reinforce standardization, concern for security, and the organizational status quo. More policy-led approaches offer organizations the potential for self-mobilization, to extend the organization into new areas and allow a higher degree of organizational self-awareness, control, and flexibility, including the use of information to change organizations.
3.  Machine-centered strategies for system development: These pay insufficient attention to the cultural factors that surround IT systems. In this technicist engineering model, system development is seen primarily as a technical process. This model assumes clarity in information needs and stability of organizational purpose and minimizes the role of humans in the information process. It places a priority on "human-proof" procedures; there is assumed to be one best solution to any given computing problem. In the contrasting cultural model, system development is seen to be a social process, one that accepts ambiguity in the conceptualization of information needs as common, change in organizational purpose the norm, and humane procedures the general goal.

Attempts to computerize are often overly promotional, administrative, and machine-centered. In Sheffield, because computerization took place within the context of an attempt to implement a new political strategy, the failures of such inappropriate approaches were more public. Less promotional, more participatory and culture-centered system development strategies already existed or could have been invented; their use was essential if policy rather than "tradition" was to determine information system structure. Like most system developers, those in Sheffield often failed to perceive these problems or to do something about them in a timely fashion. It was only in 1986, for example, that more user-centered approaches, like the study circles, became integrated into the system development process. Despite the interest of such groups as the tenant's association, regular integration into system development of ultimate information users (the citizens of Sheffield) does not yet take place.

These problems are rooted in a tendency to be technicist in approaching NIT; that is, to assume problems will be strictly technical, lacking a substantial social dimension. Although existing hardware was not particularly conducive to the goals of NMS, neither was it innately hostile. Rather, implementation of any new information systems requires choices, and such choices often have social consequences. A systematic concern for such social dimensions should be integrated into any system development process and must be a part of attempts to computerize progressively.

### Problems in Local State Policy

Some of the difficulties in implementing progressive IT followed less from narrow technicism and more from the problems of transition from Labourist to "Blunkettian" structures within the local state. To have accomplished the twin goals of effective intervention in local economic reproduction and working-class political revitalization, the roles of all involved would have to have been reconceptualized along the following lines:

- for chief officers (administrators), switching from centralizing authority in their offices (that is, fighting for department autonomy, and treating information as "capital") to participating in collective mechanisms of authority, building relations with other departments, and treating information as a group resource;
- for professional staff, switching from a "turf" approach (protection of and identification with existing programs) to developing familiarity with sophisticated new information technologies and building collective relationships with peers and service users, who will often be more politically sophisticated;
- for clerical and manual staff, learning to approach her or his job as a political activity and to develop a "career" orientation to it;
- for unions, switching from a reactive, "Them versus Us" job protection orientation to proactive participation in the formulation of policy;
- for councilors, switching from giving priority to protecting the departments under "their" committees (thinking primarily in terms of budget and developing a "job" attitude toward their own role) to giving priority to involving service users, developing a councilwide, corporate approach, and thinking of themselves as intensive but essentially short-term political mobilizers; and
- for service users, switching from the role of alienated consumer to active participation in policy formation.

## The Fate of New Municipal Socialism

NMS projects share much with other computing initiatives in Europe and North America.[7] To decide what Sheffield suggests for local computing policy elsewhere, we must analyze where the difficulties encountered came from— external factors, such as the problems of the general NMS strategy or the structures referred to in Part Three, or internal factors, flaws in conception or implementation strategy. Council NIT programs depended upon the success of NMS. To promote socially responsible new technology through loans and grants, municipal capital must be able to leverage private capital. An effective technology network implies a leading role for the council in the local economy. Progressive internal promotion of NIT and development of an effective NIT strategy means central control of council departments. Promotion of skills and awareness require effective systems for publicity, education, and popular participation. Finally, an effective technology agreement require management and workforce cooperation.

Initial success in creating NMS programs was followed by difficulty in implementation, significant narrowing of what innovation aimed to accomplish, stretching of time lines, or abandoning of programs altogether. Council attempts to influence independently the development of the regional economy were substantially altered. A major independent initiative to control redevelopment of the East End of Sheffield was turned over to academics, to be carried out in conjunction with local industry and the Sheffield Chamber of Commerce, a primary public antagonist in the early 1980s. The project was narrowed to influencing the "Urban Development Corporation" (UDC) imposed by central government.

The political climate at the national level was inimical to computing strategy. Though "local democratic planning" was important Labour Party rhetoric, it was never developed into a real alternative policy. The NMS slogans were absent from the 1987 "American-style" national election. Instead, municipal initiatives like those of Sheffield, branded "loony left" by the Tories, were seldom defended by Labour.

Blunkett himself, like his Greater London Council counterpart Ken Livingstone, became a member of Parliament, and development of NMS halted. As a prefigurative strategy—one promoting actions based on a vision of what a decentralized socialism might be like—NMS presumed that substantial extraregional resources would follow initial local interventions. NMS was ultimately as dependent on Labour control of the national state as Labourism was, but three Tory governments greatly decreased the power of local government, taking control of such areas as housing and education, placing severe limitations on local finance and control, and even abolishing whole layers of local government, including South Yorkshire's County Council.

Symbolic of the changes in NMS practice were changes in language. The 1983 pamphlet proclaims: "The proposed 'Technology Campus' in the city centre is not a 'science park' to attract capitalist entrepreneurs in competition with 50 other locations" but instead to "subordinate technical advances to community needs" (p. 15). In 1987 the same project was indeed referred to as a "science park," and although the park still contained several local authority initiatives, their influence on employment practices was only indirect. One Labour Party activist referred to the council practice on development as "low on politics but high on PR"; he was particularly bitter that changes in policy were no longer discussed with the "popular" Labour Party Manifesto groups. Talk about "the problems of building socialism in a cold climate" had replaced "the Socialist Republic," the latter phrase now attributed to a Tory.

Nor did the political economic context support NMS. Little investment capital was available to be leveraged into technology, whether it built on or replaced existing worker skills. As room for maneuver narrowed, campaigns became the responsibility of program officers and concentrated more on proper language rather than on political action. Active popular support was difficult to mobilize, and programs had to have either a high likelihood of short-term success or had to operate essentially outside of the general political discourse. All these factors mitigate against long-term popular planning through political channels.

NMS computing policy was also complicated by "Tomorrow's World" computopianism. This popular "frontiers of science" television program reinforced a machine-oriented view of computer problems and led to general impatience, since compubabble implied that technological problems were largely solved.

These economic, political, and ideological complications developed slowly in the 1980s. The result was a paradox: Although class remained an important determinant of what one experienced—for example, where one lived, whether one had employment, one's access to resources—one's ability to respond to change in the "traditional" way (as part of a collective class group) was substantially undercut.

Still, the relative failure of progressive computing policy can also be tied to internal factors. As Pete, the traffic systems engineer, comments:

"The co-op structure involves a lot of meetings, and participation. I'm sorry that the co-ops in Sheffield aren't more together—they're a bit isolationist. We did some wiring for the Women's Print Co-op and were charged with price gouging, like we should have done it for free. Ideally, we'd like something like the Mondragon [Spain] system, with networked co-ops. The ideal situation is one where co-ops get together for periodic meetings to discuss a range of issues openly, without so much structure."

David asked if the decline of "co-op togetherness" wasn't attributable to changes in the political climate, with Thatcherism and so on. Instead, Steve felt the decline was more due to the characteristic development course of a co-op: "It starts as kind of an idea, but reaches a point where you have to get determined, drop everything else—your family, your political activity—to make sure it works, because failure would be disaster. After a while, you begin to feel secure.

We're there now, and we want to get more involved with the other co-ops again. I really think it is a good way to deal with the economic crisis; large corporations won't invest in the North of England again, so it's a matter of finding new ways to service people's needs and provide them locally with goods, so that the people making them have an identification with customers and the area."

David asked if they were dependent on political help for survival, contrasting their experience with that of co-ops in the States, which had been frozen out of markets. Pete talked about the importance of the first South Yorkshire County Council order and also said, "We're very high on the support of the Council's Co-operative Development Agency and its first director. Even though he knew nothing about engineering, he were like a member in the early days. The constant publicity was a bit of a bother, but we generally enjoyed it; we even got a positive 'David versus Goliath' story in the *Sun*."

## Culture-Centered Computing and the Reproduction of the Local State

Local policy did affect the course of computerization in Sheffield. NMS computing policy posed important questions in meaningful terms, and despite difficult conditions, several initiatives were moderately successful. These culture-centered projects would not have accomplished what they did without substantial council support. Their success suggests as least some room for local computing policy.

Whatever the difficulties, Sheffield was attempting to act politically—that is, collectively—to influence the reproduction of its culture. Many of the difficulties encountered are ones that will be faced by any regional social formation aiming to equalize the benefits of new technology. By demonstrating the feasibility of computing policy, the Sheffield experience indicates that the social correlates of computerization are amenable to policy, not strictly a consequence of some technological imperative.

### Notes

1. "Policy" can be used broadly, to characterize the behavior of any group organized for consistent action, or narrowly, to refer to situations in which tight procedures insure that actions address specified goals. In discussing "the policy idea," Erve Chambers draws attention to two additional characteristics of policy: the presence of deliberate change and the involvement of institutions of control or authority, the state (1985:38–39). Thus, if politics is the study of how groups attempt to exert influence over the reproduction of their social formation, "social policy" can be usefully understood as the attempt of complex societies to use state instruments to influence social reproduction. Debates between Marxists and anarchists have turned on whether, as Marxists contend, the state can be used to accomplish progressive goals or whether the state is fundamentally flawed. The attempt to use local pol-

icy as a means to affect social reproduction is thus of relevance to a whole range of classic debates.

2. Similar politics were discussed (e.g., Cockburn 1977) and policies developed (Boddy and Fudge 1984) in other urban areas, most noticeably by the Greater London Council. These initiatives were the subject of substantial political, policy, and social science discussion (e.g., Darwin 1987a, 1987b; Goodwin and Duncan 1986; Weinstein 1985; Bennington 1985, 1986; *Local Government Studies* and *Local Economy*).

In a narrow view—for example, as a strategy to defeat Thatcherism—NMS failed. NMS was criticized by Leninists as a futile attempt to build "socialism in one county" and by the "soft" left as too class based. NMS faced negative international conditions, a consequence of the Thatcher/Reagan restructuring of the world system necessary to facilitate capital accumulation. Technicists would trace the "cold climate" for socialism to the new technologies themselves.

To dismiss NMS in these ways is wrong. The class politics of new municipal socialism maintains its appeal; throughout the 1980s, the Sheffield Labour Party raised its share of the vote, as did "left" British urban Labour Parties. NMS is similar to politics developed elsewhere: Bologna in Italy, Santa Monica and Burlington in the United States and Lima in Peru. Central American and South African liberation politics stress local politics as an important component of the transition to a new society.

Strategic local action constitutes a reasonable approach, along with Eurocommunism and urban guerilla insurgency, for effective socialist campaigns. NMS politics draw extensively on recent left critiques of both social democratic and "really existing," Second World, Leninist socialisms. In Sheffield, many people first active outside the local state—in community groups, the Communist party, and other left organizations—joined NMS battles, went to work for the local state, and joined the Labour Party. This new "urban left" is said to prefigure the political constituencies that must be created in the wake of on-going class restructuring (e.g., Gorz 1982). Important conflicts emerged in Sheffield NMS, as in the housing strike, which threatened to split local Labour politicians from their traditional trade union base.

In an important sense, such conflicts prefigure the future of mature industrial social formations. Since it is based on a broad understanding of working-class culture as a way of life, NMS is of anthropological interest; cultural intervention was the focus of the Society for Applied Anthropology symposium of Labour Party activists in York, England (Hakken and Darwin 1990). A cultural understanding of the new municipal socialism in Sheffield may contribute to our understanding of the developmental contours of future human social formations.

3. Municipal action in the transition to socialism was an important component of the program of World War I Guild Socialists such as G.D.H. Cole, inspired in part by the shop stewards' movement in Sheffield.

4. In this tradition, culture is viewed as a complex whole, containing dialectically related emic or semiotic and etic or material moments. This view of culture is different from sociological or semiotic constructs, which posit autonomous realms of culture, each of which requires analysis in its own terms. "Culture-centered" is also different from those Marxist views that reduce cultural processes to epiphenomena of a political economic base. In the neoMarxist approach, a cultural perspective interprets events in relation to the complex set

of broad contexts, of which technology is only one, involved in the reproduction of social formations (Hakken 1987b).

5. OR uses rigorous, detailed modeling as an approach to complex decisionmaking (Thunhurst 1987). Though OR became very closely tied to management in the post–World War II era, especially in the guise of cost-benefit analysis, a series of radical critiques (e.g., Rosenhead and Thunhurst 1977) suggest that OR could be put to other purposes.

6. It is only if we define "policy" narrowly that informants were right to say there was no real computer policy in Sheffield. We label what happened in Sheffield with regard to new technology "policy" because there was an articulated set of overall goals, specific programs within the local state to implement the goals, and structures to coordinate programs and measure their progress toward the goals. These criteria allow us to distinguish between interventions with substantial potential for affecting social reproduction and mere rhetoric.

7. Utica, New York, is very different from Sheffield, England, yet research on work sites there (Hakken 1986) uncovered two projects that qualify as "culture-centered," suggesting that this approach is possible in regions that manifest less social and political consciousness than Sheffield. In a legal aid office, secretaries expressed feelings of empowerment with computerization. This empowerment derives from the secretaries' control of the computerized filing system and subsequent higher involvement in legal matters, a consequence of staff participation in system development.

The Techspress program of the Utica Resource Center for Independent Living promotes use of computers to help people with disabilities cope with the world that disables them. Attention is given to both the technology and the creation of a supportive social environment through inclusion of people with disabilities in decisionmaking structures. (David's research program since returning from Sheffield focuses on disability technology.)

# 12

## Computing and Gender

New technology is a key part of Sheffield women's discourse about their lives as women, just as gender is an important dimension of computer studies professors' worries regarding the future of the field. Changing conceptions of gender are a prime example of the correlation between computing and change in symboling. Talk about computing contains significant gender ambiguities and is a primary dimension of the problems associated with developing a politics of computing.

The term "gender" refers to the differences in perception, action, and experience associated with being female and male. (The term has migrated into social analysis from linguistics, where it refers to parts of speech—e.g., the gender of a German noun determines how its plural is formed, etc.) "Sex" has been replaced by "gender," as in "gender role" versus "sex role," because use of gender underlines how these differences are primarily social constructs rather than essential, biological differences. "Gender" encapsulates the dominant message of recent cross-cultural studies (e.g., Reiter 1975).

The computing/gender link is related to change in the South Yorkshire labor market, such as the strain in family life related to the growth of service employment and the increased proportion of female and part-time workers. In Sheffield, new technology means a more precipitous decline of female than male employment in manufacturing industry. Mavis's experience in the Data Shop shows the continuity that often holds between gendered jobs, whether computered or noncomputered. Such changes are best explained by "institutional" factors—a tendency to substitute part-time female labor for male labor in otherwise separate labor markets for males and females. In Chapter 13 we present survey data indicating that women who actively pursue jobs seem to find them more easily than men but that half the jobs they find are part-time.

Gender and new technology are also linked on the terrain of Sheffield policy, as in separate SPRITE women's groups or in the WTTW itself. Program success is partially measured in terms of gendering, less gender difference indicating less hierarchy. The heavily male character of "traditional" working-class culture is criticized, and the activism of women in the miners' strike is described as positive. Clearer gender politics is a desired feature of the politics alternative to

Labourism, and women's groups are an important component of Sheffield community politics. In Chapter 13, a female community activist argues that the re-emergence of oppressive sexuality is evidence of an increasing social divide.

The patterns of gendering change summarized above defy simple explanation. Theoretically, robotizing the heavy parts of a manufacturing process should lessen the impact of, for example, strength or stamina, yet there are fewer manufacturing situations in Sheffield in which computing is more beneficial to women, in terms of wages or skill, than to men. Another gender-related finding is that women appear to lose somewhat less than men as manufacturing is replaced by service, as in building societies, in which women's relative position appears to have advanced with computing.

Such patterns are inexplicable in terms of new technology alone. Accounting for them involves addressing educational and political strategy, questions of concern to working-class and feminist activists in Sheffield. One such question is whether women, as they enter the new computer-based positions, should be encouraged to "act just like men," or should they search for a distinct, feminist approach to computing? Answers to such questions are to be found by placing computing in the context of general changes in the reproduction of working-class culture.

As the following vignette suggests, gendering change has been particularly at issue in mining culture.

On a crisp night in early 1987, the Sheffield City Hall was buzzing with a national "heroes concert" benefit for the many miners whom the Coal Board had refused to rehire after the strike. Miners and their supporters circulated among the book and badge booths and discussed the split between the NUM and a breakaway union. Everywhere the subject was politics.

Gloria, a tenant activist, was ambivalent about the "heroes" idea. "Sheffield has traditionally been a home to labour politics and a strong working-class movement, part of why the headquarters of the National Union of Mineworkers was moved to Sheffield in 1982. Most working-class people see miners as a symbol of working-class strength and independence, as tough, militant, very male working-class 'heroes.' Women who grew up in mining communities will testify to the particular form of hero worship that used to be given miners."

Gloria's comments reminded us of a previous gender-relevant experience with the miners, an Easter weekend school ten years before. The school was held at the seashore holiday camp of the Derbyshire miners. Labour was in power, and miners talked about not having room to maneuver. One suggested, "Let's let the Tories back in and have another go at them!"—a line repeated by numerous others. The miners were then regarded as the strongest, most unified union in Britain; the miner was the symbol of working-class strength and solidarity. (By 1987 the Conservatives were back in power and the "go" wished for by both sides had been had.)

A night of entertainment at the school had surprised us. The floor show included a traditional stand-up comedian whose patter was full of sexist allusions. The music was slick but primarily "old standards." The folk or political music that we had come to expect as part of the entertainment at a political event was absent.

"Miners don't want their entertainment to be political," said Gordon, a tutor and organizer for the Workers' Educational Association. "They want a break from politics; a bit of something different. In 1975, a political theatre group, The Red Mole, came to this school. During the day, they did one of their plays, and it was smashing. But in the evening, when they did their cabaret show—it was quite good, really, but the Miners weren't having it. They are very clear on what they want when they want to be entertained, and they don't want politics." In 1987 we wondered if the "heroes concert" would be different.

It certainly began differently. The emcee, a prominent Sheffield radio personality with a thick Yorkshire accent, started with a black gospel group from Sheffield. Next was "Tony Benn, a True Friend of the Working Class," former Labour Government minister, leader of the Campaign Group of M.P.s, and recently re-elected as member of Parliament for a Derbyshire mining constituency. Dressed in a plain wool jacket and trousers, the Wedgewood Potteries scion gave a ten-minute presentation on the "glorious history of the working class in Sheffield," and on why the Campaign Group, unlike other Labour M.P.s, support the demand for amnesty for fired miners.

Next, the emcee welcomed "an entertainer who was there on the picket lines during t'strike, Mal Finch." Her performance reminded Barbara of American singer Holly Near, not only because of her political lyrics and her beautiful resonant voice but also because she was dressed in trousers and a loose shirt and wore little makeup. We wondered if her strong and independent image, not at all the "traditional" woman, was a new role model, resulting from such groups as Women Against Pit Closures.

The music changed as the emcee introduced "The Castleford Cuddlies." Down the aisles danced a dozen women dressed in short pink satin dresses with bows in their hair, lip-syncing to remakes of songs from the 1950s. Their movements were those of American cheerleaders, but they lacked the youthful coordination. Fleshy thighs, pink satin stretched suggestively—Barbara shrank down in her chair. As the Cuddlies gyrated off the stage, we wondered if the applause was for the actions of these women during the strike—or was it because they had just put forward a traditional image of women? What did it have to do with Mal Finch?

"Traditional" working-class culture in South Yorkshire was heavily gendered. Life in the pit village was centered on the mine, and life in the home was centered on the quintessential male miner, working in dangerous circumstances, ale-drinking, and so forth. The wife "stopped" at home to mind the children and deal with things domestic. (Although these patterns were also the articulated ideal on the urban housing estate, there were both more opportunities and more necessities for women to work outside the home.)

Pit village gendering changed greatly during the 1984–1985 strike. The initial strategy of the miners was "flying pickets," mobile teams of striking miners to bring out all the pits. When national state action blocked this strategy, women, particularly South Yorkshire miners' wives, emerged as organizers of support, speakers at rallies, and family breadwinners as strike pay dwindled. Some formed miners' support groups closely allied to the male leadership of the National Union of Mineworkers, but others created Women Against Pit Closures. WAPC cast itself as an independent women's organization following its own course of action, its members increasingly identified with the feminist women's movement of the broad left in Britain (Winterton and Winterton 1989).

One change highlighted in the strike was the increased female labor market activity, and another was the emergence of women into more public roles in the working-class movement, as frequent participants in political events. The labor movement had been profoundly male, just as well into the 1970s women in South Yorkshire had been more peripheral in the labor market than in the rest of the country. Part of the public emergence of women was due to the development of specific women's politics, as working-class females sought out ways to change their lives, including ways to influence directly the images of women in working-class culture. A holistic analysis of the connection between gender, computing, and social change in South Yorkshire requires that systematic attention to gender politics supplement our attention to discourse, labor market structure, and general working-class politics.

## The Women's Movement in South Yorkshire

Women's sections of the Labour and Communist parties and cooperative women's guilds have existed for some time in South Yorkshire. Justified in terms of women's lack of self-confidence and experience, these organizations existed to insure women's acceptance of, and occasional participation in, the structures of the labor movement. They were not important generators of political demands, nor were they critical of male-dominated structures.

In the 1970s a distinct women's movement with explicitly feminist goals re-emerged in Sheffield. Initially, such activity was associated within the politics of "independent left" groupings, distinguishable in terms of their differing strategies–rejectionist, entryist, or showing "comradely outside criticism"—with regard to the Labour Party. Perceived as a place where people without "a working-class background" could participate, albeit with difficulty, in working-class organizations and movements, Sheffield attracted several of the more "workerist" of these groups, for whom dealing with feminism was particularly difficult. The new feminists had often been involved in higher education, and there were political and personal gulfs between them and many of the older female activists as well as the males. Communist Party new feminists chose to work both in the party and within established women's groups. In book stalls at weekend schools the older *Red "Mrs. Beeton"* found itself next to *The Female Eunuch*. Others developed new forms within existing organizations. The Working Women's Charter Campaign worked within the Sheffield District Trades Council's structure of reports and resolutions while also criticizing them.

Increasingly frustrated by the narrow political space available to them in left organizations, a third group of new feminists opted for independent feminist forms. Often organizing around particular issues—rape crisis, battered women's shelters, and so on,—they included a critique of existing working-class politics within their broader analyses. Because these politics had stifled women's ability to establish their own political identities, consciousness-raising came to be viewed as essential, complemented by citywide meetings, a women's newsletter, and participation in several national socialist-feminist conferences. Though individual politics remained disparate, the movement grew.

By the mid-1980s, women's politics in Sheffield had changed substantially. The critique of traditional structures as sexist and the awareness of distinctly women's issues were more widely shared by women and by some men in all strata of society. Working-class women were more forthright in their willingness to critique sexism within their class. However, the independent forms of the 1970s movement had disappeared, and attempts to renew traditional women's organizations had lost their energy. Like other leftists, many feminists had joined the Labour Party and local state structures.

A good example of the consequences of this "incorporation" is the Women's Employment Forum (WEF), organized in the early 1980s, WEF applied for and received a local council grant to carry out education and also committed itself to feminist activity beyond traditional employment issues. By 1986 the women involved in WEF were so heavily involved in the local authority's Women's Unit that they no longer had the energy to carry on the forum, and it effectively disbanded.

Lynne Segal's 1987 description of the British women's movement aptly captures the situation in Sheffield: "The women's liberation movement burst into the political arena of the 1970s with the energy and confidence to impress, and—could such things be?—at times even silence the male political voice. Times change. In the West, there is now no cohesive women's liberation movement (p. x)."

Segal does not mean that women's politics have died, but that feminism has adapted to the kinds of changes in labor market and social role summarized above: "[F]eminism remains a strong, if diverse political force. It remains a strong force, in my view, not so much because feminists were the most ardent and committed of rebels—though many of us were that—but because the changes in women's lives, which throw up contradiction and confusion at every turn, were the most profound and continuing (p. x)."

Segal's point here is a reproductionist, not a structural one. The changes she discusses have roots in structural change, as in the labor market, but they also involve consciousness and action—politics. In the 1980s Sheffield working-class women were more willing to articulate views similar to those of 1970s feminists and, indeed, to identify with feminism, precisely because these views provided cultural means to handle the changes taking place in their lives. By constructing alternatives to older myths of gender, ones no longer taken for granted, the efforts of feminists changed gendering as much as they were changed by it.

Women and men found themselves exploring different ways to gender. In concluding her discussion of *Divided Loyalties: Dilemmas of Sex and Class,* Anne Phillips describes the feminist intervention in working-class culture since the 1970s:

> When [feminism] introduces the conflicts of gender into a politics defined by class, it necessarily changes the terrain. Picking its way through the minefield, it makes its novel connections: that poverty is female and not just working class; that trade unions are a problem for women as well as a scourge of employers; that sexual violence is no respecter of class. The women's movement ... has allowed us to forge new kinds of alliances, and in the process had disrupted the battle lines of before. (1987:154)

At the "heroes concert," conflicting gender images were acted out. Whereas in 1977 entertainment reproduced a stable gender concept, the symbolic antagonisms—between the traditional male worker image and the new worker, as likely to be female or black as white and male—came through vividly in the 1987 cultural performance.

Yet in both cases, entertainment remained clearly gendered. Like race and ethnicity, gender is a political terrain on which the arguments for an alternative working-class politics are very effective, but also like race, gendering remains despite change in social reproduction.[1] Though gender is clearly "up for grabs," the current era is one of transformation rather than disappearance.

## Gendering and Computing

Gender was also at issue in Sheffield computing, as when Barbara visited a SPRITE club at "The Welcome," a community center on a council housing estate.

Barbara first heard about The Welcome Centre's computer club at a national conference, when a black community leader from London had referred to it when he was emphasizing the importance of politics to community computing. Tom later told Barbara how it all started. Although proud of helping to initiate the club, Tom had doubts about the direction it was taking: "I'm not sure I want a political atmosphere, leastwise not as political as the club at The Welcome. Community centres are already suffering from too much politics. We've been through a bad patch at the Welcome, and another Sheffield centre has had its problems. In both instances, the problems have to do with 'women's lib.'

"I'm personally at sixes and sevens about it all. When I was in employment, my wife did most of the housework, shopping, and so on. Since I've been on the dole, I've done more and more of what she did. Now, she's on a course at College, the burden of home responsibilities had fallen on me even more, and she's becoming a bleedin' feminist. Perhaps things needed to change, I could agree with that, but I feel like I'm being made the object of anger I don't deserve."

A few weeks later, Tom had left The Welcome Centre "to do other work."

During the mornings at The Welcome Centre computer club, a SPRITE worker taught a new group of single parents, all women. In the afternoons, there was a mixed group of more experienced computer users, a few of whom, like Tom, had been involved in setting up the original computer club. The center was bustling with activity the morning Barbara arrived. The central hall was large and open, with activity areas and the creche (day care center) opening off on the sides. In the computer club/SPRITE room, computers and printers were placed on a long table that faced a bank of windows opening on the hall, giving the illusion of computers controlling a room full of activity.

By quarter past ten, the women in the single parents group were ready to begin their class. There were five women in the group, all in their late twenties or early thirties, and all but one on Social Services Supplementary Benefit. The room had been opened earlier by Harold, a pensioner who had stayed to work on one of the machines. As the class came in, Jack from SPRITE asked Harold if he would move to one of the machines at the end. Harold balked; he didn't want to give up his machine; he didn't see why the class had priority. Suddenly, he was on about "politics, what goes on between women and men. Gore blimey, I feel henpecked. My needs are just as important as any group of young Mums."

Mary, a class member, refused to back down: "We've made way for men in many situations, we don't intend to lose our class. We have children to support. Learning about computers might be a way to a job; it is certainly a way to keep up with what's going on in the world."

The women treated Harold not as an enemy but as a man frightened by the changes going on around him. He was not denounced, though the women became angry at his twenty-minute refusal to let them get on with their work and with his repeated contention that he was being victimized by them. Jack told Harold that he was welcome to stay and that he could use the computers that the class did not need. Harold stayed but mostly watched what was happening.

The discussion did not really come to a conclusion—it simply stopped as women sat down at the computers and began work. Although they had only been in on the course for three weeks, the women began the worksheet given them without hesitation. They then went on to an introduction to programming in BASIC. Each woman worked at her own speed, using Jack—and each other—as

resources when they had problems, often teaming up to share available machines.

What are we to make of the connection between gender change and computing? It would clearly be inappropriate to attribute the gendering problems in this
vignette primarily to computing; unemployment, change in political economy,
and new life-style choices are also implicated. At the same time, computing is not
just an excuse for Tom and Harold to complain about a loss of male privilege. New
technology and new gendering are connected in the perceptions of both men and
women, both seeing higher gender "stakes" in computing.

### Compputropian Perspectives on Computing and Gendering

A strong compputropian theme is identifiable in 1980s British academic and
political writing on women and computing. Cynthia Cockburn's *Machinery of
Dominance: Women, Men, and Technical Know-how* (1985) is an effective expression of the view that new information technology means more wealth and power
for men and less for women. Cockburn's work contains some well-documented
examples of negative effects of technology on women. Besides reviewing surveys
and interviews, she presents case studies of five United Kingdom labor sites that
use new technology. In all of them Cockburn finds a consistent pattern: After the
introduction of new computer-based technology, women end up with separate
jobs, lower pay, less desirable work conditions, and with less autonomy, interest,
and mobility.

Arguing that technology is essentially biased against woman, Cockburn develops a feminist critique of several writers who have suggested that new technology
might make a more positive contribution to women's liberation than have previous technologies. Her first chapter outlines a philosophical anthropology of
gendering that implicates work technology at its inception as a primary source of
the subjugation of women. The link between technology and gendering is a very
tight one, with gendering taking place in technology, a core aspect of the labor
process. It is particularly through technological change that men actively pursue
the reproduction of gender divisions; women who fight technology are made to
pay a very high price.

Cockburn also critiques the view of women as mere victims of their own inac-
tivity in the face of personal discrimination who could break out of their situations
if they would just try harder. Rather, technology itself subordinates women, irrespective of how they behave. Because men control design, computing reinforces
existing male-female power relationships; consequently, the problem of gendered
technology cannot be solved by masculinizing women. Resolution can come only
in the cessation of gendering in the broader reproduction of society outside of the
workplace; that is, through change in the socialization of children and in the gendering of domestic life.

## Gendering and Compputropian Approaches

Much of our Sheffield experience (e.g., Mavis's description of the Data Shop) supports Cockburn's compputropian description of computing as unfairly gendered. However, we feel that at least the stronger forms of her analysis must ultimately be rejected. The patterns outlined above are complex, not simply compputropian. Women's experiences in a Sheffield academic department, where female secretaries spoke very positively about the way in which computing had broadened their working skills and the opportunities to practice them, were more computopian. The positive feelings about computers articulated by the women at WTTW and The Welcome Centre were echoed on numerous occasions, particularly in small service organizations and other offices. A computer specialist in an agency that services the cooperative sector, for example, argued that computing tended to break down gender hierarchies in offices, giving women workers control over more diverse tasks. Overall, our Sheffield results are as computopian as compputropian, most consonant with a "computing studies" point of view.

Moreover, there are gaps between the explanations Cockburn offers and the policies she advocates. She argues for obstructing technological change and concentrating on changed socialization. She never explains how change in socialization and domestic labor will solve the technology problem that exists primarily in the labor process. Further, despite her theoretical indictment of new technology as such, Cockburn supports "getting a grip on technological competence" through women-only training, explicitly identifying the WTTW as the kind of program in which women need to get involved. Yet what is the point of training women in new technology if the technology inevitably subverts them? Doesn't her argument suggest women should resist WTTWs?

In accepting that women desire to use new technology to alter their position at work, Cockburn's policy recommendations contradict her theory. The disparity between her analysis and her policy parallels the "stop-go" ambivalences—critical of computing in the abstract, supportive of it in the concrete—in Sheffield women's computing discourse. Similar ambiguity about how to relate to computing was a characteristic of discussions about women and computing in unions, community computing conferences, and educational workshops.

Part of the ambiguity is a consequence of failure to develop consistent analytic constructs. Like many analysts, Cockburn uses the term "technology" in several diverse ways—sometimes as a synonym for power, sometimes as an abstraction, sometimes as a signifier of simple technique. In failing to deconstruct technology theoretically, Cockburn reflects everyday uses of "technology," but clear analysis is necessary in order to develop a consistent technology practice. In contrast, Langdon Winner (1984) distinguishes between a technology per se and the technological *system* in which it is embedded, a particular technological artifact (for example, a computing machine) from the entire complex of machines, practices, and social relationships of which it is a part.

## New Technology and Patriarchy

It is useful to compare Cockburn's analysis to contemporary radical feminism, which places explanatory priority on patriarchy. When technology is implemented, the result is oppressive to women because of the preexistence of a powerful, generalized social system of male domination. The cause of female subordination is located outside of technology per se, in contrast to Cockburn. The accounts are similar, however, in that neither contains a developed history of the changing relationships among men, women, and technology.

A full history of gendering would need to recognize that, like technology, gendering has a complex history rooted in social evolution. It is most plausible to suppose that gendering among early humans, though increasingly extensive, was complementary but mostly egalitarian, the position taken by an important trend in feminist anthropology (Leacock 1981).[2] In contrast to both radical feminism and Cockburn, inequality between men and women appears relatively late—with the rise of the state, some 5,000 years ago. Rather than being coterminous with productive technology, repressive gendering develops in conjunction with repressive technologies.[3] There is no necessary connection between technology in general and repressive gendering. Each follows its own dynamic in relative autonomy.[4]

Distinguishing between complementary and repressive forms of *both* gendering and "technologizing" is essential to deconstructing the relationship between gendering and technology. It may be repressive technology, rather than technology "in general," that oppresses women at work. Similarly, it may be repressive gendering that oppresses women, not gendering in general. In either case, the aim for feminists need not be the dismantling of either gendering or technology as such but the elimination of their repressive forms, still a formidable task, but not to the same degree.

Recognizing the relative autonomy of technology and gendering allows one to differentiate among the sources of a technology's correlates. For example, where we find subordination of women with new information technology, we can inquire whether it is the *type* of technology (e.g., machine technology or some new, unique form) that is antiwoman, or whether it is something repressive about this particular technological *system*. Does it make most sense to see the antiwoman correlates as derived more from some other aspect of the work site, such as the repressive technologies in place—for example, the system of supervision or of labor control?[5]

The abstract technology on which a particular data processing "system" is based may itself be gender biased. Many women find the androcentric language of computer science—for instance, "hardware" versus "software"—off-putting enough to make them hesitate to get involved. Yet this aspect of computing is only one source of the negative effects for women.

Technology need not be repressive in itself, but it may be.[6] Subordination may follow from the way in which repressive technologies have shaped how productive and/or abstract technologies have been implemented. A major thrust of the recent literature on the social construction of technology (e.g., Bijker, Hughes, and Pinch 1987) has been on how factors other than technical proficiency shape decisions about which technological alternatives get developed. On this reading, an indictment of a particular technology as oppressive may be valid, but only if one can demonstrate that oppression is internal to the technology itself. For example, one must demonstrate that it is the productive technology in a computerized food warehousing system itself, rather than what is characteristic of an associated technology of another type, or interactions among these, that is the source of subordinating effects. Recognizing the relative autonomy of gender and technology also justifies deliberate collective human action, such as social policy, as a lever with which to affect social reproduction.

Consider, for example, Mavis's account of her experience in the Data Shop (Chapter 5). Admittedly abominable, her experience is as explicable in terms of repressive technology (a system of labor control that separates males and females, unionized and nonunionized, part-time and full-time) and/or repressive gendering (promoting men and not women) as it is in terms of computing technology per se. This latter possibility should not be dismissed out of hand; indeed, several early descriptions of word processing pools (e.g., Machung 1982; and Glenn and Feldberg 1979) are similar to Mavis's. However, more recent accounts of word processing based on microcomputers rather than minicomputers report more upskilling and upgrading of conditions, like those we encountered in the academic department referred to above.

In general, particular technological artifacts are only one element to be considered in accounting for female computing experience. A main conclusion of the post-Braverman (1974) sociology of work concerns the complexity of actual determinations in the labor process. Before new technology, many Sheffield manufacturing firms already employed women in shop floor positions in which they were paid less and labeled as less skilled. Often, computers made the work less physically demanding. Further, ardent Thatcherites in management perceived women to be less likely to participate actively in militant disruptive activities; for them, the elimination from the shop floor of skilled male activists was a high priority. For all of these reasons, one would have expected women using computers in manufacturing to fare less badly than men, that more women in machine operating positions already would have moved into computer-based jobs conceived to be lower skilled.

Yet in Sheffield plants women lost out when the computers came. Is this because of an antiwomen bias built into technology? Even in this case, the conjunction of the introduction of technology with the lessening of employment opportunities for women does not automatically imply that the technology was the cause. Women already working might have been squeezed out by, for example, antifemale practices institutionalized in the formal organizational structure (e.g., a deliberate management choice to "maintain good relations with the men" by firing the women). Equally plausible explanations include trade union practices based on seniority, or women's lack of confidence about working with new technology or in the firms' (generally miserable) training programs. It may even be the case, perversely, that the repression central to triumphant Thatcherism encouraged the reimposition of divisive gender differentiations. This would be consistent with Jane Humphries's argument that the recent labor market experience of women is more consistent with segmentation than buffer analyses.

A second post-Braverman finding is that the results of work change don't always meet the expectations of management implementers. In Burns's Sheffield engineering factories, employers were quite specific about why they were bringing in computerized equipment: to save money and to gain more control over production through lessening skill requirements. These aims were to be accomplished by channeling programming into a management position and taking the actual physical shop work away from skilled machinists and placing it in the hands of low-skilled machine operators.

Yet in Chapter 5 we describe a clear drift in factories toward the integration of the shop floor and office aspects of operating computerized machine tools. Over time, programmers learned to set up and operators learned to reprogram. This drift suggests that Sheffield labor sites were highly resistant to the representational desires of system designers and purchasers.

By acknowledging that technology is not unitary and must be understood in the broad context of the labor place of which it is a part, we can avoid reducing productive, abstract, and repressive technologies to one undifferentiated thing. By differentiating among them, we can understand the role of a particular technological artifact more precisely. As a system of social reproduction the labor process is complex and highly resistant to change. In resisting both compputropian and computopian generalizations about new technology and insisting upon identifying with precision the specific mechanisms by which the labor process is reproduced during any particular implementation of technology, we increase the possibilities for effective intervention to prevent the subordination of women or any other social group.

## Gender Politics and NIT

There is little doubt ... that feminist writers have produced ample evidence for why women should be miserable. We have indeed chronicled our own misery, often in detail, and sometimes convinced ourselves that the subjugation of women has been with us for so long (perhaps forever?) that remission is unlikely, perhaps impossible. Feminist anthropologists have certainly challenged such a view, detailing the fact that any particular form of oppression is not universal nor is any particular form of women's oppression an historical absolute. While this may provide us with hope and alternatives, it has hardly moved us forward in our vision of the next step, nor, some would argue, does it give us adequate understanding of where we are at the moment. (Groenfeldt and Kandrup 1985)

These Danish feminists stress that the promise of a cultural perspective on gender and computing is yet to be fulfilled. The "misery" logic, which fills the vacuum, leads to two choices: Either women withdraw and create separate societies or they become more like men, entering the world of new technology on their terms. This latter view was indeed articulated by some women and men we met. Margaret Thatcher herself is a strong symbol of this way of thinking; no analysis of gendering in Britain can ignore her influence as a masculinized female, palpably contradicting any notion of the special nature of women.

We reject the idea that these are the only choices by challenging the misery logic. When some women feel that new technology could make their work more interesting, this is not merely false consciousness, and not only because it is hard to make a deskilled and repetitive job less skilled. New technology often draws attention to work environments in which stress has been long-standing, rather than creating stress.

Our analysis stresses the indeterminacy of the gendering/technology relationship. When women suffer in conjunction with new technology, it may be that this is because the new technology is innately antifemale, but this is unlikely to be the entire story. Misery is also likely to be related to other factors, such as repressive technology, nontechnological patriarchy, or some combination of these. The relationship between technology and gender is so complex because it is highly mediated.

To avoid the misery theory, feminists have to decide what they want to accomplish and how new technologies might help them to get where they want to go. What we experienced in Sheffield—at the WTTW, in women's study circles, in SPRITE and other community computing groups, in the Sheffield Women's Unit, and in London's Microsyster—was a very different feminist approach to computerization. This approach stressed possibilities for controlling computerization socially to benefit users of all genders.

The most striking example was in the use of study circles in Sheffield and in the Scandinavian countries. These groups encouraged participants to move beyond simple bipolar thinking and to actively look for ways that technology could complement human objectives. The structure of the study circles was nonhierarchical, emphasizing the value of the contributions of every member of the work group. In their aims and structures, the study circles suggested a feminist alternative approach to technology in the workplace.

In order to plan for the consequences for women of any particular new information technology, one must pay attention to the social contexts within which the technology is to be embedded as well as the properties of the technology itself. Equally important, as suggested by women involved in the computerization movement, is the development of alternative approaches to computing that are feminist, clearly nonhierarchical and nonexploitative. Also of relevance is training in how to pressure organizations to adopt these alternative systems and implement them in ways that realize design objectives.

When women experience new technology at work, they may also be forced to work with productive technology perverted by repressive technology as well as repressive gendering or patriarchy. Ending this situation would indeed involve transforming the technology itself, purging it of the effects of repressive technology as well as the manifestations of repressive gendering. Still, this is different from eliminating technology and gendering as such. The elimination of exploitation would not come about automatically through a Luddite smashing of machines or the creation of new, nongender roles, even were these possible. The task of eliminating exploitation is a more subtle one, involving first the identification of the actual manifestations of repression, specifying for example, how repressive technologies actually shape productive technologies as well as how other repressive processes effect social reproduction in each particular case.

Feminists are beginning to realize that we ourselves have often failed to see the importance of repressive technologies because we have measured our own success by the same yardstick as men. Posing an alternative structure has the advantage of making us see the actual social process in new terms, long one of the strengths of feminist analysis. In essence, computing is better understood as a terrain on which gendering change is being worked out than as an independent cause of gendering change. Similarly, gendering is a symbolic terrain on which the dimensions of new technology are also being explored. In regard to gender issues, as elsewhere, computing is essentially a cultural phenomenon. It is the salience of computers to the way contemporary humans create and recreate their lives and life-styles, not the computing machines as such, that accounts for the important connections between computing and gendering.

## Notes

1. Concern with the contradictions of gender was an important element of our research design as well as the action research roles we constructed for ourselves. We wish we were able to present a comparable chapter on computing and race. One of the SPRITE centers, for example, was located within an Afro-Caribbean community center, and the WTTW made particularly strong efforts to recruit Asian women. However, we have insufficient data to analyze the dominant patterns of the computing/race connection.

2. Archaeology offers evidence that among early humans there was a moderate sexual duality of physical structure, as there is among humans today and our closest primate relatives, the chimpanzees. Neither the existence of this dimorphism, nor the difference in the roles of the sexes in the reproduction and nurturing of offspring, explain the position of women in contemporary societies. Dimorphism is, however, a plausible source of the extensive gendering observable among contemporary gatherers and hunters, especially in productive activities, in which there is extensive differentiation between "male" and "female" activities.

The existence of difference, however, is not a sufficient explanation of hierarchy (Coontz and Henderson 1986). It is important to realize that the gender divisions among gatherers and hunters are not rigid, with men often doing what we call "women's work," and vice versa. Cultural categories are often heavily gendered, but symbolic stress is also given to the complementarity of gender roles. Gender cooperation to overcome conflict is a frequent theme of expressive cultural performance or ritual.

Indeed, contemporary anthropologists have switched to calling the first human social form "gathering and hunting" rather than "hunting and gathering" in recognition of the paramount dependence of such social forms on the more female work of gathering. The label "gathering and hunting" is also a means of overcoming the legacy of androcentric language in anthropology. The label "hunter/gatherers" is anachronistic as well as androcentric. A distinct productive technology of animal hunting, as opposed to the opportunistic killing or scavenging characteristic of chimpanzees, is of no great antiquity, present only in the last 500,000 years of human existence, not the first three and one-half million.

3. To see why it makes sense to link repressive gendering to the rise of complex social formations, consider the gender possibilities in the earliest days of a state established through coercion (Carniero 1970), where one society institutionalizes domination over another. In one possible gendering case, dominated males may have been as exploited as dominated females, perhaps because males were conceived as a greater "military" threat by the dominators, for example, and were therefore more vulnerable to losing their lives (an extreme form of exploitation). Conversely, one can imagine an implicit "deal" cut between a conquering social group and the males of an area recently dominated. The dominators could "offer" to exploit men less than women in exchange for tacit acceptance by dominated males of the new social structure.

The first alternative conceptualized implies little substantive change in the relative status of dominated men and women, a situation continuous with the previous complementary character of gendering. The second alternative involves the replacement of complementary with exploitative gender roles, at least in the dominated group. A third alternative would be to posit the development of exploitative gendering processes supplementary to existing complementary ones.

In considering which of these three alternatives provides the best account of the origin of exploitative gender relations, the character of gendering among gatherer/hunters bears closer examination. Hunting of large animals, where it occurs, is almost universally perceived as a more male than female activity, is usually riskier in terms of its dependability as a food source than gathering, and involves tools that are more easily adapted to the requirements of repression than, for example, tools for digging roots. It also appears that the fruits of hunting labor, perhaps because of their scarceness, carry greater prestige than female products. It therefore seems likely that in state societies, where prestige itself became an important justification for the power of the dominant social group, these male symbols were appropriated by the ruling strata. Thus, techniques associated with males were likely to be more frequently adopted by the repressive technology than female-associated techniques. Furthermore, the tools of hunting and the tools of repression are similar. If a dominant social group wished to retain dominance, it was important that they control use of these tools. Similarly, the predation of one human group on another, initially an occasional rather than regular phenomenon, is also more similar in periodicity to male than female activity.

In other words, there are several good reasons to expect the emerging repressive technology to be linked symbolically to males and, consequently, to presume that repressive technologies will have a generally male character. An association of repression with male culture would have an impact on gendering. However, as our third alternative suggests, the impact might have been to distort or to complicate gendering rather than simply to replace the complementary systems of gendering that preceded the rise of the state with uniformly exploitative ones. Elements of gender complementarity clearly remain within ethnic groups as well as families. As contemporary popular music reminds us, young men and women, no matter how much "in love," establish their relationships in a complex social context, not in a vacuum. Still, such relationships do have some relative autonomy; they are not reducible to the context of social group power alone.

There are a number of other ways to conceive of the changes in the reproduction of power and gender institutionalized at the time of the rise of the state. Our basic point is that there is analytic value in distinguishing between complementary and repressive gendering and in the relationship of each to the various types of technology: productive, abstract, and repressive. Even within state-level societies, kinship and family institutions retain a degree of gender equality (Gailey 1987). One way to account for this continuing arena of equality is to see state society as supplementing preexisting complementary gender roles with exploitative ones. As in our theory of technology, such a view of gender posits the existence of multiple, somewhat autonomous, gendering systems.

4. The understanding of technology and gender that we advocate, when stated in this manner, is still overly simplistic. Because of the interdependence that is characteristic of the various types of technologies and gendering patterns in real social formations, they have to be placed into the processes of social formation reproduction within which human patterns of behavior actually exist and to which such analytic categories as "repressive gendering" apply only imperfectly. The child who knows that there is a difference between men's and women's activity is not therefore necessarily able to distinguish between complementary and repressive patterns of gendering; either of these can provide a foundation for other symbolic differentiations. Although the development of productive technologies follows an internal dialectic to some extent, it is also affected by the developmental dialectics of abstract technologies and repressive technologies. Melman (1974) and others have demonstrated how military funding of a high proportion of basic research in the United States and Britain has shaped (and limited) the process of the transfer of knowledge from science to industry.

Moreover, the changes in gendering cannot be understood in isolation from the international political economic, national state, and regional structures discussed in Part Three, as well as the local policies described in Chapter 11. Gendering is "overdetermined" in Trotsky's sense, being reconstituted in the context of massive change in external structures and local human processes.

In arguing for the relative autonomy of these different kinds of technology, we do not wish to overstate our case. Clearly, developments in each of the forms of technology affect each other; they are similar and are subject to similar conditions. Surely forms of repressive technology drew heavily on the artifacts of existing productive technologies: Axes are effective weapons against both people and plants, and early armies used many of the same tools to repress fellow humans that were used to hunt animals. Further, the elaboration and development of repressive technologies is clearly enhanced by developments in abstract technologies—gunpowered ballistics being dependent on development in mathematics, for example.

Still, it is both unnecessary and unwise to see productive technology, or abstract technology either, as therefore necessarily repressive—to treat them as theoretically the same. Each type of technology has something of an internal dynamic, so that the characteristics of an artifact are dependent on the dynamics of the form of technology within which it has developed. An understanding of these dynamics allows us to predict something of the likely social correlates of the artifact. Consider the case of the semiautomatic rifles (e.g., Uzi, AK-47, M-16) that the National Rifle Association in the United States is trying to exempt from regulation. These are artifacts of a particular repressive technological system, the modern infantry. Though it is true that these weapons could serve as tools in a hunting economy (that is, as part of a system of productive technology), they would probably be inappropriate for this use, both because they are extremely dangerous to hunters and because they would destroy the meat. This is simply not a use to which their design easily lends itself.

Most important, a theory that refuses to treat use of technology as necessarily unitary, but instead is inclined to see each use of technology as composed of multiple forms, allows us more easily to deconstruct each use into component elements. Such analysis creates much more room for recognizing the kinds of social construction factors that our Sheffield research demonstrated are of such great importance.

5. Such a possibility is based on the argument that labor sites are loci of social repression as well as production of commodities. This view is, of course, a basic contention of the Marxist perspective. Put schematically, this perspective acknowledges that a particular form of supervision (e.g., the "open" office plan) or labor control (the automated assembly line) does more than merely serve a technical (e.g., coordination) role in a technological system. As important to an analysis of the nature of a particular supervision system is the recognition that the system has a history, a developmental trajectory initiated within a particular social context. Under capitalist conditions, this social context can be stated abstractly as the transference from the situation of direct domination in a feudal society to indirect domination in a capitalist one. What takes place at many contemporary labor sites has more to do with the reproduction of capital than with work, the human production of the materials for social subsistence.

6. In our view, patriarchy may itself be dependent on the "successful reproduction" of repressive technology. It is the development within state societies of structures that give permanence to dominant social groupings that may be the essential source of gender domination. Gender domination can be understood as an insidious nuance of state domination that is particularly difficult to confront because of the divisions it creates among the dominated groups. On this reading, men do benefit from gender divisions, but often such benefits are spurious and self-damaging. Men's failure to understand the limitations of those benefits, and their positive damage, is less a consequence of their material interest than it is an allegiance to patriarchy in the absence of a clear alternative.

# 13

## Class, Culture, Computing, and Politics

*Farewell to the Working Class* (1982) is one of the more influential "post-industrial" polemics. In it, French social theorist Andre Gorz bases his argument for a radically alternative left political strategy on the idea that the working class is disappearing because of the new technology.

### Vanishing Workers?

Working-class culture in South Yorkshire today is different from that of the 1970s, and were culture primarily a matter of images, tastes, and advertising hype, one might agree with Gorz. Yet culture is also about how institutions affect the experiences people have, the reproduction of language and other symbols, and the strategies for relating to material conditions. Unlike Gorz, we left South Yorkshire convinced that class is not disappearing and that class analysis remains essential to understanding computerization.

Changes in the reproduction of Sheffield working-class culture are related to such material factors as cuts in financial support for state services; but they also involve actions to address dissatisfactions with working-class culture. Some dissatisfactions had already been articulated in the 1970s, when younger workers complained that Labourist gradualism retained too much of the "cloth caps, clogs, and tugged forelocks" social deference of the nineteenth century. Culture, like life, is reproduced, and also like life is changed in the process. Although culture does involve "adapting" to changes in material conditions, the nature of the adaptation is subject to the symboling of sentient beings. The working class, an important presence at its birth (Thompson 1963), continues to be an important presence at its reproduction.

What remains unclear is the extent to which this presence will be guided by conscious collective intervention or politics. We wish to show here how cultural analysis is necessary to proactive class politics on computing. We do this by drawing together our analysis of computing and the working class, of politics and culture.

Computers are a central symbol in contemporary working-class culture, but a symbol as much of fear as of hope. Cynthia Cockburn met some fifth-form (high school junior) girls in a London comprehensive high school who said that if you do computers at school, "you grow hair on your chest." The analysis of this kind of story or myth is at the core of modern anthropology. Though the cultural analysis provided by myths themselves is often unreliable, the guidance they offer to the kinds of things that matter to people—for example, in Cockburn's story, the trans-formative power of computers—is ignored only at great risk.

In this volume we show how computing studies—and more generally, the study of contemporary social formations—can be grounded in analysis of every-day experience, including myths. The value of such a cultural approach is more readily conceded in a "postmodern" era than in the more scientist one that pre-ceded it, yet its proper form is hotly contested. We begin sketching our approach by taking up a theme common to the computing and "end of class" literatures, the decline of employment. In its demonstration of the continued relevance of class, our analysis addresses both conceptual and statistical evidence on the boundaries of the labor form in South Yorkshire. Data regarding the collective experience of freedom from labor, related to some of the models for its analysis and manipula-tion, leads back to the centrality of new information technology, as labor site in-novation, as symbol in the lives of unwaged working-class people, and as part of efforts to create a society outside of the labor form, yet still working class.

Demonstration of the importance of culture to class and technology leads to a more general examination of cultural analysis as actually practiced by working-class people in South Yorkshire, some of the contradictions in this practice, and identification of forms of cultural analysis that effectively relate to computing. We then compare these forms to similar cultural perspectives emerging within aca-demic computer science. After summarizing our Sheffield findings in cultural terms, we return to the question of postindustrial society in our conclusion.

## Postindustrial or Labor-Free?

Our Sheffield data refute the notion that computing creates a "postindustrial" society as this is commonly understood. Nonetheless, "labor-free" working-class people in South Yorkshire are the pioneers of a potential "postemployment" cul-ture. The following vignette illustrates the importance of including in any analysis of computing and social change an explanation of how freedom from labor is ex-perienced.

It was the fourth day of a Northern College one-week residential course on "Understanding Unemployment," a "follow on" (sequel) to the one described in Chapter 1. The students were from Mexborough, a coalfield village in South Yorkshire's Dearne Valley whose economic performance was the second worst in the nation. In addition to organizing their own unemployed center, the students had organized the course and had asked for a session on "Do the Unemployed Understand the Future Better Than the Rest?" The topic was justified to the Manpower Services Commission, course funder, in terms of a major goal, increasing students' self-confidence. None of the participants had had a job within the past year.

One group discussed "the good side of being labour free, not working for wages." Mark, a slight bearded man in his thirties, summarized: "You get plenty of leisure, and you get more chance for real work, work that makes a difference. Not just a job, but like work for organisations, and you get more freedom to choose which ones. There's more Adult Education like this course, and more time with the family. There's more concessions, like at the Anvil Cinema in Sheffield, and more time for your hobbies—just more choice all around. And it helps fight inflation!"

Ann, a single mother in her forties who had "not been one of the favorites in a big family," presented a second group's ideas on "the bad side of labour freedom": "First, you're so bound up by State rules, you feel personally controlled—means tests are always separating people into different class groups. Then there's the loss of individuality, and no room for mobility, either socially or geographically. They pressure you to narrow your job choice, so's to become more employable.

"You have to live on a low standard, with a lot of uncertainty about the future, which discourages marriage and other normal social choices. You get a bad attitude from those in employment, and you feel socially inadequate, because you can't mix, due to lack of money. There's domestic tensions, due to boredom, poor health, and a lack of social activities. All together, it adds to a loss of confidence in society.

A third group had discussed what the labor-free want from new information technology. Martin, a young man who had lived in the South for several years before coming back North, read the group's list: "We want encouragement for more skills training in NIT, more further education in general, better leisure services, and a shorter working week, which will lead to more jobs."

"How important is it to you to have jobs?" David asked. "It's mixed," responded Martin, pointing to a poster on the wall that urged the students to "Fight Back with the Unemployed Workers Charter." "Like the first demand says, 'Work at trade union rates or full maintenance.' The only real problem with being unemployed is that it don't pay enough."

"The way I look at it," Ann interjected, "is that no one can afford to pay me what I'm worth. That's the problem with the rest of the demands on that poster, 'No to the Community Programme, Abolish YTS,' and so on—those programmes are not that bad, and they give us some room to make our own way. Don't get rid of them, just make sure they provide a living wage."

"Don't get us wrong," Mark said. "We do want jobs, and we come on courses like this hoping to get them. It's just that, after you've been on the dole a long time, you realize that being a slave to some wretched job is not the most important thing in life. And with all the new technology, we don't need that kind of job any more. The kind who put out that poster don't really understand the likes of us. Like the trade unions, they just can't imagine life without a job, and they patronize us.

"Knock unemployment, not the unemployed. It's not us who are wrong, but circumstances, and the most important job is for us to organize ourselves in a positive way. That's what I like about calling us 'the labour free.' It's ironic, but we've at least got some space to figure out what we want, and what things we need, like new technology, in order to get it."

### Conceptual Problems in Talking About Unemployment

For those with considerable experience of labor freedom, the need for social identities that transcend laboring roles is obvious, as is the justice of seeing their difficulties in social rather than individual terms. Equally interesting is the link they see between new technology and the construction of a viable future. Much of the discussion about the experience of those not bound to the employment form suffers from implicit ethnocentric (in this case, "laborist") distortions and other unwarranted presuppositions.

The unemployed are a social category defined in apparently economic terms. However, these terms are really based on a dubious psychologism. The unemployed are considered to be like the employed in that they desire a job—that is, they are "in the labour market"—but they are also like unwaged people in not having one. Implicit is a simplistic assumption: that the basic difference between those desiring a job but unable to find it—"the unemployed"—and those who do not desire a job—the "economically inactive"—is an individualistic "free choice." Treating the decision to search for labor as voluntary is dubious because it oversimplifies people's complex responses to their economic options, diverts attention from the reproduction of the social contexts in which they find themselves, and obscures the complex issues described by the Northern College students. (Equally dubious is operationalizing measurement of "the unemployed" by equating them with those who successfully complete a bureaucratic process, those who have "signed on at the dole" for unemployment compensation.)

Moreover, as a linguistically negative label (i.e., one that defines a group in terms of what it lacks), "unemployment" tends to reinforce the "outsider" perspective also criticized by the students from Mexborough. It is no wonder that those free of labor have a hard time thinking proactively about their situations. (Nor is it easy for the person who has had relatively secure employment for some time to empathize with those not "in work.") An anthropological desire to avoid language that implies negative evaluations, as well as a desire to include those who have not signed on for the dole, leads us to prefer the linguistically more positive "labor-free" over "unemployed."

## The "Labor-Free"

Instead of trying to find a way to separate the unemployed from others in society, we need to place their situation in a broader context. Many people not usually thought of as being like "the unemployed" share much of their condition. Children, house spouses, retired people, some of those with disabilities, and "those not actively seeking work" (because of their belief that there are no appropriate jobs available) all share with "the unemployed" the need to make decisions like those described by the Northern College students. The term "unwaged" is increasingly used in Sheffield to refer to these groups *as well as* to those in the labor market but without a job. However, "the unwaged" crosses major class boundaries. It includes those who through their wealth—for example, large property owners—have very different access to means of subsistence. Whether they have a job for wages or not, their security of position allows them to avoid the choices demanded of the insecure unwaged.

Following Marx's ironic discussion of the double "freedom" of the proletariat—freedom from both the restrictions of serfdom and the control over means of production—the labels "wage-" or "labor-free" refer to the unwaged who are insecure, those without personal wealth and unable to find an adequate job, irrespective of whether they wish to do so. To be "labor free" means to be working class but to live increasingly outside of the employment relationship.[1] For many, wage labor in the formal economy is no longer a "normal" component of the adult condition. Expansion of the group of people free from labor for varying periods of time was a major difference between the 1970s and the 1980s in Sheffield. At the same time, wage labor is increasingly important for some (e.g., housewives), although its quality (e.g., temporary, part-time) is different from the form of labor dominant throughout most of this century. Their increasing numbers meant that the labor-free, part-time workers, and "temps" are a real presence in social reproduction.

The labor-free, not subject to the particular social relationship of laboring for a wage, are not "workless." They do an increasing amount of work, including activities contributing to group subsistence in the domestic sphere or caring for each other, in what Sheffielders call the "voluntary" sector. The labor-free may also be self-employed, although despite massive national government promotion through various "enterprise schemes," self-employment in South Yorkshire has risen only marginally.[2]

The labor-free may work periodically in the so-called "black" economy; that is, engage in labor-like activities in which cash changes hands but the transaction is not recorded, especially for tax purposes. Rigorous studies of the black economy suggest that its role is generally exaggerated. Alternatively, they may work in the barter economy, where no cash changes hands (e.g., good-for-service barter). Barter work was preferred over "black" work by our labor-free informants. They do not like to work illegally and articulated elaborate codes for deciding what illicit labor they would and would not do. For example, one informant would only work "under the counter" (i.e., off the tax record) at certain times of the year, so that he could buy birthday or Christmas presents for his children. He based his unwillingness to join the black economy on an ethical principle, the desire to contribute positively to a public social surplus through paying his fair share of taxes.

In terms of security, people in low-wage jobs have much in common with the labor-free. Even some of those in full-time employment are and feel threatened by the precariousness of the current political economy. "The insecure" is an accurate label for all of these people, but again, it is a linguistically negative label. "Security-free" might be useful, except it sounds like double-talk. Still, it is useful to have a label that includes all of these while excluding the relatively secure, whether waged or unwaged—the working class. The following vignette illustrates how this basic divide between the secure and the insecure is symbolized in contemporary South Yorkshire.

On a Saturday in winter 1986, the Sheffield Town Hall was the venue for a conference: "The Growing Divide." In his opening statement, a council officer challenged the geographic terms in which popular discussion was cast: "Is there a North/South divide? No question about it in terms of jobs, but in the end, what does it matter if your only choices are unemployment in the North or homelessness in the South? Wherever they are, the working class have problems. We need to understand these problems if we are to bridge the social divide. That's why we've invited Marge Brandon from the Castle Housing Estate. Marge is a volunteer at the Castle Rights and Advice Centre for the unemployed, who's going to tell us how she experiences the great divide."

"As you know, I'm from the Castle, a notorious estate—half our kids can't even get a place on government schemes to hide unemployment! You know that the biggest mistake of the ruling class was educating the working class, but even that's being taken away. They don't even want factory fodder any more, so they don't even bother about the truants from school.

"Up on the estate, this North-South divide is just another way to fob off the real class war that's goin' on. To uz, the problem is the Victorian values of Mrs. Thatcher and the ruling class at large, the idea that working class people should be put where they belong—seen and not heard. Women are just a sex symbol—they can have a good job if they're willing to be fondled.

"The ruling class don't want to know about our real problems, like the illness in my family from lack of heat. We've an electric heater in our Council house, but we've shut it off because of the high bills. Their desperate need for housing, food, and benefits means working-class people are afraid to open their mouths. There's no unity in the working-class movement now, it's totally divided between the employed and the unemployed, the old and the young. On my estate, single mums are attacked by the Oxford fraud squad, sneakin' about to see if they can find a man! This isn't being done to the middle class—catting about is acceptable for them. If this fraud squad bunch visit me, I'll invite them in for an orgy—this body's been all over t'Castle!"

What these speakers stressed as different in 1980s Sheffield, the new divide, is the increasing proportion of working-class people who lack secure access to adequate work and means of subsistence. Another notion is also implied in their comments: Whether insecurely waged or completely labor-free, working-class people must develop a new habitus, a new politics, involving nonlaboring as well as, if possible, laboring techniques, to improve their basic subsistence situation.

Another assumption implicit in "unemployment" discourse is the idea that to be free of labor is an aberration. In reality, the majority of the population in complex social formations does not work for money, and we may well look back on the post–World War II era of relatively full employment as unusual if not unique for employment social formations.[3] The increasing difficulty that capitalist political economies have in providing social necessities is another reason for seeing the "traditionally" nonemployed (e.g., house spouses) as sharing the same fundamental condition of insecurity as those unable to find regular employment.

### Labor Freedom and the Standard of Living

What is it like to be free of employment? A December 1986 *Sheffield Journal* issue carried the following headline: "City Record as 940 Chase One Job—and It's at a Rubbish Tip!" A council survey in Walkley, "a typical inner city area," investigated "how unemployment and falling incomes are affecting people's standard of living." The main findings include the following:

- unemployment is about 40 percent, if one includes (with those "signed on") individuals not signing on because they don't get benefits, people who would prefer to work but are looking after other people, and people with disabilities;
- two-thirds of the unemployed had been out of work for a year or more;
- most women who wanted a job had one, but half of the jobs were part-time (true of none of the labor-free men);
- although the official unemployment rate for men was higher than that for women, a greater proportion of women were on short-time working or were administratively unable to claim benefits and therefore were not counted officially as unemployed; if such women were included, rates for men and women were very similar;
- average household income was one-half the national average, so that one-half of the families in which there was a wage coming in had incomes "topped up" from benefits;

- indeed, one-half of all income was from benefits, one-half of all families were totally dependent on benefits, and nearly one-half had had difficulty with the benefits system;
- one-quarter of families had gone without heat because they couldn't afford it, and one in five heated their living room only.

Of course, these conditions have differential impacts, falling particularly hard on the black (which in Sheffield includes South Asians as well as Afro-Caribbeans) and the young. Under the headline "Job Despair of the Young," a Sheffield journalist reports on recently published government statistics: "Nearly half the jobless people in Sheffield are aged under twenty-five. ... The city careers office had nearly 12,000 names on its books—and only had twenty vacancies to offer youngsters not on the Youth Training Scheme last week" (Watson 1986).

Something of how unemployment is experienced is communicated further in the same story: "[An official] of Sheffield Coordinating Centre Against Unemployment ... claimed that unemployed are now being harassed by Government. ... [A] team of officers are in Sheffield knocking on doors and spying on the unemployed. ... 'Investigators are aiming to harass the unemployed off the register and thereby fiddle the unemployed statistics downward.'"

The way labor freedom is experienced is not preordained; it is a social condition actively created by different groups in society. As the last comments suggest, among the most important participants in the creation of this social condition is the state. Working-class people in Sheffield tend to see the national state as a primary cause of unemployment, through redundancies in state-owned enterprises, such measures as rate capping, and financial policies that discourage local investment.

## The Social Construction of Labor Freedom

The unemployment statistic is perhaps the most important national number. By mid-1987 Thatcher's government had made nineteen changes in the way this statistic was calculated, according to the national Unemployment Unit. The "Restart" program, a more or less coercive measure to "get people off the dole count," was typical of such changes. By threatening to end their dole money, Restart compelled long-term labor-free people to come into the Jobcentre for counseling and training. Once involved in a training program, an individual no longer was counted as unemployed. If they didn't find a job after the training, they were counted as unemployed again, but as "newly" rather than "long-term" unemployed. The Unemployment Unit reckoned that the nineteen manipulations had lowered the unemployment statistic total by over 500,000.[4] In addition to finding new statistics and trying to bury the unemployment number inside a large volume of other statistics, the government considered doing away with the monthly number altogether (*Guardian* June 20, 1987).

The Conservative government tended to argue that unemployment was essentially a matter of personal choice. Conservative spokesperson Norman Tebbit suggested that unemployment would be solved if the unemployed person would "get on your bike" and move to where the jobs were. In fact, most interregional job mobility takes place among the employed, much within the same company; lack of information about job opportunities, tremendous differences in housing costs and access, and difficulties of settling in impede the migrant. Margaret Thatcher herself emphasized individual choice in matters like the right to obtain private health insurance. Rhodes Boyson, minister for local government, condemned people for "choosing" to live as single parents and characterized them as creating "probably the most evil product of our time."

In these views, working-class people themselves, not the state, were responsible. "Blaming the victim" is a common theme in analysis of the wage-free. Unemployment is held responsible for breaking up the civility that was so striking when we first came to Britain from urban America in 1976. A *Guardian* story headed "Jobs Divide 'Twists Morals'" summarizes an academic study of the northern city of Sunderland, which concluded that "the division between the employed and the unemployed is becoming more important than that between the working- and middle-class." This study "discovered whole communities for whom unemployment was the norm and among whom a new 'culture' was emerging ... People who have to exist on social security have a different set of values. Morality starts to change. Small-scale thieving is seen as part of a way of everyday life ... cut off from the rest of society" (Routledge 1987).

Anthropologists recognize here strong echoes of the "culture of poverty" thesis of Oscar Lewis (1966), who argued that under capitalism, poor people adapt to the absence of material resources by developing a collective life-style or culture that allows them to survive.[5] (Lewis died in Cuba in the midst of research on whether socialism altered the culture of poverty.) Through the use of phrases like "the iron-clad life style of the poor" and "the distinctive feature of the culture of poverty is the poverty of culture," Lewis legitimated a poverty discourse in which the culture concept can be used politically. As the Northern College students argue, "laborist" presumptions also make it difficult to talk about being out of labor without moralizing.

### Workers and the Social Construction of Labor Freedom

The following vignette explores some of the conflicts among the labor-free that emerged during a heated discussion in the lounge of an unemployment center.

A young man with dyed hair, a black leather jacket, and torn jeans argued, "We're the users; why shouldn't we run the centre?"

"It's not that simple," replied a female center worker. "This isn't just a drop-in centre, an ''ome away from 'ome' for those on the dole. It's set up for all people who are against unemployment and what it does to people. There are people coming in here all the time, for meetings, and classes and things—they're users as well, but they don't come here regularly. Doesn't the centre have to relate to them as well?"

"The centre is really for activists," added a bearded man in an olive combat jacket who was employed as a development worker by the local trades council. "It's a place for campaigning, to make plans for fighting against unemployment; it's for whatever needs doin' in the fight against the policies of the current government."

"You just want the professionals to run it," said the female companion of the young man—"those middle class people who make a career out of unemployment. They don't really want to do away with unemployment—it would take their jobs. It should be uz—the unemployed—who run the centre. Let us decide how much the tea should cost, whether the rooms should be used for speakers or darts, the library for books on politics or football. We don't want politics. That councilor who was here said it right—let the Council handle the politics. We just want jobs."

The vignette reveals phenomena common to ethnogenesis. Groups struggling to form a collective identity often push for their own space or "turf" and try to separate themselves symbolically from those who do not share their condition and who may impose inappropriate cultural constructions on them. Like the young man from The Welcome Centre in Chapter 12, these unemployed have difficulty defining themselves in the political terms of traditional working-class culture.

In his series of pieces published in the *Guardian* and in *Survivors of Steel City: A Portrait of Sheffield*, psychologist Geoffrey Beattie tries hard to create an inside view of labor freedom. Beattie presents the results of four years of participant observation among the labor-free by describing the coping strategies—turning into self-employed decorators, nightclub bouncers, pimps, and so on—of several individuals, people who have been made redundant. Having described his interest as concerning "how the social performance of people in a town in decline is organized" (1986:25), Beattie analyzes his results in a chapter entitled "Playing the Part." The chapter is an insightful application of the descriptive dramaturgy of everyday life developed by American sociologist Erving Goffman (1959). Beattie links his description of personal psychologies to a "political perspective." Though claiming to have documented how these social marginals have "started to claw their way back up the slippery slope, renegotiating their new levels of [personal] power" (p. 199), Beattie acknowledges that they may be powerless.

Although anthropology teaches that to understand a people's culture, one must find a way to see it from within, anthropology also places the inside view in a broader context than does Beattie. His approach to politics, like that of the young man and woman in the unemployed center and that of Labourism, is too narrow, operating at the microlevel actions of interpersonal relations, including only the panache involved in creating a new personal habitus. National state policies are analyzed only in Goffmanesque terms—for example, the "performance team of the Conservative government … keeping its strategic secrets"; they are analyzed structurally.

The culture of labor freedom is also being created more collectively, by such people as the students from Mexborough or activists in the unemployed centers. Beattie eliminates such people from his field informants; the result is a distorted analysis of the production and reproduction of labor-free working-class culture. He replicates the error made earlier by Richard Hoggart, whose justly famous *The Uses of Literacy* (1957) purports to present British working-class culture, but also deliberately eliminates from consideration activists of all sorts.

## Helping to Create Labor-Free Culture

Effective participant observation of subordinate social strata is epistemologically dependent on examination of the actions of those who intervene actively in the reproductive process. Such activists exert a disproportionate influence on the terms through which changes in social structure are perceived within the culture; it is the very construction of such terms that mark possible proactive responses.

The Dearne Valley is a region in the north of South Yorkshire. The Dearne Valley Project, a collaborative endeavor of the Northern College in Barnsley and the Workers' Educational Association, is a highly developed effort to adapt the services of adult education to the labor-free. In the first annual report (Cole, Ellis, and Grayson 1986), project participants explore the lives of those in a highly industrialized rural region hit by rundowns in both steel and coal. The Dearne is an area of low morale; its people have "a sense of decline" and feel underresourced, living in "a forgotten valley" and suffering "the stigma of unemployment."

However, the report also gives attention to numerous efforts to begin a new life. Some of these are informal, such as neighborhood support networks, and some are more formal, such as the unemployed center organized by the students, the various women's support groups organized during the miners' strike and carrying on after it, and worker cooperatives exploring life on the fringes of the capitalist marketplace. Some, like the Dearne Enterprise Centre, operate in uneasy alliance with such state bodies as the MSC, on the one hand, and with new organizational forms like the Yorkshire and Humberside Alliance of Unemployed Centres, on the other.

Adult educators recognize that education cannot on its own bring about the core socioeconomic changes that must take place if a materially decent and humane new culture is to emerge in the Dearne. Given the importance of educational failure in legitimating poverty in the valley, the approach of education must be indirect, involving a pedagogy of community development and "cultural competence." Learning must take its cues from the emerging new informal and formal organizations; it must involve the unemployed in developing policy, relate to social issues, such as the need for welfare rights advice, and work to develop new groups as well. It must pay particular attention to those who have already "broken the mold" laid down by the previous community process, like the women's support groups. The report points out the shortcomings of traditional views of women's adult education. An experience-led educational program must address immediate problems, such as the need for sharpened campaign skills, and it must support the creation of new forms of group identity.

With this volume we aim to accomplish a cultural redirection of analysis of the computing/social change connection. The informants' conversations to which we draw attention below provide a vehicle for summarizing the various ways that notions of culture can be used in the ethnography of computerization and the illustration of the negative consequences of overly narrow cultural perspectives. Instead, we draw together the strands of the several "cultural" approaches into a consistent framework.

## A Symbolic Conception of Culture

The following vignette shows one way in which culture is consciously at issue for the contemporary British working class.

They carried the same petition box as the original "crusaders for jobs" fifty years ago, but the 1987 Jarrow marchers were dressed in trainers (running shoes) and nylon anoraks (parkas) rather than clogs and cloth caps. Supported by politicians of all political parties, the 1937 march received publicity all the way to London, but the 1987 march lacked this support. At a rally at the Sheffield Coordinating Centre Against Unemployment, one of the marchers, in a heavy Jordie (Northeastern/Newcastle) accent, explained why: "For the capitalists who rule this country, any attempt of workin' people to speak out is a danger, and their hired lackies of the so-called 'free' press are just as afraid. They don't want people to know the truth about unemployment, because they're afraid that the workers will unite and claw back some of what's been taken from them by the present government. The things we want, like a job for every person, must be revolutionary, because the capitalist system can't provide that any more. We've got to change it, so we're taking our march to London, like they did in 1937, so that the people there can see what it's like up here, without work, on the dole with no hope. We don't want that much, just the culture that working people deserve."

The explicit culture concept used here has an ironic sense, a riposte to Mathew Arnold's ultimately class-based notion of culture versus anarchy. Although the marcher explains the actions of his class opponents in terms of their particular way of life, he justifies working-class action universally, invoking the premise that all people deserve a certain level of "culture." Culture is equated with some very general form of human opportunity, an abstract good.

The next part of the rally involved a more particular use of the culture construct. Here, working class culture is equated with a particular aspect of class, the values or symbols that are (or should be) characteristic of working-class life:

By 1987 Arthur Scargill was the most popular target of national press's favorite sobriquet, the "dinosaurs" of the trade union movement. The National Union of Mineworkers had moved its headquarters to Sheffield shortly after Scargill became president in the early 1980s. In the heart of the coalfield, among militant union supporters, the leader of those Margaret Thatcher called "the enemies within" greeted the marchers: "On behalf of the NUM, I want to welcome the Jarrow Crusade to Sheffield. We congratulate you for what you are doing, most importantly for building solidarity in the working class. There have been strains in that solidarity, as in the mining industry, which people in this audience will know about. But the Jarrow March is a splendid example of the determination of working people to stand up for what they believe in. We need this determination even more to win the fight against those selling off the noble birthright of every English working man and woman.

"Many people ask me where I get the strength to soldier on against the powers that the ruling class array against us. One was the American evangelist Billy Graham, in Sheffield for a crusade during the strike. I had a long discussion with him about the hardships being faced by miners and their families—the pit closures, the communities disappearing. Near the end, Billy said to me, 'Arthur, there's one thing I don't understand. Through all the troubles of the strike, through all the personal attacks, how do you remain so cheerful?'

"I looked him straight in the eye and said, 'Billy, you've got to have faith. The cause of working people is noble, a way of life whose righteousness I believe in.' And that's the way I see it with the Jarrow marchers and all the other working people who continue to demand the right to a job from the uncaring capitalist system. No matter what the doubters may say, the trendy leftists with their plans to broaden the appeal of the Labour Party by selling out the working class, I believe that we will prevail, if only we have enough faith in our cause, the faith being shown by the Jarrow marchers, true heroes of the working class."

The notion of "way of life" or culture is invoked here (also ironically) in modified form. The focus is placed on values, a particular element of working-class culture, and contains an evaluation. Scargill professes "faith" in the "cause" of the working class, thereby linking general notions of humanism and human destiny with a particular *aspect of* the working class.

Though the specific content may change, something is taken for granted by this kind of "working-class" analysis: that there is something essentially good about working-class people and experience. This underlying essence, often referred to by the phrase "working-class culture," transcends any particular political perspective, although there clearly is room for debate over what are its most salient characteristics. Such uses equate culture with widely shared collective self-perceptions, as with particular ethnic or class cultures. In such discourses as Scargill's, attention is directed to the set of symbolic categories and constructs—what anthropologists call a semiotics—that underlies the shared ways in which a given people perceive of, and through which they act on, their experience.

## A Situational Conception of Culture

A different approach to class culture emerges in the following vignette. With Mary, a team leader in a Sheffield council department, we were talking about how to promote a working-class policy on both jobs and computing:

"Before you can come up with a working class strategy, you need to figure out who is in the working class. There are obviously different components today. There's the scholarship culture like myself, those who in one sense had gotten out of the working class through education, but who in other ways are reluctant to give up our working class identity. Even though like me—for example, I shop on the Moor rather than at the [municipal] Castle Market, like my mother. Then there's the Bennite working class, those from the middle class with a political identification with workers. There's also the 'still' working class, those who have not changed very much. These are all different from those working class people who rose outside of education, perhaps through large incomes like the miners of the 1970s. These last see themselves as middle class much sooner than the others."

"Do computers change class?" Barbara asked. "Are they seen as a way out of the working class?"

"They seem to offer an alternative, in my experience at least," Mary responded. "Hackers—we call them that, too—seem to come from every level of society. The cult of the home computer is a major thing in all classes. But still, the best selling software is not games of skill but fantasy games, like 'Hobby,' which is inspired by Tolkien. They're an escape, but into fantasy, not out of your social situation.

"England remains much more a class society than Europe. Sheffield particularly—being 'Labour's home' is still an important part of the local identity; people are suspicious of all the changes in jobs, in mobility, even geographic mobility. If class is defined in the appropriate way, to include people's dreams and goals, and their expectations, all these groups are still part of the working class. They still share the same dreams of community. Class is really a matter of which you're more willing to give up—family and friends or money and jobs."

Mary's first concept of class culture is based on "situation"; that is, those who share similar positions in relation to major structures (like the labor market and educational institutions) are in the same group. She later encapsulates the situational view within a broader, more humanistic concept of culture.

## An Expressive Conception of Culture

Humans are unique among animals not only in that they supplement their physical beings with "artificial," "cultural" devices but because they also examine themselves and their devices through various forms of "expressive culture." These forms—songs, plays, paintings, and so on—themselves often articulate both the values of a culture and a general cultural perspective.

Consider *The Stirrings in Sheffield on Saturday Night,* a perennial Sheffield dramatic production. We saw *The Stirrings* during the Sheffield festival, the fourth production we had been to as a family in a week. Most of the plays had been put on in the city center Crucible Theater, but this production was in a community hall. The walls were covered with pictures of previous productions of the drama troupe, one of several amateur groups in the city. The stage itself was small and the hall was filled with folding chairs. The audience was a mixture of pensioners, local people, and Boy Scout and Girl Guide groups. During the intermission, tea was served with biscuits and popular sweets. A leaflet on our chairs described the play:

> *The Stirrings in Sheffield on Saturday Night,* is far and away the most successful piece of theatre ever staged in Sheffield. [There are] … two stories in the play, the first dealing with the activities of William Broadhead, the saw-grinders' [Union] leader in the 1860s. At that time the unions were not recognised by law, and the only way they could coerce their members into paying their dues was by intimidation and physical violence. It was a worrying time for the union. Automation was rearing its head in the cutlery trade: a machine could take over the work formerly done by a roomful of men, and some "little mesters" [small workshop owner/operators] were unscrupulous in taking on too many apprentices to do the work of fully-flegged union members.
>
> Broadhead, with the connivance of the union committee, used his own methods to discipline both the grinders and the employers.
>
> The second story concerns Isaac Ironside, who formed the Consumers' Gas Company to compete with the established United Gas Company, which was charging too much for its product. Prices came down, although the two companies were ordered by the government to amalgamate, and Ironside went off to throw his enthusiasm into other aspects of civic endeavor, such as sewerage.
>
> [Local author] Alan Cullen's interpretation of these events is studiously based on historical fact, but by using the media of comedy, song, and music hall, these sometimes tragic episodes become family entertainment.

As we watched the play, it was difficult not to think about the parallels with contemporary events implied by the leaflet: the current wave of technical change with information technology, hard times for the unions, the conflicts engendered by forceful union response, as manifest in the miners' strike, and the complicated interrelationships between working-class and middle-class advocates of social change. Expressive culture can open eyes to new perspectives, and the play combined celebration of culture—in this case, local history—with challenging presentations of social issues. When we asked our children on the way home if the play was against violence, our eleven-year-old replied, "Yes and no. It didn't like the violence of the union people, but it also understood that they saw no other way." "Family entertainment" is found in a community theater performance that examines the complexity of regional working-class culture.

Expressive culture involves those forms of activity in which humans strive to portray explicitly what they understand to be the distinctive features of particular events. The intent of such expressive culture may be to celebrate, to denigrate, or merely to contemplate these features. Such moments, in which particular aspects of a group, be they values or situations, are deliberately raised to consciousness through performance, are common to all cultures. In employment social formations, "culture" is most frequently used to refer to expressive culture like *The Stirrings*—"the arts," education, or other nonwork, "play" activities.

Thus the culture constructs actually used by South Yorkshire people reference several different things: general "way of life"; semiotics, including symbols and embedded cultural categories; situational, complex conjunctions of patterns of behavior and social relationships; and expressive, more or less self-conscious performances. In everyday speech, use of a construct in multiple ways is common, probably inevitable, and cultural analysis of the relationship between computing and change in the lives of working people in Sheffield can begin with any of them. Before it can become a prime mode of analysis in computing studies, however, ambiguities in what it means to take a cultural perspective must be eliminated and the analytic and the popular must be connected systematically. We begin by showing the analytic problems that arise when the culture constructs noted above are used in isolation.

### Semiotic Approaches and Semioticist Fallacies

The symbolic type of cultural approach privileges "values," equating culture with cultural constructs (semiotics). The identification of distinct values is an important stage of a group's ethnogenesis. Often invoking the humor of caricature—cloth cap wearing, forelock tugging, ale-drinking, dialect speaking, and so on—such uses identify the traditional with important social values—for example, courage, perseverance, commitment. A graspable identity is created through the use of specific "traditional" symbols, but there is a concomitant tendency to identify any deviation from these symbols as *rejection of* the group identity, for example, as *not* working class. Values are abstracted from the situation in which they are created, and a "semioticized" class construct stresses continuity alone, irrespective of change in the rest of the social formation. Culture as values can justify suppression; by stressing "their right to cultural self-determination," South African whites continue apartheid. Static views of working-class culture mythologize continuing class realities and inhibit development of successful strategies for extended class cultural reproduction.

### Situational Approaches and Situationist Fallacies

Another conception of working-class culture treats it in static situational as op-posed to semiotic terms, but the result is the same: Culture is hypostatized into a metaphysical structure of its own, treated as a mechanical set of reactions com-pelled by unchanging situations. An example is the strategy operative in the min-ers' strike. The outcome of the confrontation was ultimately a matter of which so-cial force, the miners or the national state, had greater power. The miners' difficulties were partly a result of not recognizing the extent to which the relations of class force had changed. Deliberately escalating the application of implicit social power worked to the miners' benefit at Saltley Gate in 1972, but in 1984 and 1985 the government was quite willing to apply stronger forces, more preemptively and in new ways.

The only way to counter such greater social force was the application of new so-cial forces on the side of the miners. In the course of the strike, potential new sources of power—for example, support and miners' wives groups—developed. However, the tactics used by the miners were limited by *traditional* conceptions of class and class power, which meant that the new groups' potential power remained underused.

In mechanistic semiotic or situational views of culture, the role of class in social reproduction tends to be conceived as follows: First, a time in the past when con-scious class action had an impact is identified. Second, a celebration that stresses the class's characteristics at the time of successful action abstracts from time and process. Third, current events are compared to the heroic past and differences be-tween it and the present are explained as deviations, current realities being con-ceived structurally rather than processually. (It is of course difficult to maintain this perspective consistently; cultural contradictions, like those manifest in the "heroes" concert, tend to arise.)

As in the miners' strike, mechanistic fallacies damage agitation. Strategic think-ing is limited to what worked in the past. Even in 1987, trade union strategies tended to presume an expanding economy, as in the most successful periods of Labourism, when it was possible to exchange improvements in terms and condi-tions of work for management control over the labor process. This approach is not likely to be adequate as a strategy in the current conjunction of new technology and transforming economic conditions.

### Expressive Approaches and Expressivist Fallacies

Among the joys of Sheffield as a field site were the numerous opportunities to participate in "expressive culture" linked with the working class. The events that took place, from the playing of the World Snooker Championship to the presenta-tion of *The Stirrings*, broadly reflect the concerns of Sheffield regional working-class culture. Many performances, especially those sponsored by the Sheffield Festival organized by the Council Arts Department, deliberately stressed the interrelationships between art, perception, and the dominant life-style in the city.

The range of events itself says something noteworthy about cultural self-consciousness among working-class Sheffielders. "The Esteli Splash," a benefit for a project to supply the city of Esteli in Nicaragua with a new water supply, involved a range of progressive singers, dancers, and comedians. Two pantomimes—raucous dramatizations of fairy tales—were also produced during our year's field study. One, the annual *Christmas Pantomime,* was one long paean to regional South Yorkshire culture. It featured Bobby Knut, a famous local comedian. The second, *Margarella, the Moles, and the Money Tree,* about Margaret Thatcher, underground miners, and the 1984–1985 strike, was written and produced by strike supporters. The live drama, *Here We Go,* dramatized a strike incident between miners and police in deepest Grimethorpe, South Yorkshire. The play borrowed liberally from the work of Italian Dario Fo and ran for more than three weeks in 1987. *In Deepest Red* portrayed South Yorkshire working-class activists in the period between the wars. One afternoon during the festival, dramatist Stephen Lowe addressed "the importance of imagination as a creative force in a working class society under systematic attack" at a wine and sandwiches session sponsored by the Sheffield Arts Department.

*The Stirrings* was the most complex, and the most satisfying, class portrayal of all the events we observed. Other performances were less successful, victims to a greater or lesser extent of an "expressivist" fallacy, one in which celebration of distinct class symbols leads to abstraction from the contradictions of real social life. "Expressivist" performances (one is tempted to say "ritual") give priority to the correct presentation of the symbol rather than to the understanding of the processes to which the symbol refers. *In Deepest Red,* for example, was close to hagiography, an uncomplicated celebration of traditional working-class virtues peppered with disparaging contemporary parallels (e.g., the nonsupport of the miners by the rest of the Labour movement). *Margarella* ... contained a bit more dramatic dialectic, but this was largely a consequence of the ambivalent attitude communicated toward Arthur Scargill. (The audience responded positively to the caricature of his personal style contained in the performance. This attitude was encouraged by comments before the "panto" began that hinted that having Scargill's personal signature on a book for sale might actually *lessen* its value. The result verged on blaming Scargill personally for the failure of the strike.)

Expressivism follows from the semioticist and situationist fallacies critiqued above. Paradoxically, it was the most "historical" of the expressive culture events, *The Stirrings,* which best avoided the expressivist fallacy. Our eleven-year-old was able to see that the attitude of the play to the events that were its dramatic core was complex. On the one hand, the violent "stirrings" were more than just lamentable: They were condemned by the working-class characters in the play as getting in the way of class solidarity. At the same time, the stirrings were explicated by the play, presented as the only strategy open at the time to the class's primary organizational form, the unions.

As expressive culture, the play both communicates the difficulty of the dilemma of violence and reaffirms the necessity of action in the face of such dilemmas. The values presented are contextualized, not essentialized. The expressive dynamic is broadened to show the links between working-class activism and middle-class concern over public utilities. In this way, the issue of the future of working-class culture, approached within a historical context yet relevant to current options for human action, is itself "expressed" and raised to conscious contemplation.

## Integrative Conceptions of Culture

Ultimately, the most valuable cultural analyses are integrative, tying together elements of all three of these views. This is the approach of Raymond Williams in an important 1958 essay entitled "Culture is Ordinary." In an earlier vignette, Mary, the council team leader, critiques static views that present the working class as disintegrating due to changes imposed on it from the outside. Like Williams, Mary finds continued unity in shared visions of the possible, those that include "dreams of community" as well as shared economic conditions. She finds in culture so conceived something that both explains and supports continuing unity.

In more holistic usage, the culture concept refers to a social totality, a whole "way of life," one in which culture is what happens as semiotic constructs interact in situations with material and physical forces. In some "way-of-life" approaches, primary emphasis is placed on material limitations, whereas in others it is placed on overcoming material limits through action; in either case, culture is capable of both transforming and being transformed. It is this "created" way of life or "culture in action" that underlies Mary's comments about dreams. From another perspective, it is also relevant to the comment of the Jarrow marcher about "the culture which working people deserve."

We have in mind this fourth conception of culture-as-process when we speak of "the reproduction" of a class culture. If Raymond Williams is best at articulating this kind of conception theoretically, the work of Barnsley's own Barry Hines (e.g., *The Gamekeeper* 1979a; *The Price of Coal* 1979b) is particularly successful at expressing it literarily and through television film. It is not surprising that the BBC chose not to show Hines's piece on the miners' strike, despite the fact that the organization itself had commissioned it.

It is such integrative conceptions of culture that are needed in political analysis. An integrative cultural approach combines in a single frame an understanding of the situations people share, the ways they perceive their identities, and their articulations, as in performance, of these things. How they actually live their lives is of course inexplicable without an understanding of the broad contexts within which these lives are lived—the structures of state, political economy, and region.

## Cultural Roots of the Failure of NMS

Labourism, the approach to building socialism that has been the dominant trend in the British working-class movement since 1945, required only the periodic involvement of most working-class people, such as their voting and participating in strikes that did not involve the public sector. NMS rejected this part of the Labourist perspective, calling instead for active worker participation in decisions regarding investment, labor processes, and so on, an involvement in production very different from that of traditional adversarial Labourism.

Participatory, popular planning was also contradictory to more traditional bureaucratic notions of the role of planning in the building of socialism. Worker participation in the direction of enterprise and citizen participation in forming policy both require a more proactive working class. A different working-class culture, one involving a high enough level of shared consciousness to allow for rapid changes in tactics, a more political, less mechanistic culture, was a prerequisite of NMS.

The Sheffield experience suggests that this higher level of participation cannot be forced or finessed; it must be actively developed. One important block to such development was the use of the same static "them versus us" semiotics of class difference explored above. Hanging over from Labourism was a permanent separation, for example, between the "working-class" service recipient and the "middle-class" council program officer. This was particularly evident during the Sheffield housing strike, when the National Association of Local Government Officers (NALGO), the organization of the striking workers, was described by some councilors as "not a real union" because its membership was "middle class." The kind of flexible, sophisticated union response to challenges required by an NMS policy depended on using the analytic and conceptual skills in which teachers, program officers, and technicians are trained. Equally important were the solidarity and collectivity experienced and promoted by both manufacturing and "pink-collar" sectors of the working class.

Only a small proportion of left thought continues to deny the existence of extensive sea changes in working-class culture and consciousness. The fundamental differentiation in the contemporary British left is concerned with whether existing trade union and Labour Party structures, based on a "traditional" conception of the working class, are sufficient to attract the support of a changed populace, or whether new organizational structures based on appeals to different self-conceptions are needed. Like Albert the computer programmer, another long-time Labour Party activist has difficulty shifting his perspective: "The concept of Local Authorities becoming vehicles for economic revival got lost as you got further away from the industrial base of the Party. As Labour was not in power [nationally], other factors were introduced, such as women's rights, gay issues, etc.,— legitimate in themselves, but clouding the original thrust."

It may be accurate to see economic revival as the goal of new municipal socialism. However, popular mobilization, the mechanism through which revival was to be achieved, was just as essential. If, because of changing relations of power, the industrial base is not able to be sufficiently mobilized or, even if mobilized, is not a source of sufficient social force on its own—new appeals have to be made. In part because of increased unemployment, it is necessary to recognize the varied character of the contemporary working class, the necessity to mobilize all of the insecure, whether waged or labor-free.

Another problem of NMS, also traceable to fallacious cultural constructs, was lack of clarity over basic goals. As described by the program officers quoted in Chapter 10, goals were articulated differently in different contexts: restructuring the local economy radically in order to serve the needs of the working class; mobilizing the working class by involving it more actively in the defense of services; and probing the limits of reform within a capitalist economy. As discussion raged over what to do about a program that *strengthened* capital, not merely *aided* its simple reproduction (and thereby weakened the working class), it became increasingly difficult to find resolution in older conceptions of the working class as unified and industrial.

Structures for popular planning should have provided answers to such questions, but it was difficult to balance the need for *authentic* participation with the need for a unified strategy in the face of a hostile national state. Such questions have obvious parallels in Eastern Europe. The failure to resolve them got in the way of policy implementation, as in SPRITE discussions of politics.

## NIT and Ethnogenesis Among the Labor-Free

Like Mary, we wish to bring an integrative cultural analysis to computing studies. In 1987 Sheffield people perceived being "out of work" as having much to do with new information technology. Computers are a palpable (and for some, more palatable) symbol of a new social formation, one in which the basic social relationship is no longer the wage, because wage labor has ceased to be the most important means of creating a social surplus. In discussing "Plans for the Future," the *Dearne Report* comments: "Informal discussions with unemployed men and women have also revealed that they have an interest in information technology and in acquiring computer skills" (p. 58).

The first vignette showed what students hope to get: more encouragement for skills training in NIT, more higher education in general, better leisure services, and a shorter working week, leading to more jobs. These views are more computopian than compputropian. From the perspective of "the computer as Rorschach" (Turkle 1980), these students are using the computer to fashion a collective vision of an alternative future around freedom from wages, a future with both more jobs and more leisure.

These students wish to use new information technology as an aid to constructing the new world and new morality they seek. Is it possible for computerization to be a positive, humane process? Boyson and other Thatcherite ministers might recoil in horror at Marge Brandon's "invitation to an orgy," and some academic researchers might, like Lewis, label her expressions of defiance "an inversion of values." In Sheffield her comment was responded to differently, as a statement of belief in the continuing vitality of her class.

Thus, when young working-class people in South Yorkshire eschew "traditional" working-class identities and create new ones centering on computers, they are not automata driven by a technological imperative. They are best understood as active participants in the creation of computing culture, their actions making most sense when viewed in cultural terms. The connections being more cultural than technological, the results of their actions are often unanticipated because understanding of the computing/social change connection is often misdirected. In this regard at least, NMS succeeded in directing attention to issues that must be confronted if a nonmechanistic working-class politics is to be discovered.

## Simplistic Concepts of Culture and Computerization

The working class itself was not the only object of misleading cultural practice. In working-class performances and in public political speeches, computing appeared as an entity abstracted from context and treated as independent. As in the *Morning Star* poster described in Chapter 7, computers appeared at the symbolic margins as objects of dark humor, compputropian symbols of a clouded future. Even within progressive computerization activities like the SPRITE weekend school, trade union and political activists often began presentations with a ritualistic statement of their personal ignorance and suspicion of computers. The formulaic quality of such performances suggests roots in mechanistic views of culture. They manifest a static view of the daily lives of working-class people, one in which people's actions are seen as effectively determined by external conditions alone.

The consistently expressivist construction of computing is linked to the failure of unions to respond proactively to computerization. All the fallacious approaches we have described separate culture from technology. In Chapter 7, however, we argued that the nature of technology varies from social formation to social formation. The regularization of practice that we know as technology comes in different forms, each of which has emerged at a different point in history. Productive, abstract, repressive, and machine technologies each have their own relatively distinct dialectic, a consequence of the place of each in relation to the reproduction of the particular social formations of which they are a part. Computerization is manifest in each of these domains of technology.

As a process with its own "relative autonomy," (Burrawoy 1979), computerization is important new terrain over which various social groups are struggling to accomplish their basic goals. The government of Margaret Thatcher, for example, made explicit its determination to eliminate socialism from the British social landscape, just as it branded striking miners "the enemies within." Its activist, uneconomic use of computerization in mining and social service, while abandoning or undercutting programs for computerization in education and research, only makes sense in relation to its broader political agenda. Equally, trade unions and local labor groups in such areas as Sheffield have had great difficulty even articulating their policy objectives with regard to computerization, let alone attaining them, because other industrial relations or political goals or structures have had higher priority. Similarly, change in gendering is related profoundly to technology; this may be the cultural point of the story about computing studies putting hair on girls' chests.

Yet in advocating a cultural approach to computerization, we also assert that one can't understand structure without understanding action. New technology is no more to be understood as some external political economic determinant than as an external technological one: How working people consciously conceive of themselves, how they perceive the world, and how they experience their lives are also important to the creation of computer culture.

## Cultural Approaches and Computer Science

Although computers are not a juggernaut technology, changing all before them, neither should they be seen as a contentless medium, a vessel shaped primarily by other social forces. Though computerization is often associated with deskilling, disemploying, and antiwomen results, more positive and successful examples of the uses of computers are discernible in areas of cooperative work in which hierarchies are diminished in favor of shared skills. One can find in Sheffield some important examples of progressive computerization, as with Traffic Systems Co-op and the SPRITE, where the character of computerization has been affected clearly by policy. This reality runs counter to the ideology of the male authoritarian and hierarchical image of the computer scientist or the individualist image of the computer hacker.

One can now begin to discern the outlines of a cultural approach to computing (Hakken 1991b). Anthropologists like Lucy Suchman, for example, have developed a critique of the reductionist, rationalist models of human practice that dominate cognitive science (1987). She argues instead for ethnographically based models of information activity and for developing an anthropological theory to provide a more effective basis for computerization. Sociolinguistic perspectives are integrated into network systems recently developed by Winograd (1987) and his computer science colleagues at Stanford.

Still, such perspectives have yet to come to prominence. Although not necessarily unmindful of the broader consequences of computerization, computer professionals have tended to ignore the broader consequences of computing, concentrating instead on the technological/engineering problems at hand. System designers were taught to see any negative correlates of computing as due to muddle-headed social policy or anachronistic tradition. Unpleasant results were labeled unintended "by-products" of technology, to be engineered out after the basic design phase is over.

Yet as we indicated in our introduction, some voices (e.g., Kling 1974; Weizenbaum 1975) were raised against such narrowly technicist, "machine-centered" perspectives. When the pace of the spread of computerization failed to reach expected levels (e.g., as with robotization—see Hunt and Hunt 1983), more computer professionals (e.g., Emery 1982) began to acknowledge that sociocultural factors had to be dealt with more directly and effectively. Adequately complex sociocultural models had to be developed and integrated into system development.

It is by now standard practice among computer professionals to acknowledge that some attention should be given to nonmachine or "human" factors in information system development. For a variety of reasons, the full implications of accommodating computing to a sociocultural perspective are being worked out only slowly among technologists (Hakken 1991a). In general, human factors approaches are conceived within the framework of individualistic psychology, as relevant primarily at the level of the physical individual rather than that of the social group. This is particularly true of ergonomic studies (e.g., Tijerina 1984). Alternately, human factors are presented as relevant to only a part of the system development process—for instance, implementation trials—rather than throughout the entire system development and implementation process. Systems approaches like structural systems design (Long 1986) and the sociotechnical approach (Mumford and Weir 1979) attempt to include system users more fully. The former is flawed by its tendency to deal with users only as individuals. The latter recognizes the importance of the organizational culture into which the information system is being introduced, but it tends to treat the organization as a given, ignoring the way in which diverse class, cultural, and political economic structures affect the reproduction of the organization and therefore how any particular system is implemented.

A few computer professionals have taken a broad approach more consistently. Niels Bjorn-Andersen argues that system support is not just a matter of supporting "the individual user and his/her machine" but involves providing "information support to groups and collectives rather than individuals" (1986:65). He conceives of system development as a *sociocultural* process, one of which system design is only a part. Bjorn-Andersen is one of several Fenno-Scandians (e.g., Nygaard 1983; Bjerknes, Ehn, and Kyng 1987; Ehn 1988) who practice a "socio-technical" approach in their own technical system development work.

The weaknesses, strengths, and ambiguities of the current situation among computer professionals are well reflected in Shackel's "Ergonomics in Design for Usability" (1986). Shackel initially casts the human dimension of the system development process in mechanical and individualistic terms: "[T]he first process ... is to define the system aims and the various functions needed to achieve those aims and then to examine and decide which functions within the whole system should be assigned to human elements and which to machine elements. ... [S]uch factors as cost, weight, size, reliability, safety, and efficiency must be assessed and compared" (p. 45) in order to find "the optimum fit of the people to the jobs" as part of "setting limits within which humans can be used" (p. 51).

After initial use of such mechanistic terminology, Shackel goes on to use very different language to discuss the features of the "Design for Usability" that he advocates. Among these features are:

1. user-centered design, which is based on study of who the users are and their tasks, study "requiring direct contact with users at their place of work and learning their tasks";
2. participative design, in which "a panel of users should work closely with the design team, especially during the early formulation stages";
3. experimental design, in which users actually use prototypes of the system for real work;
4. iterative design, in which difficulties identified by experimental users are corrected through as many redesign steps as are necessary; and
5. user-supportive design, in which user supports are included all through the system development process, not just at the end through help-screens, and so forth (pp. 57–58).

Two very different conceptualizations of the role of humans in information systems, one mechanical, one humanistic, underlie the two parts of Shackel's argument. He does not address how these two views are to be reconciled, and his argument appears almost schizophrenic.

The current practice of computer professionals illustrates a broad consensus that an integrative approach to system development is desirable but an absence of consensus over *how* to blend sociocultural considerations into system development. Discussion of this issue is only slowly benefiting from attention to data from the empirical social scientific study of the social correlates of computerization. Although information on the social correlates of computerization has accumulated, differences in tactics and strategies have complicated its use, as have continuing ambiguities about exactly what it means to take a broader approach to computerization. Still, at least some computer professionals (e.g., various authors in Briefs et al. 1983) look increasingly to collaboration with social scientists for the knowledge with which to build computer systems that are fully cognizant of human social process. Moreover, there is an increasing awareness among social scientists and computer professionals of the extensive room for collaboration in computer system development.

## The Sheffield Research and Computing Studies

At least in part, broader acceptance of the cultural perspective depends on clear demonstration that computing based on it is feasible on a wide scale. Conclusions about feasibility based on a single field study are necessarily tentative; much remains to be learned from culturally informed efforts in other field sites. Nonetheless, we feel that several conclusions follow from our examination of computing in Sheffield. First, computer systems work better when conscious attention is given to the broad cultural dynamics within which they are embedded. Second, the existence of projects like these show that culture-centered computing is feasible, even in regions that lack the supporting local environment manifest in Sheffield. Third, a more sophisticated general awareness of the potential implications of computerization, and a commitment to influencing these implications in line with articulated policy objectives, can encourage the spread into popular consciousness of less mythical, more instrumental attitudes to computing. A proactive attitude toward computerization underlies the views of many individuals presented in vignettes throughout our book.

Culture-centered computing is self-conscious, and proactive approaches to computing are best encouraged when the information task at hand is approached critically. Our research on culture-centered computing suggests the following activities should become regular parts of developing a new information system:

1. Early on, a thorough analysis of the actual activities of the organization for which a system is intended should be instituted. Often this will require interviews with people at all levels of the organization, as well as direct observation of work processes, in order to separate organizational myth from reality. For example, if the organization is a for-profit enterprise, it is essential to understand the specific nature of the labor process within it and the extent to which this process is shaped by broader social forces. The frank involvement of all participants in the work process, especially direct producers, is essential.

2. Similarly, a critical analysis of the information activities and needs of the organization should be developed, including collection of data on how current information practices developed historically. Because of the danger of presuming that the best solutions are technological—that is, the technicist "dazzle" effect—it is often first necessary to formulate information needs independent of computer options.

3. Consideration of technology options should be separated from initial analysis of information needs. Often, such consideration requires education and hands-on experience with new systems. For "dazzle" reasons, it is important that those providing such "computer literacy" training have no self-interest in the options from which choices must eventually be made.

4. Finally, and most importantly, a collective, collaborative perspective on the nature of the organization and the interests of those within it should be developed. This involves reaching an understanding of the broader social dynamics within which individuals and organizations develop particular patterns and choose goals and the strategies for achieving them. Particular

attention needs to be given to the class cultures within which individuals participate and the existing class strategies among which they can choose, since these have great influence over individual choices and eventual group dynamics.

These activities would build upon the procedures contained in the second part of Shackel's "Ergonomics" that we described above. Shackel's list is essentially chronological, suggesting the various steps that need to be taken at the appropriate time. Our list of implications from culture-centered computing projects aims to make explicit the underlying objective of the procedures involved. In an important sense, neither list can be considered complete. First, though they express goals, the appropriate methods to attain them are not adequately articulated. Second, the extent to which specific historical, national, class, and ethnic factors influence the course of information system development in each particular place means that a search for "one best approach" to culture-centered computing is futile. Nonetheless, further comparative research can help identify the kinds of factors that are important to take into account in most system development.

In effect, three options with regard to "the cultural dimension" confront the system developer: (1) to try to ignore the cultural context, in which case broader structures and processes will impact information system development in unplanned and frequently disruptive ways; (2) to select priorities other than information and knowledge maximization, as with the United Kingdom national government's approach to computerization in the mining industry; or (3) to approach the contexts of computing proactively, as in many of the Sheffield cases.

## Culture-Centered Computing and Microcomputer Technology

The spread of microcomputing has altered the course of computerization. Yet the microcomputer is not an example of technology determining information practice. As argued by Siegal (1986), the radical decentralization made possible by the microcomputer was the outcome of a deliberate attempt by computer professionals to develop information system technology with the potential to empower people rather than big institutions.

In fact, microcomputer technology substantially increases the possibilities for culture-centered computing. The Sheffield data suggest a sociocultural perspective on information system development that complements the flexible potential of microcomputing machinery. Additional study of culture-centered computerization will lead both to broader knowledge of successful techniques and to closer specification of the social and political contexts most conducive to successful development of information systems. The progressive local authority computer policies and the culture-centered computerization projects described in Chapter 11 were created by people who tried to develop a positive working-class politics of computerization. These politics contain an awareness of and concern for the impacts that new information technologies might have, as well as optimism about what policy could accomplish. The economic depression and a hostile, powerful national state placed limits on what was actually attained, but they do not mean that action was pointless, and they certainly do not invalidate humanistic policy goals.

Efforts such as those of cities like Sheffield can be viewed as social "experiments," attempts to bring about change that are based on a developed model of contemporary social practice. As such, the experiments provide substantial evidence against which to test the promises of computopians and the fears of compputropians. Such attempts to influence computerization through regional democratic institutions, from county government to the computer club, also serve as a cultural beacon, offering vivid images of how computerization can aid creation of a more humane society. This is only likely to happen in the context of an integrative, broadly cultural approach to computerization. Such concepts as "socially responsible production" and "broad participation in decisionmaking" provide a positive basis for a truly universal futurist strategy.

The course of computerization is not determined by technology but *through* social reproduction. Reproduction is a process subject to both structural constraint and human action. To the extent to which computerization is viewed processually (as reproduced on an extended scale) and in accurate detail, its effects on social formation reproduction can be influenced and the quality of human life can be enhanced. "Computer culture" will exist in the fullest sense, as a true human social formation, when people who use computers have developed sufficient means to have conscious influence over the way computers spread.

The following propositions summarize what we learned about computerization from research in Sheffield:

1.  Computers as a technology, as this term is normally used, are not the primary cause of the substantial changes in the nature of jobs and social life in Sheffield. Though involved in several major changes, computer technology is only one of several, structural and/or processual, implicated factors.
2.  Preexisting structures of the state, political economy, and region, which can be taken together to constitute class, constrain the course of computerization. The contours of computered society are determined in the interaction between such class constraints and responses to them. For example, despite the loss of the miners' strike, disruption continues in both NUM and non-NUM areas. Most frequently, these actions center on introduction of the new technology; indeed, NUM staffers argue that it might have been possible to maintain unity during the strike had its focus been on the technology as opposed strictly on pit closures.
3.  Further, computerization as a legitimating, mythological and/or ideological process is highly implicated in Sheffield social change. Interpretations of

computerization—such as the notion that traditional forms of trade union struggle are an anachronism in an information age—justify a broad range of social initiatives. Such interpretations, though based more on ideology than on careful research and examination, have wide impacts. Consequently, analysis of computerization must give attention to what the technology is perceived as doing as well as to what it does.

4. Although the computerization policy efforts of the Sheffield District Council have not had a major economic impact, such policies and programs do affect how people think of and act in relation to computers. New technology programs have clarified what integrative computerization policy can accomplish and how to implement the approach more effectively in the future.

5. As with all humans searching for new identities, what working-class people do about computing has much in common with what they used to do. Paradoxically, it is the very cultural rather than technological character of these connections that provides the space for action and even transformation, as well as reaction and adaptation.

In sum, despite the numerous inconsistencies to which we drew attention in Chapter 1, Sheffield workers belief in the importance of new information technology is essentially correct: There are indeed significant connections between computing and the changes in working-class life that we have described.

## Computerization and Future Policy

In her articulation of a "best case" view of computerization, Shoshona Zuboff (1988) coins the phrase, "to informate." She uses this to refer to those situations in which computerization makes a positive contribution to what we call social formation reproduction. "To informate" or "inform" a particular aspect of social life, then, is to create a humane computer culture. It is appropriate that we end our discussion of computerization with what we learned in Sheffield about how to "informate" South Yorkshire:

1. The most important political task is to find ways to mobilize not just the "traditional" but also the "insecure" working class. These include: those in jobs whose continuation cannot be normally assumed; those in marginal jobs; those looking for jobs; and those who are insecure and not looking for jobs, for whatever reason—from discouragement to those with life roles generally incompatible with employment (e.g., that of "child"). As Chapter 14 suggested, these groups may be more successfully mobilized around multiple cooperative strategies to provide social security than through a stress on the re-creation of jobs alone.

2. Such insecurity already characterizes the situation of the bulk of the population, and it is a condition likely to spread. Future economic growth, to the

extent that it is based on computerization, is unlikely to change this situation but will likely reinforce it. As people adapt to and challenge this condition, basic characteristics of life-style change and new patterns become the
norm. Through studying the adaptations and challenges of those already
living the future, we come to perceive the dynamics of future social organization as well as to increase our prospects for effective social self-
mobilization.

3. "Informating" the working-class movement may itself play a significant
part in solving the crisis manifest in increasing wage-labor freedom. First,
this may come about through experiences with new information technology
that undermine narrow, sectional, ideological uses of computerization.
Informating can demythologize computerization in many ways, such as
undermining ideological justifications for the necessity of alienating labor.
Second, computerization has potential for helping wage-labor-free groups
and individuals identify more effective personal and group strategies
through revealing alternatives. Third, computerization can contribute to the
development of a proactive and truly postemployment culture.

## Conclusion

In Sheffield, the strong history of working-class culture and consciousness can
continue to be an important means through which a large group of people is able
to influence social formation reproduction for their mutual benefit. The effectiveness of popular institutions—the Employment Department, the Labour Party, the
women's movement, and so forth—depends on the extent to which their strategy
is based on a view of class that is dialectical. An appropriately cultural strategy
could provide working-class people the means to participate actively in creating
the world of computing. In such a strategy, worker education is of increased importance. As the "labor-free workers" of this chapter show, computers present a
powerful image of a future society in which humans don't waste their time in repetitive production of either subsistence or profit. It is by specifying real work
practices to replace the pseudowork of alienated labor, and by providing new positive postlabor identities, that the study of computerization can suggest a positive
way forward for human culture.

In this volume we have developed a broadly cultural approach to computerization. We have explained how the problem of computerization is at base as much
cultural as technological. Such a recognition places a responsibility on, as well as
provides an opportunity for, anthropologists to apply their knowledge of culture
to programs to develop progressive forms of computing.

Computer systems informed by a cultural perspective are often useful in and of
themselves in that they result in more effective as well as more humane information systems. Involvement in the development of such programs is important for
another reason: As in Sheffield, they can have a positive impact on the symbolic

content or meaning of computerization as well. The symbolism of computing is implicated in, among other things, the way working-class people in Sheffield are trying to forge a new identity. If they master computers, learning to use them to pursue their own objectives, this may support the maintenance of a viable oppositional culture as long as necessary into the future. Such computer use would indeed transcend the social relations of wage-labor. Only such a development would constitute a real opening to "postindustrial" civilization.

## Notes

1. Hiring wage or salary labor for the production of commodities remains central to the accumulation of capital, and capital/labor remains the dominant social relationship in contemporary social formations. The institutions of employment continue to mediate the reproduction of the broader regional, national, and international social formations that they inhabit. Another alternative term, following Marx more closely, would be "wage slavery-free." Just as the notion "wage slave" demystifies the notion of free labor (not really "free" because compelled to sell its labor power), so "wage slavery-free" draws attention to the absence of a compulsion to sell labor power, thereby suggesting that there might be something positive about the situation. Unfortunately, the term's "double negative" quality makes it too opaque for analytic purposes.

2. There is much to recommend "the working class" as a label for all of the insecure. Whether laboring or labor-free, working-class people do increasing amounts of work outside of wage labor. The term "working class" also draws attention to a major social fault line discussed in Chapter 7, the division between those relatively secure because of the nature of their employment (the "middle class") and the insecure "working class." This still allows one to distinguish both of these groups from those with secure nonemployment access to wealth. The main problem with "the working class" as a term is the difficulty of dissociating "working" from being "in employment."

3. The view that unemployment is temporary or unusual may be a consequence of abstracting thinking about the political economies of overdeveloping core nations from those of underdeveloping peripheral ones. The illusory kind of security manifest in Sheffield in the mid-1970s has been greatly dissipated by the 1980s, and a good case could be made that conditions in major parts of the overdeveloping world are becoming much more like those in the underdeveloping areas.

4. The national government was quick to take credit for the slight decline in unemployment that took place during 1987. However, much of the decline in unemployment is reflected in an increase in the number of people "economically inactive." The proportion of people of working age who were considered active had declined from 75.1 percent in 1979 to 70.0 percent in 1987.

5. There are fascinating parallels between the way that culture of poverty theory came to be applied to the culture of black urbanites in the United States by such authors as Daniel Patrick Moynihan (1965) and the sociolinguistic theories that Basil Bernstein applied to the British working class. The latter, according to Bernstein, are handicapped in their competition in school with middle-class children by their "restricted codes."

# Bibliography

Althusser, Louis. 1971. *Lenin and Philosophy.* London: New Left Books.

———. 1977. *For Marx.* London: New Left Books.

Andrews, Barbara, and Hakken, David. 1976. "Educational Technology: A Theoretical Approach." *College English* 39(1): 68–108.

Ardron, Alan. 1986. "Information Technology Strategy." Sheffield: Information Technology Panel (Policy), Sheffield District Council.

Attewell, Paul. n.d., ca. 1985. *The Deskilling Controversy.* Stony Brook: Department of Sociology, SUNY.

Attewell, Paul, and Rule, James. 1984. "Computing and Organizations: What We Know and What We Don't." *Communications of the ACM* 27:1184–1192.

Barratt Brown, Michael. 1972. *From Labourism to Socialism.* Nottingham: Spokesman Books.

Barron, Iann, and Curnow, Ray. 1979. *The Future with Micro-electronics.* Milton Keynes, United Kingdom: Open University Press.

Beattie, Geoffrey. 1986. *Survivors of Steel City: A Portrait of Sheffield.* London: Chatto and Windus.

Bell, Daniel. 1973. *The Coming of Post-Industrial Society.* New York: Basic.

Bennington, John. 1985. "Local Economic Initiatives." *Local Government Studies* 2(5):1–8.

———. 1986. "Local Economic Strategies: Paradigms for a Planned Economy?" *Local Economy* 1:7–24.

Benson, Ian, and Lloyd, John. 1983. *New Technology and Industrial Change: The Impact of The Scientific-Technical Revolution on Labour and Industry.* London: Kogan Page.

Berg, Ivar, ed. 1981. *Sociological Perspectives on Labor Markets.* New York: Academic.

Bernal, J.D. 1965. *Science in History.* London: C.A. Watts.

Bernard, H. Russell, and Pelto, Perti. 1986. *Technology and Social Change.* Prospect Heights, Ill.: Waveland.

Bernstein, Basil. 1971. *Class, Codes, and Control.* New York: Shocken Books.

Best, M. 1984. Summary of "Human Aspects of Computer Based Monitoring and Control Mining Operations," pp. 15–19. In Anon., ed. *Results from Community Ergonomics Action Projects.* Sheffield: National Union of Mineworkers.

Bewsher, Jim. 1987. "Working Men ... Working Lives" Presentation at the "Men and Women: Working Together" Conference, Islington.

Bhasker, Roy. 1979. *The Possibility of Naturalism.* London: Harvester.

———. 1989. *Reclaiming Reality: A Critical Introduction to Contemporary Philosophy.* London: Verso.

Bijker, Wiebe; Hughes, Thomas; and Pinch, Trevor; eds. 1987. *The Social Construction of Technological Systems.* Cambridge: MIT Press.

Bjerknes, Gro; Ehn, Pelle; and Kyng, Morten; eds. 1987. *Computers and Democracy: A Scandinavian Challenge.* Aldershot: Avebury.

Bjorn-Andersen, Niels. 1986. "Understanding the Nature of the Office for the Design of Third Wave Office Systems," pp. 65–77. In M.D. Harrison and A.F. Monk, eds., *People and Computers: Design for Usability.* Cambridge: Cambridge University Press.

Bjorn-Andersen, Niels; Mumford, Enid; and Novotny, Helga; eds. 1982. *Information Society: For Richer, for Poorer.* Amsterdam: North Holland.

Blauner, Robert. 1964. *Alienation and Freedom.* Chicago: University of Chicago Press.

Blim, Michael. 1988. "Hegemony and Development: The Role of the State in Post-War Italian Development." Paper presented to the Ninety-First Annual Meeting, American Anthropological Association, Phoenix, Ariz.

Blunkett, David. n.d., ca. 1981. "Alternative Economic Policies: A Socialist Local Government Response." Sheffield: Labour Group, Sheffield District Council.

Blunkett, David, and Green, Geoff. 1983. *Building from the Bottom: The Sheffield Experience.* London: Fabian Society.

Boddy, Martin, and Fudge, Colin. 1984. *Local Socialism?* London: Macmillan.

Bourdieu, Pierre. 1978. *Outline of a Theory of Practice.* Cambridge: Cambridge University Press.

Braverman, Harry. 1974. *Labor and Monopoly Capital: The Degradation of Work in the Twentieth Century.* New York: Monthly Review.

Briefs, U.; Cibrolla, Paulo; and Schneider, Leslie; eds. 1983. *Systems Design: For, with, and by the User.* Amsterdam: North Holland.

BSSRS (British Society for Social Responsibility in Science) Technology of Political Control Group. 1985. *TechnoCop: New Police Technologies.* London: Free Association Books.

Burns, Bernard. 1985. *The Impact of New Technology on Job Design and Work Organization.* Sheffield: Sheffield University MRC/SAPU.

Burrawoy, Michael. 1979. *Manufacturing Consent.* Chicago: University of Chicago Press.

Burrows, Roger. 1987. "Some Notes Toward a Realistic Realism." Paper presented to the British Sociological Association Conference on Science, Technology, and Society, Leeds University.

Carniero, Robert. 1970. "How Did the State Evolve?" *Science* 169:733–738.

Cassell, Catherine, and Fitter, Mike. 1987. "The Impact of Organizational Characteristics on Computer Education in Community Centres: An Evaluation." Sheffield: Sheffield University SAPU Memo No. 834.

Central Policy Unit. 1986. "Sheffield: Putting You in the Picture." Sheffield: Sheffield District Council.

Chambers, Erve. 1985. *Applied Anthropology: A Practical Guide.* Englewood Cliffs: Prentice-Hall.

Clarke, Alan. 1987. *The Rise and Fall of the Socialist Republic: A History of South Yorkshire County Council.* Sheffield: Sheaf Publishing.

Clawson, Dan. 1980. *Bureaucracy and the Labor Process.* New York: Monthly Review.

Clifford, James, and Marcus, George E., eds. 1986. *Writing Culture: The Poetics and the Politics of Ethnography.* Berkeley: University of California Press.

Cockburn, Cynthia. 1977. *The Local State.* London: Pluto.

_____ . 1985. *Machinery of Dominance: Women, Men, and Technical Know-How.* London: Pluto.

_____. 1987. "Working Men ... Working Lives" Presentation at the "Men and Women: Working Together" Conference, Islington.

Cole, G.D.H. 1973. *Workshop Organization.* London: Hutchinson.

Cole, Pam; Ellis, Ed; and Grayson, John. 1986. *Annual Report 1985–1986; Dearne Valley Project.* Barnsley: Northern College.

Conference of Socialist Economists Micro-electronics Group. 1980. *Micro-electronics: Capitalist Technology and the Working Class.* London: CSE Books.

Cooley, Mike. 1982. *Architect or Bee?: The Human/Technology Relationship.* Boston: South End Press.

Coontz, Stephanie, and Henderson, P. 1986. *Women's Work, Men's Property: The Origins of Gender and Class.* London: Verso.

Cornes, Deirdre. 1986. "Retail Boom in Steel City.*" Chartered Surveyor Weekly,* 20 November.

Curran, Ken. 1986. *Rotherham in Crisis: Determining the Future.* Wakefield, South Yorkshire: National Union of Public Employees.

Darwin, John. 1982. "City of Sheffield Employment Department." Sheffield: Sheffield District Council.

_____. 1983. "Review of the Work in the First Year." Sheffield: Department of Employment and Economic Development.

_____. 1987a. "Property-Led Versus Employment-Led Development Strategies." Brighton: Brighton Technology Conference.

_____. 1987b. "Economic Development: Value, Wealth, and Job Creation." Sheffield: John Darwin.

_____. 1989. *The Enterprise Society: Regional Policy and National Strategy.* Manchester: Centre for Local Economic Strategies.

Darwin, John; Fitter, Mike; Fryer, David; and Smith, Leigh. 1985. "Developing Information Technology in the Community with Unwaged Groups." Presented to Aarhus Conference on Development and Use of Computer-based Systems and Tools.

Dearne Valley Project. 1986. *Annual Report 1985–1986.* Barnsley: Northern College.

Department of Employment and Economic Development, Sheffield (DEED). 1983. *Women in Sheffield: In Work, Out of Work.* Pamphlet.

_____. 1986. *Industrial Decline in Sheffield: Where Will We Be in* 1990? Pamphlet.

_____. 1987. *The Retail Revolution: Who Benefits?* Pamphlet.

Dertouzos, Michael, and Moses, Joel, eds. 1979. *The Computer Age: A Twenty-Year View.* Cambridge: MIT Press.

Dobrianov, V. 1986. "A Paradigm for Assessment of Technological Impact on Society." In Lina Zhiansks and Maya Dimitrova, eds., *Society and Social Change.* Sofia: Svyat Publishers.

Draper, Hal. 1977. *Karl Marx's Theory of Revolution: Volume One: State and Bureaucracy.* New York: Monthly Review.

Dunford, Michael. 1987. (Untitled) Paper on Grenoble, France, presented at the Technology Conference, Brighton, England.

Ehn, Pelle. 1988. *Work-Oriented Design of Computer Artifacts.* Stockholm: Almquist and Witsell.

Ellul, Jacques. 1964. *The Technological Society.* New York: Alfred A. Knopf.

Elster, Jon. 1983. *Explaining Technical Change.* Cambridge: Cambridge University Press.

Emery, J. 1982. "The Promise and Problems of Computer Technology," pp. 23–27. In W. Michael Hoffman and Jennifer Mills, eds., *Ethics in the Management of Computer Technology.* Cambridge, Mass.: Oelgeschlager, Gunn, and Law.

Evans, Peter; Rueschemeyer, Dietrich; and Skocpol, Theda; eds. 1985. *Bringing the State Back In.* New York: Cambridge University Press.

Feldberg, Roslyn, and Glenn, Evelyn N. 1983. "Technology and Work Degradation: Effects of Office Automation on Women Clerical Workers," pp. 59–78. In Joan Rothschild, ed., *Machina ex Dea: Feminist Perspectives on Technology.* New York: Pergamon.

Field, John. 1985. "The Unmaking of the English Working Class? Socio-Economic Change in South Yorkshire and Derbyshire." Paper presented to the Community Education and Unemployment Conference, Belfast.

Fitter, Mike, and Garber, Bob. 1987. "General Practice at the Crossroads." SAPU Memo No. 846. Sheffield: MRC/ESRC Social and Applied Psychology Unit, Sheffield University.

Forester, Tom, ed. 1985. *The Information Technology Revolution.* Cambridge: MIT Press.

Fothergill, Stephen, and Vincent, Jill. 1985. *The State of the Nation: An Atlas of Britain in the Eighties.* London: Pan Books.

Frates, Jeffery, and Molderup, William. 1983. *Computers and Life: An Integrative Approach.* Engelwood Cliffs: Prentice-Hall.

Friedrichs, Gunter, and Schaff, Adam. 1982. *Micro-electronics and Society: A Report to the Club of Rome.* New York: New American Library.

Gailey, Christine. 1987. "Culture Wars: Resistance to State Formation." pp. 35–56. In Thomas C. Patterson and Christine Gailey, eds., *Power Relations and State Formation.* Washington, D.C.: American Anthropological Association.

Garfinkel, Harold. 1984. *Studies in Ethnomethodology.* Cambridge: Polity Press.

Geertz, Clifford. 1973. *The Interpretation of Cultures.* New York: Basic.

Giddens, Anthony. 1986. *Development in Sociological Theory.* Palo Alto: Stanford University Press.

Gill, Colin. 1985. *Work, Unemployment, and the New Technology.* Cambridge: Polity Press.

Glenn, Natalie, and Feldberg, Roz. 1979. "Proletarianizing Clerical Work: Technology and Organizational Control in the Office," pp. 51–72. In A. Zimbalist, ed., *Case Studies on the Labor Process.* New York: Monthly Review Press.

Goffman, Erving. 1959. *The Presentation of Self in Everyday Life.* Garden City: Doubleday Anchor.

Goodwin, M., and Duncan, S. 1986. "The Local State and Local Economic Policy." *Capital and Class* 27:14–36.

Gordon, David; Edwards, Richard; and Reich, Michael. 1982. *Segmented Work, Divided Workers.* Cambridge: Cambridge University Press.

Gorz, Andre. 1982. *Farewell to the Working Class.* London: Pluto.

————. 1985. *Paths to Paradise.* London: Pluto.

Gramsci, Antonio. 1971. *From the Prison Notebooks.* London: Lawrence and Wishart.

Groenfeldt, Janet, and Kandrup, Susanne. 1985. "Women, Work, and Computerization, or 'Still Dancing After All These Years,'" pp. 205–221. In A. Olerup, L. Schneider, and E. Monod, eds., *Women, Work, and Computerization: Opportunities and Disadvantages.* North Holland: Elsevier.

Gutman, Herbert. 1977. *Work, Culture, and Society in Industrializing America.* New York: Random House.

Hakken, David. 1978. *Workers' Education: The Reproduction of Working Class Culture in Sheffield, England and "Really Useful Knowledge."* Ann Arbor: University Microfilms (Ph.D. diss.).

_____. 1980. "Workers' Education and the Reproduction of Working Class Culture." *Anthropology and Education Quarterly* 11(4):211–234.

_____. 1983. "Impacts of Liberation Pedagogy." *Journal of Education* 165(1):113–125.

_____. 1985. "Class and Computers: The Reproduction of Working Class Culture and New Information Technology (NSF Grant Application)." Utica: SUNY College of Technology.

_____. 1986. "Class and Computers: Factory and Society in the Micro-Millenium." *Cultural Futures Research* 8(3):23–31.

_____. 1987a. "Studying Work: Anthropological and Marxist Considerations," pp. 57–80. In David Hakken and Johanna Lessinger, eds., *Perspectives on U.S. Marxist Anthropology.* Boulder: Westview.

_____. 1987b. "Culture and Reproduction in Complex Social Formations." *Dialectical Anthropology* 12(2):193–204.

_____. 1987c. "Introduction," pp. 1–23. In David Hakken and Johanna Lessinger, eds., *Perspectives on U.S. Marxist Anthropology.* Boulder: Westview.

_____. 1988a. "The Vanishing Worker of the Information Age? Technology and Culture Change in Sheffield, England." Unpublished manuscript.

_____. 1989. "Has There Been a Computer Revolution? An Anthropological View." *Journal of Computing and Society* 1(1):13–30.

_____. 1991a. "Thoroughly Postmodern Milling: The Challenge to Technology Education." *Research and Creative Expression* 3:3–10. SUNY Institute of Technology.

_____. 1991b. "Culture-Centered Computing: Social Policy and Development of New Information Technology in England and the United States." *Human Organization.* Fall 1991.

_____. 1992. *Disability Technology Policy: Report of A Conference to Identify the Issues* 45:15–35. Newsletter of the Special Interest Group on Computers and the Physically Handicapped, Association for Computing Machinery.

Hakken, David, and Darwin, John. 1990. "Shall the North Rise Again? The Politics and Practice of Local Economic Development in Britain." Panel presented at the Annual Meeting, Society for Applied Anthropology, York, England.

Hakken, David, and Lessinger, Johanna. 1987. *Perspectives on U.S. Marxist Anthropology.* Boulder: Westview.

Hall, Stuart. 1987. "Gramsci and Us." *Marxism Today* 31(6):16–21.

Harris, Marvin. 1968. *The Rise of Anthropological Theory.* New York: Thomas Y. Crowell.

Harrison, Joan. 1987. "The Cumberlege Report—Some Thoughts from the Sidelines." *Radical Nurses Newsletter.* Spring 1987:2–5.

Harrison, M.D., and Monk, A.E., eds. 1986. *An Introduction to People and Computers: Designing for Usability.* (Second British Computing Society Conference on Human/Computer Interaction.) Cambridge: Cambridge University Press.

HEW Panel. 1972. *Work in America.* Washington, D.C.: U.S. Government Printing Office.

Hilferding, Rudolf. 1910. *Das Finanzkapital.* Frankfurt: Springer Verlag.

Hines, Barry. 1979a. *The Gamekeeper.* Harmondsworth: Penguin.

_____. 1979b. *The Price of Coal.* London: Michael Joseph.

Hoffman, W. Michael, and Mills, Jennifer. 1982. *Ethics and the Management of Computer Technology.* Cambridge, Mass.: Oelgeschlager, Gunn, and Law.

Hoggart, Richard. 1957. *The Uses of Literacy.* New York: Oxford University Press.

Hoogeveldt, Angkie. 1987. "A Tale of Two Economies, or Is Socialism Dead?" Presentation to the Sheffield University Policy Studies Centre.

Howe, Louise Kapp. 1977. *Pink Collar Workers: Inside the World of Women's Work.* New York: Avon Books.

Humphries, Jane. 1987. "British Women in a Changing Workplace, 1979–1985: Female Labour and Enabling, Disabling, and Exploiting Measures of Employers and the State." Paper presented to the Conference of Socialist Economists, Sheffield Polytechnic.

Hunt, H. Allan, and Hunt, Timothy L. 1983. *Human Resource Implications of Robotics.* Kalamazoo, Mich.: W.E. Upjohn Institute for Employment.

Huws, Ursula. 1982. *New Technology and Women's Employment: Cases from West Yorkshire.* Leeds: Leeds Trade Union and Community Resource and Information Centre.

Johnson, Deborah. 1985. *Computer Ethics.* Englewood Cliffs: Prentice-Hall.

Johnson, Deborah, and Snapper, John W. 1985. *Ethical Issues in the Use of Computers.* Belmont, Calif.: Wadsworth.

Jones, Barry. 1982. *Sleepers, Wake! Technology and the Future of Work.* Melbourne: Oxford University Press.

Kling, Rob. 1974. "Computers and Social Power." *Computers and Society,* Fall 1974:6–11.

———. 1980. "Social Analyses of Computing: Theoretical Perspectives in Recent Empirical Literature." *ACM Computing Surveys* 12(1):60–110.

Kusterer, Ken. 1978. *Know-How on the Job: The Important Working Knowledge of "Unskilled" Workers.* Boulder: Westview.

Leacock, Eleanor Burke. 1981. *Myths of Male Dominance: Collected Articles on Women Cross-Culturally.* New York: Monthly Review.

Lenk, Klaus. 1982. "Information Technology and Society," pp. 261–296. In Gunter Friedrichs and Adam Schaff, eds., *Micro-electronics and Society.* New York: New American Library.

Levitan, Sar, and Johnson, C.M. 1982. "The Future of Work: Does It Belong to Us or the Robots?" *Monthly Labor Review* 105(9):10–14.

Lewis, Oscar. 1966. "The Culture of Poverty." *Scientific American* 215(4):3–9.

Leyard, Richard, and Clark, Andrew. 1987. "Those Who Want to Work and Those Who Don't." *Financial Times,* 19 May.

Liebowitz, Leila. 1980. "Double Entendre: Or, Yet Another Model of the Origins of the Division of Labor Along Sex Lines Which Tries to Integrate Biological and Social Factors." Paper presented to the Twenty-First Annual Meeting, Northeasthern Anthropological Association, Saratoga Springs, New York.

Linn, Ian. 1985. *People, Jobs, and Industry in South Yorkshire.* Barnsley: Northern College.

Long, John. 1986. "People and Computing: Designing for Usability," pp. 3–23. In M.D. Harrison and A.E. Monk, eds., *An Introduction to People and Computers: Designing for Usability.* Cambridge: Cambridge University Press.

Lucas, Henry C. 1975. *Why Information Systems Fail.* New York: Columbia University Press.

Machung, Anne. 1982. "Word Processing: Forward for Business, Backward for Women," pp. 124–139. In Karen Sacks and Dorothy Remy, eds., *My Troubles are Going to Have Trouble with Me.* New Brunswick, N.J.: Rutgers University Press.

Malinowski, B. 1932. *Argonauts of the Western Pacific.* New York: E.P. Dutton.

Marcus, George, and Fisher, Michael. 1986. *Anthropology as Cultural Critique: An Experimental Moment in the Human Sciences.* Chicago: University of Chicago Press.

Marx, Karl. 1967. *Capital. Volume Two: On the Circulation of Commodities.* New York: International Publishers.

Massey, Doreen. 1984. *Spatial Divisions of Labour: Social Structures and the Geography of Production.* London: Macmillan.

Massey, Doreen, and Meegan, R. 1985. *Politics and Method.* London: Methuen.

Melman, Seymour. 1974. *The Permanent War Economy: American Capitalism in Decline.* New York: Simon and Schuster.

Miller, Roger, and Coté, Marcel. 1985. "Growing the Next Silicon Valley." *Harvard Business Review,* July–August 1985, pp. 114–124.

Milliband, Ralph. 1973. *The State in Capitalist Society: The Analysis of the Western System of Power.* London: Quartet.

Mills, C. Wright. 1959. *The Sociological Immagination.* New York: Oxford University Press.

Miron, Wilfred. 1973. (Untitled.) Memo to Sir Derek Ezra, Chairman, British National Coal Board.

Montgomery, David. 1979. *Workers' Control in America.* Cambridge: Cambridge University Press.

Moody, Robert. 1987. "City Is Dragged into the Age of Technology." *Sheffield Star,* 19 March.

Moynihan, Daniel Patrick. 1965. *The Negro Family: A Case for National Action.* Washington, D.C.: U.S. Department of Labor.

Mumford, Enid, and Weir, M. 1979. *Computer Systems in Work Design—The Ethics Method.* London: Associated Business Press.

Mumford, Enid, and Henschel, Don. 1979. *A Participatory Approach to Computer System Design: A Case Study of the Introduction of a New Computer System.* London: Associated Business Press.

Murray, Fergus. 1987. *Reconsidering Clerical Skills and Computerization in UK Retail Banking.* Sheffield: Sheffield City Polytechnic.

Nash, June, and Fernandez-Kelly, Maria. 1983. "Introduction, pp. iii–xii." In Nash and Fernandez-Kelly, eds., *Women, Men, and the International Division of Labor.* Albany: SUNY Press.

Newson, John. 1986. "The Myths of New Technology." *Local Government Policy Making,* March 1983, pp. 23–33.

Noble, David. 1979. "Social Choice in Machine Design: The Case of Automatically Controlled Machine Tools," pp. 18–50. In A. Zimbalist, ed., *Case Studies in the Labor Process.* New York: Monthly Review.

_____ . 1984. *Forces of Production: A Social History of Industrial Automation.* New York: Alfred A. Knopf.

Nygaard, Kristin. 1983. "Participation in System Development: The Tasks Ahead," pp. 19–25. In U. Briefs et al., eds., *Systems Design; For, with, and by the User.* Amsterdam: North Holland.

Offe, Claus. 1985. *Disorganized Capitalism: Contemporary Transformations of Work and Politics.* London: Polity Press.

Ortner, Sherry. 1984. "Theory in Anthropology Since the Sixties." *Comparative Studies of Society and History* 26:126–166.

Pemberton, Brigitte. 1986. *Management and Trade Union Responses to the Perceived Implications of Micro-electronic Technology in Selected Areas of the Service Sector.* Sheffield: Sheffield Polytechnic.

Pfeiffer, J. 1982. "How Were Cities Invented?" pp. 79–84. In David Hunter and Phillip Whitten, eds., *Anthropology: Contemporary Perspectives.* Boston: Little, Brown and Company.

Phillips, Anne. 1987. *Divided Loyalties: Dilemmas of Sex and Class.* London: Virago.

Poulantzas, Nicos. 1978. *State, Power, Socialism.* London: New Left Books.

Rains, Howell. 1988. "Laborites Head for a Leadership Battle." *New York Times,* March 25:A3.

Rainwater, Lee, and Yancy, William L. 1967. *The Moynihan Report and the Politics of Controversy.* Cambridge: MIT Press.

Reiter (Rapp), Rayna, ed. 1975. *Toward an Anthropology of Women.* New York: Monthly Review.

Rosenberg, Nathan. 1982. *Inside the Black Box: Technology and Economics.* Cambridge: Cambridge University Press.

Rosenhead, Jonathan. 1986. "Operational Research for Community Groups." Presentation to the Yorkshire Branch, Operational Research Society, Northern College, Barnsley.

Rosenhead, Jonathan, and Thunhurst, Colin. 1977. "Operational Research and Cost Benefit Analysis: Whose Science?" pp. 289–304. In John Irvine, Ian Miles, and Jeff Evans, eds., *Demystifying Social Statistics.* London: Pluto Press.

Routledge, Paul. 1987. "Job Divide 'Twists Morals.'" *Guardian,* 24 March.

Rule, James. 1974. *Private Lives and Public Surveillance.* New York: Shocken.

Russell, Stewart, and Williams, Robin. 1987. "Opening the Black Box and Closing it Behind You: On Microsociology in the Social Analysis of Technology." Paper presented to the British Sociological Association Conference, Leeds.

Sahlins, Marshall. 1976. *Culture and Practical Reason.* Chicago: University of Chicago Press.

Saxian, AnnaLee. 1987. "The Experience of Silicon Valley: Myth and Reality." Paper presented to the Technology Conference, Brighton, England.

Sayer, Andrew. 1984. *Method in Social Science: A Realist Approach.* London: Hutchinson.

Scarborough, Harry. 1986. "The Politics of Technological Change at British Leyland," pp. 95–115. In Otto Jacobi, Bob Jessop, Hans Kastendiek, and Mario Regini, Eds., *Technological Change, Rationalization, and Industrial Relations.* Beckenham, Kent: Croom Helm.

Schaff, Adam. 1982. "Occupation vs. Work," pp. 322–334. In Gunter Friedrichs, and Adam Schaff, eds., *Microelectronics and Society.* New York: New American Library.

Schneider, David. 1968. *American Kinship: A Cultural Account.* Englewood Cliffs: Prentice-Hall.

Segal, Lynne. 1987. *Is the Future Female?: Troubled Thoughts on Contemporary Feminism.* London: Virago.

Servan-Schreiber, Jean-Jacques. 1981. *The World Challenge.* New York: Simon and Schuster.

Shackel, B. 1986. "Ergonomics in Design for Usability," pp. 44–64. In M.D. Harrison and A.E. Monk, eds, *People and Computers.* Cambridge: Cambridge University Press.

Shaiken, Harley. 1985. *Work Transformed: Automation and Labor in the Computer Age.* New York: Holt, Rinehart, and Winston.

Sheffield Health Authority. n.d., ca. 1986. *Health Care and Disease—A Profile of Sheffield.* Sheffield: Sheffield Health Authority.

Sheffield People's Campaign for Health. n.d., ca. 1984. *Sheffield's Health—Could We Care Less?* Sheffield: People's Campaign for Health.

Sheffield Policewatch. n.d., ca. 1984. *Taking Liberties: Policing during the Miners' Strike, April–October 1984.* Sheffield: Sheffield Policewatch.

Sherman, Barrie. 1985. *The New Revolution: The Impact of Computers on Society.* New York: John Wiley and Sons.

Siegal, Lenny. 1986. "Microcomputers: From Movement to Industry." *Monthly Review* 38(3):110–117.

Simons, Geoff. 1986. *Silicon Shock: The Menace of the Computer Invasion.* Oxford: Basil Blackwell.

Spenner, Kenneth. 1983. "Temporal Change in the Skill Level of Work." *American Sociological Review* 48(6):824–837.

Starr, Chauncey. 1983. "The Growth of Limits." Edison Electric Institute Symposium, pp.2–3.

Stone, Katherine. 1974. "The Origins of Job Structures in the Steel Industry." *Review of Radical Political Economics* 6(2):61–97.

Suchman, Lucy. 1987. *Plans and Situated Actions: The Problem of Human Machine Communication.* Cambridge: Cambridge University Press.

Thompson, E.P. 1963. *The Making of the English Working Class.* New York: Random House.

Thunhurst, Colin. 1985. *Poverty and Health in the City of Sheffield.* Sheffield: Sheffield City Council.

————. 1987. *Community Operational Research at the Northern College.* Barnsley: Northern College.

Tijerina, Louis. 1984. *Video Display Terminal Workstation Ergonomics.* Dublin, Oh.: Online Computer Library Center.

Toffler, Alvin. 1980. *The Third Wave.* New York: Morrow.

Turkle, Sherry. 1980. "Computer as Rorschach." *Society* 172(12):15–24.

————. 1984. *The Second Self: Computers and the Human Spirit.* New York: Simon and Schuster.

van der Pijl, Kees. 1987. "Some Notes on the Transition from Capitalism to Socialism in the Current Period." Paper presented to the 1987 Conference of Socialist Economists, Sheffield Polytechnic.

Vehvilaeinen, Marja. 1986. *A Study Circle as a Method for Women to Develop their Work and Computer Systems.* Tampere, Finland: University of Tampere Department of Computer Science.

Wallerstein, Immanuel. 1976. *The Modern World System: Capitalist Agriculture and the Origins of the European World-Economy in the Sixteenth Century.* New York: Academic.

Watson, Brenda. 1986. "Job Despair of the Young." *Sheffield Journal* 199:2.

Weinstein, Jeremy. 1985. "Angry Arguments Across the Picket Lines: Left Labour Councils and White Collar Trade Unions." *Critical Social Policy* 6:41–60.

Weizenbaum, J. 1975. *Computer Power and Human Reason.* San Francisco: Freeman and Company.

Wilkinson, Barry. 1983. *The Shopfloor Politics of New Technology.* London: Heinemann Educational.

Wilkinson, Frank, ed. 1981. *The Dynamics of Labor Market Segmentation.* London: Academic.

Williams, Raymond. [1958] 1989 reprint. "Culture is Ordinary," pp. 3–18. In Robin Gable, ed. *Resources of Hope: Culture, Democracy, Socialism.* London: Verso.

Williams, Robin, and Moseley, Russell. 1982. "Technology Agreements, Consensus, Control and Technical Change in the Workplace," pp. 231–245. In Bjorn-Andersen et al., eds., *Information Society.* Amsterdam: North Holland.

Winner, Langdon. 1984. "Mythinformation in the High Tech Era." *IEEE Spectrum* 21(6):90–96.

Winograd, Terry. 1987. "A Language/Action Perspective on the Design of Cooperative Work." *Human-Computer Interaction* 3:3–30.

Winterton, Jonathan, and Winterton, Ruth. 1985. *New Technology: The Bargaining Issues.* Leeds: Leeds University and Nottingham University.

———. 1989. *Coal, Crisis, and Conflict: The 1984–1985 Miners' Strike in Yorkshire.* Manchester: Manchester University Press.

Wolf, Eric. 1982. *Europe and the People Without History.* Berkeley: University of California Press.

Wood, Stephen, ed. 1982. *The Degradation of Work? Skill, Deskilling and the Labour Process.* London: Hutchinson.

Wright, Eric O. 1979. *Class Structure and Income Determination.* New York: Academic.

Zeitlin, Jonathan. 1987. "The Third Italy: Inter-firm Cooperation and Technological Innovation." Paper presented to the Technology Conference, Brighton, England.

Zimbalist, Andrew, ed. 1979. *Case Studies on the Labor Process.* New York: Monthly Review.

Zuboff, Shoshana. 1988. *In the Age of the Smart Machine: The Future of Work and Power.* New York: Basic.

# About the Book and Authors

This study of computing in an economically transforming city in the north of England looks at how new information technologies effect and are affected by a historically vibrant working-class culture. Stressing the complex interplay between technology and culture, especially notions about work and labor, the authors examine how this dynamic is manifest in computer-related jobs, in social relationships, and in the reproduction of local culture. They analyze the structure of computing in Sheffield, placing it in the contexts of national state policy, world political economy, and the regional labor market, and they explore the processes of computing in relation to the reproduction of gendering, the rise of "labor freedom," and local attempts to influence the course of computerization. The experiences of the people in Sheffield and South Yorkshire have much to teach us about what technology does and what we can do to control it. *Computing Myths, Class Realities* will be of interest not only to anthropologists and sociologists but to all scholars interested in the social correlates of computing.

**David Hakken** is an American anthropologist and worker educator who teaches computer science and sociology of work, as well as applied anthropology, at the State University of New York Institute of Technology. **Barbara Andrews** is currently the director of educational programming for the Central New York Community Arts Council.